BEYOND THE MIRAGE

Novels by Arthur W. Upfield:

1 The Barrakee Mystery
2 The Sands of Windee
3 Wings Above the Diamantina
4 Mr Jelly's Business
5 Winds of Evil
6 The Bone is Pointed
7 The Mystery of Swordfish Reef
8 Bushrangers of the Skies
9 Death of a Swagman
10 The Devil's Steps
11 An Author Bites the Dust
12 The Mountains Have a Secret
13 The Widows of Broome
14 The Bachelors of Broken Hill
15 The New Shoe
16 Venom House
17 Murder Must Wait
18 Death of a Lake
19 The Cake in the Hat Box
20 The Battling Prophet
21 Man of Two Tribes
22 Bony Buys a Woman
23 Bony and the Mouse
24 Bony and the Black Virgin
25 Bony and the Kelly Gang
26 Bony and the White Savage
27 The Will of the Tribe
28 Madman's Bend
29 The Lake Frome Monster
30 The House of Cain
31 The Beach of Atonement
32 A Royal Abduction
33 Gripped By Drought
34 Breakaway House
35 The Great Melbourne Cup Mystery

BEYOND THE MIRAGE

AN AUTOBIOGRAPHY

ETT IMPRINT, SYDNEY
Exile Bay

First published by ETT Imprint, Exile Bay in 2020

Copyright © William Upfield 2020

This book is copyright. Apart from any fair dealing for the purposes of private study, research, criticism or review, as permitted under the Copyright Act, no part may be reproduced by any process without written permission. Enquiries should be addressed to the publisher, or through the official Upfield website on www.arthurupfield.com

ETT IMPRINT
PO Box R1906

Royal Exchange NSW 1225
Australia

ISBN 978-1-922384-14-0 (paper)
ISBN 978-1-922384-15-7 (ebook)

Text design by Hanna Gotlieb
Cover and internal design Tom Thompson
Photographs courtesy of William Upfield, Alan Whyte

Half-title photograph shows Arthur Upfield feeding a young kangaroo, 1925

Upfield's dray, with in-built writing desk, about 1928.

CONTENTS

One	The Great I Am	7
Two	Another Planet	25
Three	Beyond The Mirage	60
Four	Men And Jobs	93
Five	Fog	124
Six	A Phase Of Life	153
Seven	Embarrassing Moments	178
Eight	Ambition	208
Nine	Fur	243
Ten	Concerning A Plot	261
Eleven	The Second Act	288
Twelve	Interval	318

ONE

The Great I Am

I

Almost everyone is a snob, and people who write their autobiographies are not free from conceit. They are among the millions of ancestor-snobs; and, if they are unable to trace their ancestry back for more than three generations, they invent the details of a family tree or pay others to do it for them. I, too, am a snob, but not an ancestor-snob. I am a motor car snob. I look on the owner of a cheaper car than mine with contempt and I can hardly refrain from pulling my forelock to the owner of a Rolls.

However, there is much for which to feel pride and for which to thank the Almighty. I am not a house-snob, a society-snob, a title-snob, a hotel-snob, or of the many other kinds of snobs of whom by far the worst is the literary-snob.

As the title of this chapter might infer, I am a Pommy, meaning of course, that I am English by birth and parentage. I consider the English people to be the salt of the earth, and I have equal right to think it as the Australian who believes that those born in Australia are the earth's salt. We have here another form of snobbery, of which I am guilty equally with many millions. Yet after all, this salt of the earth theory is merely an opinion the vocal expression of which no longer creates a brawl although the collective expression of the opinion sometimes leads to a war.

People nowadays appear to realize that the subject provides poor ground for argument in a workaday world so filled with the doings of film stars.

There is a belief that no good came from the last Great War when, in fact, certain good did come from it. The Australians and the Pommies learned tolerance for each other, and since the last Great War the word, Pommy, is much less used and seldom as a taunt. This despite the jokes and drawings appearing in several weeklies depicting the Englishman as a rabbit-faced imbecile. As these same weeklies love to depict the Australian farmer, as Dad or Dave or both, as an ill-mannered, badly-dressed lunatic I for one cannot understand anyone objecting to the word Pommy. Still less can I understand myself for filling space by writing about it.

Among the many classes of snobs is the publicity-snob, a type of snobbery which sometimes produces mania demanding constant headlines in the papers. At some period of their lives publicity-snobs, generally by accident, are featured in the press. Therein lies the genesis of their mania. Henceforth they simply must have publicity. Several addicts have committed murder to obtain the publicity of a trial. Others have been known to slander with a book review some unfortunate author in order to figure in an action at law.

All of which must account for those English men and women of position and means complaining, on their return from a visit to Australia, that the Australians are bitter towards the migrant and persist in calling him a Pommy. They do not know the meaning of the word, but it is a dreadful word, anyway. And the feeling of superiority over those horrible colonials is so immensely satisfying.

Both Australians and the vast majority of Pommies in Australia experience the same exquisite feeling of superiority over the returned publicity-snobs, but there are Pommies who are excessively sensitive. They have not long been in the country and it is clearly evident that they suffer from an inferiority complex created in them by the publicity-snobs. Once I almost bought a fight with two specimens of this type.

I was living at a hut outback midway between the station homestead and the out-station, and one afternoon there arrived in a car two obvious new chums. They intended to camp that night at the outstation, and they wished to know what the cook there was like - for a hand-out.

"He'a a dashed good cook," I replied "But he's one of those ignorant ruddy pommies."

Two faces abruptly became suffused with anger. One stepped close to me and striking a belligerent attitude, demanded to know:

"What d'you mean by that? We're Englishmen."

I laughed at him, saying:

"So am I."

At one period in Western Australia I used to barrack for an association football team composed of players originating from the British Isles. The hunting cry of Englishmen, Scotchmen and Welshmen was: "Come on the Pommies!"

Oh yes, the war effected a vital change of outlook in all blessed with a modicum of intelligence. Before the war it was different. There was bitterness in the heart of many an uninformed Australian against the stranger who was thought to be a rival for jobs. Then, too, very many of the migrants were conceited asses.

In fact, I have met in not a few of them, both before and after the war, the most objectionable persons imaginable: equally as objectionable as the Australian who has won fame in London and on revisiting his or her own country tells us all where we get off.

I arrived in Australia when, in addition to this native intolerance, there was definite antipathy of the people of one State towards those of another.

It still exists but is not nearly so strong as it was a few years before the war. I have seen many brawls - and joined in some of them - brought about by the subject of Sydney Harbour and St. Kilda Road. I have witnessed private fights produced by one man calling another a Victorian Scab, and by a Victorian calling a South Australian a Crow Eater. The same men do not feel any hurt at being called a bastard. When a new chum, this condition of affairs interested me much. In fact this ugly word became used in later years as a term of endearment.

The writer of an autobiography is supposed to write nothing but the truth about himself. It is true that I took to Australia and the Australians like a hen to its chicks. I never once felt any revulsion of feeling towards either the country or the people, and I have never met an Australian who wanted really to be sick because of my birth and parentage.

And so, in order to cringe to literary tradition, let me get along with - and over with - the ancestors and come to grips with the real damper and salt mutton.

2

If the boys of today did those things which we of my boyhood days did, magistrates and court officials would swoon with fatigue and special reformatories would have to be built. The wowser era of today would say that we boys were vicious blackguards: and the wowsers would be wrong. Mischievous, adventurous, daring and obstreperous we certainly were, but no boy of my acquaintance ever went wrong in after-life. We committed extraordinary sins and we expiated many of them in thrashings received.

The Upfields lived for centuries in and near a charming Sussex village named Wisborough Green, the hundred acres of common land being surrounded by ancient white-washed cottages, the shop, the inn, the blacksmith forge and the tall wood-built windmill. The Upfields were yeoman farmers and traders, and my grandfather, being the seventh son of a seventh son, left Wisborough Green early in life - probably because he considered that there were too many Upfields asleep in the churchyard - and he migrated to Gosport situated on the west aide of Portsmouth Harbour.

At Gosport he founded a drapery business, controlled today by his grandsons, beginning in a small way and leaving a large shop above which is a house containing thirty-three rooms in three stories. Here my father was born: here did I first see the light.

In course of time my father became a partner in the business and married a Barmore of Birmingham. My mother's father was an inspector in the Small Arms Factory and a most important political lieutenant to Joseph Chamberlain. He was a fluent speaker, and during an election he contracted an illness which developed into pneumonia from which he died two days after 'Joey' was returned to Westminster. A Barmore married a canon of York Minster. Another was gifted with an extraordinarily retentive mind. He could recite any one of Shakespeare's plays throughout and not make one slip.

He could read a newspaper article and then repeat it word for word.

My mother bore five sons of whom I am the eldest.

Her early married life was hard, indeed. In those days the shop and dress making staffs totalled over forty hands, of whom six or seven lived in and half the others had meals served in the assistants' dining room as they lived at a distance. What with the labour of cooking for all these people, overseeing three servants and managing five boys, she could not always see what Arthur was doing. Neither could my father, whose business day began at eight-thirty and closed with the shop at nine o'clock at night and at eleven o'clock on Saturday night. On Christmas Eve the shop was opened at eight, and it remained open until one and two o'clock Christmas morning, when every assistant was invited to select from the stock any article which pleased him as a Christmas gift, and then were sent to their homes in a cab.

Arthur needs must possess a catapult, and a brother had only to suggest a competition to prove which of us could shoot the farthest. Away across the roofs, to be seen from the large rear yard, was a doctor's private observatory having many tempting windows. We made of this a target but failed to get the range. Then Arthur thought of finding out how high he could shoot a large coloured ally. Up went the ally, out of sight, whilst five boys waited expectantly to hear the bounce of it on a neighbouring roof. It fell through the skylight giving light to a part of the shop.

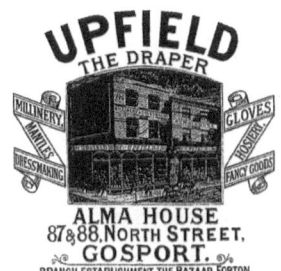

The main store at 87-88 North Street. c.1900.
Photo: Gosport Museum collection

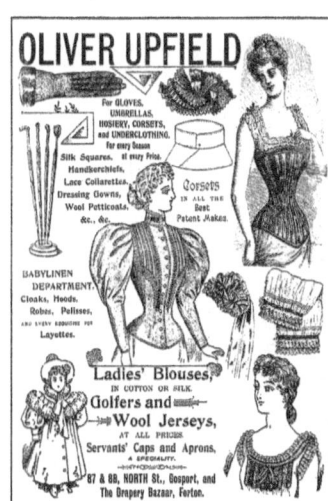

Advertisements for Upfields.
Everything for the lady of the house and her family.
Photos: Gosport Museum collection

Five bandits rushed to cover as presented by the stables and the coach-house, sheds and store-rooms opening on to the yard. My father came into the yard and called my name. Said he:

"Some blackguard of a boy has fired this glass ally into the air with a catapult. I want you to take it round to Superintendent Brown with my compliments and explain to him all about it."

So taking the glass ally I presented it to the Superintendent of Police and told him what it had done at the end of its aerial flight. The superintendent was a big, red-faced, bluff man of whom no boy in all the town was afraid.

"Humph!" he grunted, eying the ally which he held to the light as though searching for finger-prints. "This is a bad business. The projectile might have fallen on somebody's head, and, of course, you know what that would have meant. Ah, well? Tell your father I will do what I can to find the guilty party."

I had turned to leave him, and had reached the office door, when he called me back to ask with a look of pretended fury:

"What is that in your hip pocket?"

Guiltily did my hand flash round to my pocket - to feel dangling from it about a foot of catapult elastic. Speechless, I produced the lethal weapon and, mastered by the man's cold stare, I put it down upon his desk. Then he jumped to his feet. "You come along with me," he said invitingly, and he took me out and locked me into a cell.

Now I was small and the cell was cold and looked very big. I was scared and miserable and on the verge of tears when I heard in the corridor without the protesting voice of Mrs. Superintendent Brown. She was as large as her husband, and she entered the cell like a whirlwind to snatch me to her ample bosom and carry me off to the living room of their quarters where with delighted grins her husband welcomed us.

What a high tea that was which followed! There were sponge cakes and cream. There were two bottles of ginger beer which the Superintendent had gone out to get whilst I was incarcerated. He cracked jokes and his wife waited hand and foot on the gaolbird. They even gave me back my catapult when I was about to leave.

Oh, yes! In those days they knew how to manage boys without the aid of magistrates and prisons. My father had seen the elastic dangling from my pocket when he called me to him in the yard, and on my way to the Police Station he had telephoned to the Superintendent and had suggested the term of imprisonment.

I was ever a good marksman with a catapult, but as a thrower I was an absolute dud.

One of my brothers came running to report that standing on the curb opposite the shop was our arch enemy, a tea-swilling old loafer who seized every opportunity of reporting our sins to our father, a gent whose name was Budd.

Someone suggested an over-matured potato. There was a ton or so of these tubers in one of the storerooms, and now and then these were picked over by the yardman. He had, however, not carried out this task for some time, and we selected half a dozen potatoes that were in just the right condition suitable for our purpose. We rushed up three flights of stairs and then up a ladder and through a skylight on to the roof. Leaning over the parapet, we could see the detestable Budd far below, still standing at the edge of the opposite pavement. He was wearing his usual grey hat with its narrow brim and high crown. His grey beard fell down his shirtless chest as speculatively he watched the cabs and trollies pass him by. With thrilling eagerness I selected a beautiful ' spud.'

"Don't you shoot: you'll never hit him!" cried my confederates. "You can't throw for nuts. Let Ted throw."

But I would not be restrained. I felt inspired. I threw the missile and created a mental picture that will never fade. I can still see that potato curving outward and downward. It turned over and over in its flight, one end swelling dangerously as velocity threatened to burst it. Even before it began to fall on Budd I knew he would receive it. How slow did its downward flight appear to me! And how inevitable its course to the bull's eye!

Minutes seemed to pass before the tuber disappeared in the distance. It seemed, too, that all movement in the street halted, that every living thing stopped to stare at Budd. Only he was unconscious of impending doom.

Then dark-brown matter squirted outward from the centre of his chest. The victim threw up his arms and staggered back-ward to the shop front behind him. Then with furious action he scooped his eyes clear and wrang out his beard into the gutter, drivers and shoppers regarding him with no small amount of interest.

Budd, of course, was not hurt. We were not quite so stupid as to throw a solid potato. And so, after clearing his eyes and beard of the watery matter he straightened his tall frame and glared about and then looked up - to see me hanging over the parapet and rendered helpless by uncontrollable laughter.

The affair cost my father a tip of ten shillings and me a sound thrashing. Pray have no sympathy with Budd. He got his own back with compound interest.

Then there was the affair of the sixpenny sky-rocket and the tram.

They were extraordinary trams, somewhat like the hinder part of the Melbourne cable trams, and were drawn by two horses. The line extended to a suburb named Brockhurst where at the time my father owned a house. There was, I remember, a high hedge fronting the road and a gap in this hedge taking the low gate. The idea of the stunt was to fire a rocket low over the gate and timed to hit a passing tram. No thought was given to the probability of striking the unfortunate horses.

Accustomed to the noise of these vehicles it was not difficult to judge the exact moment when a tram would pass opposite the gate, but the difficulty was to judge the exact time when the fuse had to be lighted, a matter of one to three seconds before the rocket began its flight. The only point in my favour is that the chance of the rocket striking the tram was about one in a million.

The first rocket sped into the hedge. The second one roared high over the hedge across the road and into a field. The third rocket failed to act at all. The fourth rocket was a boomerang one. But the fifth! It sailed low over the gate and was just in time to crash through a window of the tram and there speed round and round the small interior until it exploded with a reverberating boom.

The horses stopped without command and out from the tram staggered one by one three hefty British navvies who were the only passengers. They and the conductor saw three heads poked through holes in the hedge.

Now we know what would have resulted in such a prank today.

Police, magistrates, a court, much publicity and a reformatory. The whole world would have been shocked and Pro Bono Publico would have written to the newspapers forecasting the end of civilization. In those days boys were treated much more sanely. The tram passengers and the conductor entered my father's premises, seized the boys and there and then thrashed them. If that had happened today they would be summoned for assault and fined by a magistrate who would have no hesitation in sending the boys to a reformatory and thus apprentice them to a criminal career. My father thanked the conductor and the navvies for their action and presented each with five shillings. He paid the tram company for the damage and then began work on us. Thus ended an affair which after all was a mere storm in a tea cup - or rather in a tram car.

3

My father's views on education might be considered unorthodox today but were, nevertheless, sound. It was his belief that if his boys were well grounded in the three R's and bookkeeping they could undertake a course of higher educa-tion if they had any aptitude for it. Thus he did not needlessly waste money on me by sending me to college.

Yet I know I never had my proper chance, due not to my father but to my school masters. Throughout the three years I attended at a technical school I was top of the form in class work and term examinations for history and geography, and I was bottom in all and every other subject.

While at this school I wrote political letters to the editor of the local newspaper as from two irate political opponents, let-ters which were published. I also wrote a story covering some four hundred pages of foolscap, a story in which I detailed the emergence of China into a military power which invaded Europe. A chapter of this book, when being written during a maths class, was confiscated by the master and read with interest - after he had given me four hundred lines.

The heading of the matter confiscated was Chapter 29, and I

confessed that the pile of foolscap already covered amounted to some 340 pages. I was then fifteen years of age and it was actually pointed out to me that I was sinfully wasting my time.

If only that school master had reasoned thus: "Here is a seeming numskull who invariably tops his form in history and geography and bottoms it in every other sub-ject. To say the least, that is peculiar. Here is this numskull who has covered some three hundred and fifty pages of foolscap with what is asserted by him to be a novel-type of story. This is still more peculiar because he cannot add two algerbriac signs or parse a simple sentence. He is like a man trying to play the piano by ear.

"Now I will endeavour to drum it into his thick head that, as his ambition is to be a newspaper reporter, and rise to sit in an editor's chair, he must learn to make bricks before he begins to build the house of his career, which means that he must master grammar and earnestly study English literature."

But no - he piled on the lines and I was articled to a sur veyor-estate agent auctioneer for three years, my father paying one hundred guineas at the time the articleship docu-ment was signed.

During the period of this articleship I was supposed to pass three examinations to obtain the degree of Fellowship of the Auctioneers Institute at London. The first examination was a mere school one about equal to the Intermediate of these days. Did I pass it? Of course not. I was far more concerned with the doings of an engineer-scientist who, inventing a space ship, visited Mars and there experienced extraordinary adventures. What with novel writing and courting a young woman my spare time was too fully occupied to spare any of it studying for a beastly examination. I sat for it and thus received my first impression of London. Like all subsequent impressions, that first one was bad. Even in those early days I preferred the scent of flowers and trees to the stinks of human crowds.

4

Not only is a man the product of his time: he is, too, the product of his early background.

One of the oldest castles in England is Porchester Castle situated at the head of Portsmouth Harbour. It was, I think, built by the Normans, but long before the Roman occupation the site was a defended one. The castle was occupied till quite recent times, being used for the destination of Napoleon's soldiers and fishermen.

Protected by the castle, Hampshire fishermen founded a village on the west shore of the harbour which was named Gosport. In course of the centuries Gosport became a moated town, a huge ditch being dug around it and the mullock piled high into a steeply sided rampart the two ends of which abutted the harbour water.

Within this moated town was my father born. When I was born there were many houses built outside the moat and rampart under which ran two roads, one to the ancient village of Alveretoke and the other, through Brockhurst, to Fareham and to the west of England. The road tunnels beneath the rampart were guarded at each end by heavy oak iron-studded doors which in times of civil strife or threat of military danger could be closed.

Within the tunnels, too, were guard-rooms occupied by those who, in the days long gone, questioned all who wished to pass through from sunset to sunrise. The rampart and moat still remain but the roads now pass through wide open cuttings.

The railway to Gosport stopped outside the rampart and

moat, but a government track extended from the station to the Victualling Yard, passing through a tunnel in the rampart similar to the road tunnels. It was in consequence to something said or done by a mayor of Portsmouth that Queen Victoria always came this way to board the Royal yacht which took her to Osborne. I saw her twice when her train crossed the road to enter the Victualling Yard, and I saw the casket containing her remains as it passed from the Victualling Yard to disappear into the rampart tunnel.

Large military barracks are built within the rampart which in those early times always housed the King's Royal Rifles. As small hero-worshipping boys we would stand to gaze upon General Sir Redvers Buller riding at the head of his men in their dark green uniforms faced with black. Earl Roberts was familiar to us, too, and so were Lord French, Lord Kitchener and other generals.

However, we owned to two loyalties, the greater being to the Navy. We were familiar with all types of warships and could tell from their markings to what division and fleet they belonged.

There were always great doings in the Navy: reviews at Spithead; the raising and bringing into harbour the ill-fated submarine A1; the escorted Ophir bringing home the Prince and Princess of Wales from opening the first Commonwealth Parliament; the visit of the Czar of Russia and the Emperor of Germany, warships constantly arriving from and going out to foreign stations; the sailing of the first dreadnought which made all other navies obsolete.

The majority of the boys attending school with us went into the Navy or to the dockyard. I can recall a dozen at least who died in the Great War: real, tough, fighting fellows they were. A schoolfellow whose parents were exceeding poor was in

1920 earning two thousand a year as a naval designer, whilst another is very high up in the Foreign Office. They were the times when clever boys were not retarded simply because they had not attended at an university. Other school-mates became chemists, engineers, parsons and civil servants. Two of my brothers entered my father's business. Another went into a bank. The fourth was articled to the agent managing the country estate owned by the Singers of sewing machine fame.

All these lads did well bar me. I was the only idiot among them.

5

Now to finish with these (apparently necessary) ancestors. The earliest recorded Upfield was a certain Oliver Upfield who was a captain in one of Cromwell's armies, whilst of the others only three or four stand out. There was that William Upfield who migrated to America in the days when ironmongery was worn as trinkets. It was written of him that he was remarkably quick on the draw. About the time of Charles Dickens' first visit to that country, this William Upfield invented a patent clothes prop, and when the Civil War broke out he was peddling this prop from North to South and South to North. To make easy money he gathered and sold to the opposing armies military secrets - and was duly hanged. Another Upfield lived to the age of 104, some said because he lived only on potatoes and pork and drank only his home-brewed beer. There was nothing wrong with the beer because I used to sample it when visiting him. The visits were always short, not on account of the plenitude of the beer but by reason of the fact that pork and potatoes became too much of a good-thing after three days. Another ancestor, on the maternal side, became the Chief Justice of South Australia and, at the time of my arrival, was the Lieutenant-Governor. However, he was a little above me.

From the Queen Victoria-General Buller atmosphere I emerged into an era of Naval Reviews, Nelson's Relics, The Blue Post Inn, made famous by Midshipman Easy, Dickens' House, the site of the murder of the Duke of Buckingham, and the ruins of Porchester Castle and Netley Abbey. In this era I was the companion of uncle who died worth tens of thousands. It was thought that he made his money as a kind of pirate in the Straits Settlements. Anyway, during his closing years he was vastly interested in historical relics, and, with me, he travelled from place to place, and pub to pub, in an ancient cab drawn by an ancient horse that was driven by an ancient Weller.

My uncle was never satisfied with just looking at a place having historical interest. For instance, when I showed him the plaque high up on a wall stating that here was the Duke of Buckingham murdered in the year which I forget, he would stand back in the middle of the road to read the inscription on the plaque and hold up the traffic, then to return to the pavement and stoop over the flags immediately beneath the plaque as though hoping to see the bloodstains. He was not satisfied with just looking at the bed in the George Inn, old Portsmouth, in which Admiral Nelson last slept ashore. He had to pummel the mattress, shake the frame to ascertain if it were still sound, and look under the bed to see if Nelson had left behind his boots. And then back to the Blue Post Inn would we go to drink old ale whilst I told him of incidents in the lives of Nelson and Buckingham which are never printed in the popular history books.

The pirate uncle's influence over me has always been

strong: otherwise an aversion to top hats and tail evening suits cannot be accounted for. When I was out of my articles and the author of three unpublishable novels, I suffered a craving to emulate him.

But the days of piracy were over - not again to return till 1937 - and the wearing of ironmongery as trinkets had gone out of fashion. We must have been an extraordinary family; for, at that time, 1909, I had no illusions about Australia and America as being places suitable for budding pirates. We knew that white people occupied Australia, but we were sufficiently naive to believe the politicians when they said that anyone could get land in Australia for the asking.

Arthur's younger brothers Frank (left), and Edward (centre) alongside young women who worked for Upfield's Drapery.

TWO

Another Planet

I

Australia was not extraordinarily blessed when in 1911 a young man landed in Adelaide, his mind filled with illusions of a beautiful farm and a rose-clad cottage easily created from land even more easily obtained from a Government which, figuratively, had gone on its knees to implore him to migrate.

However, that migration was dictated less by immigration propaganda than by a doctor's views on the probable state of my health if I remained in England a further three years - as well as by two considerations of almost equal importance.

The doctor was wise in his generation. He pointed a way out. Only fools wrote novels. Only youthful idiots wasted time courting a girl. Send this particular idiot to Australia. Australia will either make or break him.

Followed then a short but intensive study of official immigration literature, more elaborate, more beautiful than any gold brick prospectus, further money spent on a passage, and lo! the fool arrived one spring morning in Adelaide.

During a short stay in the City of Churches I met several young men who had left my home town a year or so before I did to become Australian farmers. One was a tram conductor; another was a delivery van driver; and a third was preparing for the Methodist ministry. From them I received most pecu-liar views about farming in Australia - peculiar because dia-metrically opposed to all those facts and figures and pictures I had assimilated from Australian literature. My inexperience prompted me to reject such opinions as having been given by men this country had proved to be without backbone.

Those were the years when Australia really and truly was a workingman's Paradise; when there were about two jobs vacant for every man offering. At every station to Pinnaroo, farmers waited on the off chance of persuading a new chum to leave the train to work for him instead of going on to his assigned destination. It was all comparatively new land when wheat was selling at 4/2 a bushel, and when machinery, horses and labour were cheap. Another thing which was plen-tiful was loan money.

My employer was a German, farming five miles out of Pinnaroo, and whilst we drove to the farm in a springless buckboard, I failed to see any lush pastures, any fat and glossy cows, and not one sweet little rose-clad cottage of which my girl and I had dreamed in England. The German's house amazed me. It was built of hessian stretched on a bush frame which supported a corrugated iron roof - all delightfully cool for that time of the year.

Even more amazed did I become at my own quarters - a 2,000 gallon rain tank turned upside down, and having an opening cut for a door. Within was a roughly-made bush bunk.

"It's pretty hot in here just now," remarked my employer. "But you won't notice it because we don't live indoors much."

He was right. We did not live indoors much. I was aroused at 3 o'clock every morning. By the first glimmer of daylight the horses had been fed and harnessed, our own breakfast eaten. We carted hay until 8 o'clock, and at 9 o'clock, or when it was hot enough to strip, took out a second team to strip till noon. It was 8 o'clock in the evening before I had washed up the eating utensils, and 9 before I crept to bed.

Alas! like my friends, I had no backbone. I determined to be a tram conductor, or a delivery van driver, or a minister.

And one of the hardest letters ever I wrote was that bitter disillusioned outpouring to the girl in England. All the way out into and back from the Pinnaroo country I saw not one farm which came any where near the ideal painted on my brain by that immigration literature.

I secured a job in one of Adelaide's largest hotels as "fourth cook..."

My, what a job that was! If only I had stuck to it! The chef was drawing £20 a week. He liked me, and offered to teach me all he knew - which would not be in five minutes. We worked from seven to one and from four to seven o'clock. We ate just what we liked, and in less than a fortnight the beat was not good enough.

"There will be overtime for all hands tonight," was one day announced. "A Colonel is giving a special dinner to commemorate some battle or other."

"Do you know how to make iced coffee royal?" I was asked by the chef who had called me into his office. "No? Well, I'll show you. Go down to the bar and get this order. Bring it here."

On the order was rum and vermouth and brandy and twelve bottles of beer. It occurred to me that vermouth might possibly go into coffee royal, but I was sure that bottled beer did not. "The beer? That's all right! Put all the order in my office. The beer, you idiot, is for the staff."

Eight tall Cleopatra needles of iced coffee royal went into the private dining room, and about six came out. Beside we cooks, the waiters had a share in the beer, but they had no share in the iced coffee royal. That night the chef slept on the first back landing to his room, the second cook chose the ice chamber for his resting place, whilst I found the bread table good enough.

Yes, I was mentally deficient to leave that job, but, you see, I was young; I still retained sane illusions. I knew that beyond the horizon was adventure and romance. Wheat! Pouf! Gold - opals - cattle - sheep - riding horses - camp fires, and the long long track awinding.

The door to this alluring world was shown me by an advertise ment which read:-

Boundary Riders

Wanted for Northern Stations. Apply Younger Jones and Co.

"How long have you been in the country?" asked the poker-faced Secretary to a Pastoral company.

"Two months, sir."

"Oh! Can you ride?"

"Yes. I was in the Hampshire Yeomanry."

"Oh! Can you kill a sheep?"

"I think I can manage that all right - even if I have to take an axe."

"Oh! I don't think you have enough experience yet to go north as a boundary rider."

"You give me a chance and see," I pleaded.

"Nothing doing. Good day."

At the same time the next day I again applied.

"I told you yesterday that there's nothing doing."

The next day I applied at the same time - with the same

result. The following day I was snarled at and ordered to keep out. At the sixth successive application I won.

"Confound you! I'll send you to get rid of you," the poker-faced man actually howled.

Among pastoral companies there then was a system in vogue to send young men to cattle and sheep stations, paying their fares, which were deducted from their wages, and repaid if they remained twelve months. As a man who had been legally bound to an employer for three years, I discovered in Australia the admirable custom of being sacked or leaving a job at a moment's notice. Oh! Here was democracy! Here was freedom!

The hotel manager smiled, and gave me advice with the pay envelope. The French-Australian chef swore, then wept, at losing a pupil, and sent out a coffee royal order which did not contain vermouth and rum - only beer. He gave me a hamper which must have cost the hotel a fiver, and, standing beside the poker-faced secretary, watched me slide out of Adelaide as though I were Sydney Carton riding away to the guillotine.

The jumbled hills of the Barrier Range were my first glimpse of the Australia which was to become the passion of my life. Broken Hill was then in its heyday, but I saw little of it, for I arrived at 8 o'clock, and left for Wilcannia, on the Darling, at 10 o'clock, on the box of a Cobb and Co.'s coach.

The driver knew and recited every poem written by the immortal Lawson.. His father drove coaches stuck up by the Kelly heroes. The coach, the vast, flat saltbush plain, beyond the horizon of which, as the day wore on, the hills sank like blue-black rocks, the immensity of this world of space, all spelt romance. The grooms at the horse changes, set 20 miles apart, were the real thing in Texas gunmen, although their clothes recalled bargees. The Toper Hotel, situated at the edge of the mulga lands, at which we arrived at dusk, was the original saloon at Dead Man's Gulch.

All that night, and until 2 o'clock the next afternoon, I rode the box of a jolting coach. Without sleep on the train, without sleep on the coach, the people of Wilcannia witnessed the arrival of a stunned youth. Not then did I know that in the Queen City of the West there were nearly twenty hotels, a very fine gaol, and a brewery, and that on Saturday nights one had to elbow one's way along the sidewalks.

Lashed to the seat of a buckboard, I left with the Wanaaring mail at 4 o'clock. Every time the horses stopped, I slept; every time they started, an iron-hard elbow was dug into my ribs to awaken me.

At midnight I was informed that here "I got off." Together with the Tearle Station mail and my suitcase, I fell off. The buckboard vanished in the darkness of a calm, hot night. The ground beneath my feet was yet warm, soft, sandy. No feathered bed ever was so welcomed.

And then a voice, drawling and compassionate, said: "Better get up and have some breakfast. If you stops there the sun'll burn the whiskers off you." The man who had spoken was to be my breaker and my maker.

2

To One-Spur Dick I owe a debt never to be repaid. Here on Tearle Station, western New South Wales, set down in the middle of the night by a mail driver, blurred into obscurity by lack of sleep, it had been One-Spur Dick whose drawling injunction to "Get up before the sun burns the whiskers off you," which awoke me to this new world.

Fully dressed, I arose from the soft sand beside the track

where I had collapsed like a pricked balloon into unconsciousness on alighting from the buckboard, to observe four men regarding me with amused eyes.

"Another parcel post bloke," one observed as though I were a beetle.

"Yass. English or Orstralian?"

"What are you, young feller?" inquired a one-eyed, thick-set, whiskery, sun-blackened man, dressed in blue shirt and moleskin pants, and wearing but one draggled spur.

"English," was my reply, then to gaze around me at the stone built bungalow house and the skirting corrugated iron buildings.

I slept part of the time I ate breakfast, and retained a dim memory of being escorted by the whiskery man to the men's hut in which I slept that day and night. The following morning, with the others, I presented myself to the manager for orders, and was told to assist the tinsmith. He was making two 4,000 gallon iron water tanks, and my work was to hold a hammer-head against which he riveted the curved iron sheets. It was mid-February and the sun was trying.

For two weeks I lived in close contact with Blue Evans, a 14 stone Welshman; Mick Conolly, a tall, flashily dressed stockman; Sam No. 2, a half-caste who shot galahs on the wing with a 0.22 bore rifle; the Wandering Burglar, wife of one Charlie Monger, and the mother of eight children, only two of whom were not half-castes; and One-Spur Dick, then the bullock driver.

Never before had I met such people; never have I met their like beyond outer Central Australia. Their language was terrific, saved from crudeness by its artistry. Their leg-pulling was severe; tempers quick, and fists hard. Their hearts were big, their humour dry, and the standard of general knowledge surprisingly high.

The tanks having been made, I was sent as offsider to One-Spur Dick to fetch in the winter wood supply, with fourteen bullocks drawing an ordinary wagon; and during the morning of the first day, when we then were among dense mulga, it occurred to me how would I get back to the homestead were my companion to drop dead.

The one-eyed driver - he had lost an eye in a fight at Mt. Brown - sternly repressed a leering grin and commanded me to use my brain. For half-an-hour I endeavoured to do this, my cursed imagination producing vivid pictures of a lost man dying of thirst. Eventually admitting my failure to use my brain, Dick said with grave deliberateness:

"I like a bloke who arsts questions. I got no time for a bloke, be he new chum English or new chum Australian, wot thinks he knows everything and arsts no questions to hide his ignorance. Now you see them wheel tracks? You go and stand in one of 'em with your back towards the wagon."

Having done as he ordered, he said: "Now shut your eyes. Got 'em shut."

Receiving my affirmative answer, he said:

"Now you keep your eyes shut and walk in that track for twenty minutes, and you'll knock out your mosquito brain against the store wall."

Here is an illustration typifying the character of this great man. When assured that in me he had a willing pupil, nothing was too much trouble to explain, and nothing was ever explained unless accompanied by a lesson which could not be forgotten. He taught me how to bake a damper, how to kill and dress a sheep, how to make horse hobbles, how to ride in the Australian fashion, and how to use my fists. He demonstrated that neither bullocks nor mules nor horses understood pure English or pure Chinese, but would pull like the devil when addressed with a proper mixture of all the oaths of both nations, topped up, as it were, by the worst oaths favoured by the Afghans.

"Here, have a go at 'em," he urged on our first 120 miles trip to Broken Hill with wool. He stopped the team. I took the eight-foot whip. He climbed to the top of the mountain of wool and pretended to go to sleep.

I called to the team of sixteen mules. The leaders looked around with bored curiosity. Twice I almost managed to choke my self to death with the whip. When I managed to lash the shafters, they pulled the wagon forward, I put the front part of the team one and all yawned. Three times I fell flat, tripped by the whip. I played on a simple variation of two bad words, but they were seasoned, hackneyed, British oaths, and of no earthly use. The team was enjoying a quiet siesta whilst I became very hot.

And then, over them, rushing outward through the quiet bush, roared a flood of language of such artistry as to be unequalled in any other part of the world. The effect was electrical. Sixteen animals, a huge table top wagon and ten tons of wool abruptly sped towards Broken Hill. As the wagon passed, I managed to grab an eye-bolt at its rear, and, despite entanglement with the whip, kept with it.

Without using the single near-side rein - Dick scorned such aid excepting when negotiating the steep hills of the Barrier Range - my chief pulled up the astounded mules as easily as he had started them - with his voice.

Eventually, having learned the language, I got on better. My memories of Dick are still vivid. I see him trudging beside the team, an old felt hat set back on his head, the one clanking spur, the long-handled whip over his shoulder with the thong trailing along the ground making a snake track. The whip he seldom used; it was seldom necessary. Swags unrolled on the ground, my head towards the fire which he carefully fed to keep a good light, I read aloud for hours Sexton Blakes, and the work of Stanley Weyman and Charles Darwin. Unable to read, his memory was prodigious, his appetite for any quality of food contained between covers insatiable, equalled only by that for beer when that kind of food was available.

Three trips we made to Broken Hill that winter, going south with a mountain of wool, returning north with a mountain of cased rations and fencing wire. The two leaders and the two shafters were allegedly broken in. The twelve body mules we broke in on the track. Twice I saw a pair of hoofs presented one foot beyond my face; once the sleeve of my dungaree jacket was torn away.

Towards the end of the trip the team was settling down, but the end of the third trip dictated a change of employment. It so happened that camping a night on the Wilcannia Common, coming back we failed to find two of the mules the next morning and were compelled to go on without them. I was sent to the Common Ranger to report the matter, and, having done this, I found the team drawn up outside the Globe Hotel and poor Dick very drunk within.

"Best thing to do is for us to plant him on top of the load, and for you to drive out of town and camp," said the publican. "You can't pull the team out here."

I thought that the best thing he could have done was not to permit Dick to become drunk. I was not a mule driver. I was a new chum. There were four mules which even then required our united efforts to unharness and harness.

So they shifted the load a little and made a hole in the top of

the mountain into which Dick was dumped; and, picking up the whip, I whistled to the team, uttered some of the Esperanto of the bush, and away we went.

Now we were bound for the Tearle outstation, to reach which it was necessary to cross the dry Parroo River a few miles out of town. There were two ways of crossing it; over the bridge, or by taking the track twisting down one bank and up the other. Twice before we had come this way; and, because Dick feared that the team would be frightened by the bridge rumble, he had chosen the twisting river bed track.

Discovering that I was getting along famously, knowing that this part of the Common was as bare of feed as a city street, I determined to push on until Dick regained consciousness. And now there was the white-painted long bridge making me debate which crossing I would take, and before I had made any decision the leaders reached the bridge.

Now they were on it, their hoofs sounding hollowly on the loose flooring. One of the body mules snorted. Now the shafters, now the wagon itself was on the bridge. I clung to the brake handle, praying that if they bolted they would not draw the wagon over the bridge on my side. And then, when halfway across, Dick roared, and the team instantly stopped.

I looked up. I saw his face peering over the edge of the mountain. His frozen eyes were gazing down, down beyond me, down to the river bed fifty feet below the bridge. The team was halted. Several of the mules were snorting like donkeys. The leaders looked likely enough to turn and rush back. Dick's voice was a faint whisper.

"Go on - get 'em off the bridge," he implored, incapable of any other thought, mentally and physically frozen with horror - in a place where angels would fear to tread. Six feet either aids of the wagon was a fifty-foot drop.

We would have been across the bridge ere then had he not come to. I was now as windy as poor Dick enduring a nightmare, but with unmeasured luck, although three of the team began to plunge, the leaders pulled straight as did the shafters.

Once clear of the bridge, Dick stopped the team and very nearly fell down off the load. In Chinese he described my ancestors back for five hundred years, danced with rage, and rushed away to return to the hotel.

Thereabouts was no place to camp even if I did successfully manage to unharness the team, and, even had I done this, it would have been impossible to harness them in the morning, new chum as I was. There was nothing else for it but to accept the gamble and push on to the outstation single-handed, despite two bad creeks to cross.

Babies, drunken men and new chums seldom come to harm.

Taking that team on to the outstation I thought was something heroic, but the fellows could not see it. All they could visualise was Dick looking over the edge of the ration mountain down to the dry bed of the river.

But to One-Spur Dick I owed a thorough breaking-in, the acquisition of a new and up-to-date foreign language, and the opal gouging fever.

3

The six months spent under the tutorship of One-Spur Dick did more for me than to remove the rawness of a new chum. The constant travelling over those 120 miles between Tearle Station and Broken Hill banished forever any longing for city life, delayed for twenty years the final and compulsory settling down. After the one terrible period of nostalgia, hastened by the letter from a woman in England in reply to mine describing the falsity of the immigration literature we had studied together, a letter asking to be released from her vows of fidelity, I found a mental peace never to be described with mere words. In me was born a passionate love for the Australian bush which will burn until the end, a love stronger than love of family, so strong that even now it threatens to cl aim me.

In this respect I am not singular by a long shot. Cities bore me. Farming country leaves me cold. Neither cities nor the farming country is Australia, the real Australia adequately described only by the immortal Lawson. It has been written by literary folk that the great Australian novel will come out of the cities of Australia. Impossible! There are a dozen Melbournes in

the world, a dozen Sydneys. There is only one Australia, a virgin, living Australia unspoiled by brick and cement, axe and plough, the Australia which can reveal a thousand facets of beauty, and never fail to reveal at least one.

Lucky the man to be broken in by One-Spur Dick who, when lounging beside the camp fire amidst the mulga or on the horizonwide saltbush plains around Broken Hill, would recite Lawson's poems, name the glittering stars which belonged to us, teach a simple philosophy born of that soft, warm earth and soft, bright sky. And, too, lucky the man to live and to labour with Jack Musgrove from Tasmania, who drank hard, laughed hard, fought hard, and worked hard; when one is feeling the old accustomed world of dependence and bodily comforts and habit slipping away far beyond the skyline of a new world of independence, selfreliance astounding interest, tolerance and content.

"Let's go opal gouging for a spell," urged Jack Musgrove, six feet three inches in his socks - when he wore them, which was seldom - three feet wide, a face like Atlas, and a fist like a ham.

Go! It was impossible to do anything else. We demanded our cheques at five o'clock one afternoon, and could not wait until the morning to start away. Twenty-one miles we tramped that night with our heavy swags, water bags, and billies, and Marie Lloyd clinging to Jack's neck.

The real Marie Lloyd would have loved Jack Musgrove as much as did that black and white cat who rode him like Sinbad's Old Man of the Sea. Jack's love affairs provided a mine of doubtful anecdote, which he would relate with winks and nods and thumbjerks after the great Marie's inimitable fashion.

And wherever Jack went, the cat was sure to go.

At this time White Cliffs had passed its high water mark of production. Like Mt. Brown and Tibooburra, the goldfields not far distant from it, it was a poor man's show, never being taken over by powerful companies. In the nineties men went to White Cliffs, dug out pockets of opals, sold their stuff to German buyers, rushed to Sydney, Melbourne, or Adelaide, for a space lived at the millionaire rate, and then went back to dig up a second pocket; to repeat the process and find a third, and even a fourth pocket.

Naturally, that was before my time. It would be! Twenty six pounds an ounce was paid for some of it, and when Queen Victoria declined to wear opals and British fashion slavishly followed suit, the harems of India provided a fresh market. Save for investment, I see no beauty in diamonds, and but little in rubies and sapphires in comparison with the flickering green and blue and yellow and red fires in the heart of an opal. Neither did Jack Musgrove. He had opals in a shammy hung from his neck which he loved almost as much as he loved Marie Lloyd, stones with which he would not part when years later he tramped for work, the soles of his boots gone, his gunny sack empty, and with not one flake of tobacco to press into a cold and empty pipe. Opals fascinate. Diamonds are to be bought and sold, fought for, and murdered for their money value. Opal lights remind me of sunsets, of flowers, of the hope of Paradise. Diamonds recall to mind, ice, and hate, and a knife in the back.

At White Cliffs it was as easy to start opal gouging as to pay a Chinaman five pounds for a pack of cards, and receive from him five shillings for every card "got out" in solitaire. From an urbane celestial we hired picks and shovels and windlass gear. For a sheer gamble, opal gouging stands alone. You may strike a pocket just under the surface or take over an abandoned shaft and strike a pocket after continuing it downward one foot.

We selected a site not far distant from an old partly wrecked hut which we utilised as a camp windbreak. I used to wonder what kind of a man built it and first lived in it, and at night I used to fancy hearing the heavy tread of men going and returning to it; always going away steadily, often returning slowly wearisome, sometimes returning at the double announcing the making of a strike.

The weather was hot, being the month of March, but what cared we for heat and flies and the dust-storms? Were we expected to work for others as we worked for ourselves, Musgrove, I am sure, would have started a revolution. He sank the shaft.

I laboured at the windlass. Marie Lloyd lay stretched in a little stone-made sun-shelter erected specially for her, from which at times she would saunter to the shaft edge and look down to be assured that Jack was not asleep, or gone on a journey.

Down went the shaft, foot by foot. Father Ryan came one morning to ask how we fared. He knew more of geology than all the geologists in Australia. Round-faced, thick-set, bespectacled, he lived among his flock which included every living soul whether he be Christian or heathen, or had no religion at all.

"Don't be swearin' so down there," he commanded Jack, then in the bowels of the earth. "Don't be sayin' who the, what the! Just say, Who is that? Brevity be the soul of wit, me bhoy. I always fine a man a penny for every swear word I hear him say."

"Oh - is that you, Father Ryan," Musgrove shouted. "Good day to you, Father. Hey! Arthur! slip across to the hut and dig out a fiver from me swag. Give it to the reverend gentleman on account of me swearing fines."

"Afterwards, me son," Father Ryan requested me. To Jack: "An' how's things down there? Any luck, yet? Come on up and let me have a looksee."

I wound up Jack in the bucket, and Jack lowered Father Ryan foot by foot whilst he examined every square yard of the four walls.

"Ye might be finding a trifle by going deeper. But it's not impressed that I am," he said, when he finally reappeared. "Well what the---!" remarked Jack conversationally. To which Father Ryan chuckled and said:

"I think I'll be after reminding you of that fiver, me son.

It won't be long before you will owe me another, I much fear." So we laboured sinking a new shaft, and when we had sunk it about ten feet there arrived at our camp two new chums. They were dressed in ready-made suits, starched collars, and cloth caps. They had left their suit cases at one of the hotels, hired a pick and a shovel, wanted to dig somewhere, and would bring out a windlass the next day. Where could they dig?

We were eating morning lunch in the shade of the old hut. They accepted a pannikin of tea, and yet were anxious to get to work. Musgrove suggested the hardest piece of ground within fifty miles - a place but a few feet beyond the hut doorway, beaten and tramped into almost solid rock by countless boots.

They went to it.

"Bet you a quid the bloke takes off his collar within two minutes," implored my companion, referring to the one who began to use the pick.

It was quickly evident that those two were miners. That they hailed from Yorkshire was evident, too. That they had arrived at Adelaide on the Orsova they told us.

I won my bet, for the pick man did not take off his collar before the expiration of the time limit. He loosened a square of earth and his mate shovelled it away. Still wearing his collar he began on the second layer of rock-hard earth.

Then his pick crashed through what sounded like a bottle. A roar from Musgrove stopped the pick descending again into the "bottle". As though we were financially interested we showed them how to lift a pocket of wonderful opal, for which a German buyer paid £377.

So stunned by their fortune, they left White Cliffs without even thanking us, but they recovered a little in Adelaide, from which city they sent both of us ten pounds; said they were leaving by the Orsova on her return trip, and wished us luck.

"Blast opal gouging?" Musgrove shouted when sure Father Ryan was not within hearing. "Let's get back to the station."

"Do me", I agreed. "I'm wanting a holiday badly."

4

Have you ever noticed that the sum total of a man's life may be expressed by one short and simple word? Take the failure -

Mr If. If he had not done this or that, he would have been such and such. Then there is the man, stolid and solid, both physically and financially. Mr Yes is unable to bow, he is so solid and stolid. He is the antithesis of Mr No, poor and starving, weak chinned and watery-eyed. The difference between these two is that Mr Yes never accepted the negative answer, and Mr No could never do ought else but accept it.

Success in life depends wholly upon the ability to accept the little word "no", or the ability not to accept it. Were I a normally intelligent person, I would have grasped this profound truth when, as described earlier, I got my first bush job because I would not take "no" for an answer. After a further exhibition of this gift of stubbornness which, of course, was rewarded with success, I deserve logging every Monday morning for not making the refusal to accept "no" an unbreakable habit.

When Strike-a-Light George told me there was a vacancy on the vermin fence surrounding a pastoral company's holdings of about one and a half million acres, I said that that job was mine. And because I said it, it was so.

The manager was short and plump and fiery, but kindly enough he pointed out that my bush experience was far short of that necessary for the work for which I asked.

The next day when I applied, he said:

"I told you yesterday why I won't give you the job."

The third day, he said:

"It is no use bothering me."

The seventh day he yelled:

"Oh, curse and doubly curse the fools who permit new chums to enter the country! You'll go and get bushed or the camels will roll on you, and I'll have to send out search parties, and waste my time and write reports! Get out! Get out, I tell you! Go to the job and be damned! If ever I see you alive again, I'll sack you."

Strike-a-Light was the only strong expression ever used by the tall gaunt man who showed me the 78-mile section of rabbit fence I was to "ride". His section of about eighty-miles was further on, and, each fully equipped with a riding camel and a pack beast for transport, it was not with regret that we parted. Strike-a-Light was born tired, and he will never die because he will be too tired to do so. He was so tired that he loathed cooking, abhorred washing and reading. In one respect only was he energetic. He never grew tired of grousing. He groused at the most beautifully browned and cooked damper ever I made. When I asked him what was wrong with it, he said:

"I always like my damper perfectly rolled."

Having parted from Strike-a-Light, I faced the Bush alone, thrown entirely on my own initiative, beyond policemen and ambulances, sign posts and water taps. After but a slight apprenticeship to the Australian bush, I was about to be tried before Judge Solitude and a jury of two camels, prosecuted by Mr I-told you-so, and defended by Mr Pride. The trial occupied, to my credit I still think, fifteen months.

Day after day and never a human voice but my own. Night after night lying on a stretcher beneath a mulga tree, watching the stars and the moon and the clouds, if any; imagination stirred by the wailing howls of a dingo pack, nerves shocked by the terrible scream of a curlew. Fighting a way along the fence in a dust storm, listening for camel bells to ascertain which direction they took when freed, fearful always of possible accident which, in those conditions, would have but one result. Little matters, one and all, to be laughed at today.

I came to regard the Bush as the blacks do. To me it was, and still is, a watching spirit waiting - waiting for a lonely man to make one slip to claim him for its own. Then I regarded the Bush as a dreadfully malignant spirit; but with the passage of the years, it gradually changed to one of placid maternity, calmly waiting to take me back, whispering in the trees, singing above the sand:

"Dust thou wast, and dust thou shalt become."

The loneliness was less felt when I again began to practise novel writing, and still less when I bought for ten shillings a wall-eyed cattle dog called Hool-em-up. He had formerly belonged to a man who had a passion for dog fights, and at every opportunity urged this animal to violence. One day, however, the owner of a kelpie sheep dog overheard the cattle dog's owner sooling him to fight, resulting in the dog owners themselves fighting, with ill results to the sool-em-on-er.

To obviate further unpleasantness, the sool-em-on-er rechristened the cattle dog Hool-em-up, and consequently, it was only necessary for him to shout: "Come here," and yell, "Hoolem-up" to precipitate a dog fight.

That dog might have been good at heeling cattle, but he was not good at catching rabbits or kangaroos. Yet what he lost in "toe" he made up in determination. Once started he went on until the rabbit reached a burrow or a hollow log, or the kangaroo reached Queensland or South Australia.

Always did he scout ahead, unless chasing something, which was about twenty times in the hour. He would suddenly stop to glare at something with his one eye, his one ear pricked - the other the owner of a licked dog had shot off - his tail stiff and his hackles raised. Then off he would go with murder in the timbre of his yelps and quite inconvenienced by the three-cornered jacks in his feet. But never did he bring anything back from the chase.

Where the fence crossed the dry Paroo, that alleged river was two miles wide. Nothing, of course, grew on it other than spindly, spiny rubbish. The ground was cracked like mosaic work - cracks many feet in depth and sometimes six inches in width.

Heaven help the man caught there when the flood waters, instead of rolling along, rise up from the bowels of the earth.

And on this country, Hool-em-up must needs chase an iguana which, to this day, I swear was yards in length. When the dog first sighted the land alligator, he was ahead. With interest, two animals and a man watched the race, an interest which increased when the iguana, instead of climbing a fence post, or ducking down one of the cracks, left the fence and circled back, passing us about one hundred yards distant.

The camels stopped, and I waved my hat and cheered. Hool-em up ran well, but the iguana took matters calmly - until it hit the fence from which it rebounded with astonishing velocity.

No longer calm, with Hool-em-up in sight of his only victory, the iguana ran along the fence towards us. At their approach the camels became frightened. The pack camel charged between the riding camel and the fence, leaving thus her mate to meet the charge. Like a ray of dark green light, the iguana thought only of escape from the slavering jaws but two feet astern. It appeared as though, when yet several feet away, the reptile sprang off the ground to reach the riding camel's near shoulder. There was no passage of time between then and when it was clawing its way up to me to reach the top of my head.

Followed an earthquake. It seemed like coming down from a balloon and seeing the four legs of each camel spread outward as though they were dun-coloured beetles. On awakening, I found myself on the wrong side of the fence; and, enclosed in a circumference of one hundred feet, was scattered everything which those two camels habitually carried. They were not in sight, but Hool em-up was - peacefully sleeping in the shade cast by a fence post.

What a mess! Here in a ten by ten miles paddock in February! Fortunately, I knew that the vermin fence made the southern boundary of the paddock, and that in the south-east corner was a dam and two stockmen in their hut.

It was then that counsel at my trial began argument. Mr I-told-you-so rose to say that I was an absolute failure. Then Mr Pride arose to say that failure was not yet proved, Judge Solitude, like Brer Rabbit said nothing.

So, most rashly, with the undamaged water bag filled from one of the water drums, I began to track those camels. By dusk I had followed them barely six miles, and would not have reached that far had not the country bordering the Paroo been soft and sandy.

The night was spent on a clay-pan that recalled a doctor's advice to sleep on a billiard table to cure insomnia. The fool! Daylight the next morning, hungry but fed with hope of catching up to the camels beyond the next of the eternal sand ridges, on I went, noting how Hool-em-up appeared to be running fast this day, yet never losing sight of the tracks.

At about two o'clock, when I was at fault in hard mulga country, the manager drove up in his buckboard accompanied by a black boy driving two extra horses. Looking at me as a doctor might look at a dying victim, he said:

"Better get up."

Relating what had happened, I pointed out where last I had seen the camels' tracks.

"Oh! you followed them to there," he said, wonderingly. "I thought you were just walking about admiring the scenery."

The black boy he ordered to hobble the spare horses and then ride to a clump of cabbage trees I had pointed out, from which he was to track and bring back the camels. No longer angry, the manager assisted in making a fire on which the billy was boiled.

The black boy presently returned with the camels, and we all went back to the scene of the disaster, where, after a little while, everything again became orderly. When he was about to drive off, I said to the manager:

"I suppose this means the sack?"

"I have never sacked a man in my life," was his reply. "When I want to get rid of a useless man I set him to work scrubbing floors. Just now the floors at the homestead don't need scrubbing." With a twinkle in his eyes he drove away.

And Judge Solitude smiled at the prisoner.

5

In the far north-west of New South Wales, there is a sheet of water, created by heavy rains, named Moonamurtee Lake, and, as evaporation in that country accounts for five feet of water every year, this beautiful lake goes dry after a lengthy rainless period.

Right on the west shore two Chinamen used once to occupy the hut, and they made a garden in which they grew vegetables to supply the diggings twenty miles away. Eventually, one Chinaman hanged himself, or was hanged by the other - I forget which - and the garden quickly was claimed by the native tobacco bush which there grew prolifically.

Within a furlong of the hut runs a vermin fence which I rode for nearly a year; and, because of the fish in the water and the countless water birds on its surface, the lake and the hut became a favourite camp, despite the latter's reputed haunting. Usually arriving in the late afternoon, the camels would be unloaded outside the hut door, and then freed to hobble to the water and take in about eight gallons each before making their way to the neighbouring sand dunes among which grew the delectable pig-weed and other herbage. For camels will not eat grass.

During the red hot weeks of summer, the first task, after unloading the three camels, would be to gather wood for the billy and the camp oven, erect the stretcher and the mosquito net over it on the side of the hut farthest from the water, and then rush for the lake. A swim, and then dressed in clean pyjamas, one would be wonderfully refreshed after a fortnight during which the daily ration of washing water could not exceed two pints.

The reason for sleeping on the far side of the hut was logical enough, for the following morning I would creep into the iron building, and from the living-room shoot several ducks with a double-barrel shot gun; the ducks and the water hens being so accustomed to the place that they would be feeding at early morning along the lake edge within fifteen yards range.

In mid-March, the first evening of my stay at this fine camp the bunk was fixed outside the hut, the camels were contentedly feeding, the fish lines were set, and the damper and salt meat cooked by sundown. With the incessant quackings and honking of the water birds drifting in through the open window, I wrote for several hours before slipping under the net on to the bunk, with matches and rolled cigarettes.

Lying peacefully, with no covering over me, placidly smoking a cigarette, without warning a red hot dagger was thrust into my ankle. I smacked the part with my hand, and struck a match, and found, still very much alive, a red-brown scorpion almost the size of a man's palm.

Experts tell us that scorpion stings are not fatal, and I do not presume to argue with them further than to state that to a man whose blood is in ill condition through living on soda bread and alkaline-filled water, and whose menu does not contain green vegetables, a scorpion sting is sometimes fatal without any outside or subsidiary conditions to make it so.

Naturally, I did not have with me an antidote, nor did I have any antiseptic. With all speed I got the slush lamp going inside the hut, and with a blunt knife gashed across the stung part deeply. Into the wound made, I poured the blue-black tea from the billy, and then plugged it with a wad of tobacco before bandaging it with a torn up shirt.

Doubtless this procedure would be frowned upon by a modern surgeon to whom life would be incomplete without a case of knives and a range of antiseptics, but I have known of snake venom being defeated by nicotine, although I must confess that the application of strong tea has not been proved efficacious or otherwise in surgery. It is when a man is placed out of sight of a hospital, beyond telephones and policemen, when his food supplies are low and tobacco down to the last ounce, that he will try anything to prevent incapacity for incapacity in itself can be more fatal than ten cobra bites.

Unable to sleep, I heated water as day was breaking, removed the tobacco wad and scalded the wound. I know an aboriginal who, when his foot was bitten by a tiger snake, thrust that foot into a camp fire and held it there, but he was no more stoical than I was, and no more frightened. The colour of the ankle would have perturbed Zeno himself.

At breakfast, I had ample opportunity to survey the situation. The camels were gone; I could not hear their bells. I was 26 miles from the homestead, and knew not the country between the lake and the diggings. At that time, I could not expect the chance arrival of motor car explorers.

All that day, I nursed a blue-black leg, and listened for the camel bells; three or four times crawling to the lake on hands and knees with the billy can. Towards evening, the ankle had become the size of the thigh. No sleep that night, or the following day; pain up to my armpit throbbing as though a rope ran down through my body and was incessantly tugged by a devil. I would have been less wretched had I had tobacco.

The third night the moon rose about eleven o'clock, and shortly afterwards I imagined I heard the camel bells, having for so long strained my ears to hear them. Ten minutes later, I realized that it was not imagination. On the far side of the lake, the camels were coming back to water, and even now I was in no better state, for it was out of the question to crawl the full mile round the lake's edge.

Gradually the bells became louder. They rang with the rhythmical timing of travelling animals, and presently I under-stood that they were coming back to the place before the hut to drink. There the shore surface was hard, whilst at many other places the surface was soft. Fear of being bogged dictated a familiar watering place.

When they emerged from the surrounding scrub to hobble across the sandflats, I was at the riding saddle clutching the riding camel's noseline. Three huge putty-coloured shapes finally stood drinking at the edge of the silvery water, and in my white pyjamas I crawled to them calling endearing names, hoping they would not take fright at the strange white beetle, and rear on their hind legs to bring down their ponderous forefeet upon it. When a man is up against it, he will chance anything.

"Buller! Buller, you old scoundrel!" I cried tremblingly; and, on reaching his forefeet, Buller lowered his grand old head to my level, waggled drops of water from his split upper lip, and allowed me to slip the end of the noseline over the plug drawn through a nostril. I am sure he asked:

"What the devil do you think you're doing at this time of night?"

To appreciate Buller, please visualize an old gentleman set in his habits, strong in his convictions, and emphatic in his opinions. At twelve-mile intervals along the section of fence, I had erected windbreaks at temporary camps used by many riders before me, and never could Buller be induced to pass one of them.

To him they represented a full day's work, and, being a good unionist, he struck work when arrived at one of these camps.

Unhobbling him and the two cows, I hooshed him down, slung a filled canvas waterbag from his neck, and climbed across him behind his hump, to which I clung. With the cows following, we set off for the homestead. One cross gate I opened after putting Buller to ground and crawling to it. Another was but a low one which he was persuaded to step over.

At the first of the two camps, he half-heartedly attempted to stop, but firmly I urged him on, and after a rumbling growl at this overtime, he went forward. The two cows hung back at the camp and bellowed, but he kept going, bellowing angrily back to them for attempting to mutiny at his decision. They did not stay back at the camp for long.

At eleven o'clock the next morning, we passed the second camp, and this time Buller really objected. I believe that my mastery over him was due to the fact that he was not saddled, and that his cows were not loaded with pack-saddle and gear. Of all animals, the camel is the most sagacious, and Buller appeared to know that the then procedure was very irregular but wholly necessary. We reached the gate in the vermin fence at noon, and through this gate we had to pass to reach the homestead two miles distant.

I remember hooshing him to his knees and getting off his back before the gate I had to open. Then exhaustion claimed me. I awoke as the sun was setting, my feet and one leg badly sun-blistered. Either the sun, or my body itself, had defeated the venom, for the swelling had gone down. My foot had regained its natural color, and no longer did it pain.

The two cows had wandered off to the nearest shade, but Buller all that afternoon had not stirred from beside me - which was as well, for in each of the surrounding trees were watching and impatient crows. To a wad of tobacco, blue-black tea, and a wise old gentle man, did I owe my escape from the Bunyip, the ever watching spirit of the bush.

6

According to the Lombroso school of criminology, which maintains that a criminal is born with certain physical traits - such as projecting ears, prominent brows, a protruding chin, etc. - George Bycroft was a villain of the deepest dye whose certain end would be through a trap door. He had all those physical characteristics with which villains were endowed by the great Victorian novelists.

Six feet three inches in height and massively proportioned, beetle browed and iron fisted, the stranger might as well be forgiven for shrinking when in his presence; and yet, as you shall see, George Bycroft had the tender heart of a swooning woman.

For several years, he and a man known as The Midnight Mail - a sobriquet earned by his preference for carrying his swag during the night - drove two camel teams from Kyle station, near Mount Brown, to Broken Hill with the wool clip. Each man's team comprised twenty-two camels which drew a table-top wagon carrying a mountain of wool.

After the first trip one spring, The Midnight Mail fell sick, and George Bycroft, knowing of my breaking-in by One-Spur Dick, suggested to the manager that I take the sick man's place.

"But," I objected, "I may be able to drive mules across the Paroo bridge when up against it, and I know something of pack camels, but when it comes to pushing twenty-two camels ahead of ten or twelve tons of wool I'd fall down on the job."

"That's the worst of your Englishmen," Bycroft roared - his normal voice was a bellow. "You're either Know-alls or Shrinking Violets. Now, look! We puts the humpies in here and we drives 'em for ten days before we strikes the grades of the range. For ten days they don't want driving. All they wants is flogging. If they bolts - well, all the better. The quicker they gets there. Anyways, they'd sooner sleep than bolt. They're always sooners. Sooner do anything than work."

"Well, I'm telling you I know nothing about team camels."

"You'll know all about them when we gets back. I'll do the camel hunting and you can do the cooking. Come on, now. Never let the world beat you. Never let old One-

Spur Dick know that one of his lads turned up his toes at a few measly camels."

The reference to One-Spur Dick banished further hesitation. If there was any man's respect I desired to retain, it was him.

The empty wagons were drawn up outside the woolshed and the loading proceeded whilst Bycroft and I laid out on the ground the forty-four sets of harness placed just where each camel would be "hooshed" down between the long chain lines.

Being the cook of the outfit, it was my task not only to draw rations for six weeks, but to kill three sheep and salt the mutton. And, too, early on the morning of our departure I placed two live ration sheep in the crate slung from the rear of one wagon.

I was given a man to offside for a mile or so, and when Bycroft had gained a half-mile start, I whistled to the team as I had once whistled to mules, cracked the long-handled fourteen-foot whip with a little luck, and got the team off the mark with the offsider - an experienced bullock driver - straight-ening them up on the far side.

After the first day, the journey became governed by routine. As neither had a watch, Bycroft would arouse me before dawn, timing by the stars. When day broke, we had eaten breakfast, and, mounted on the chaff-fed stock horse which followed his wagon all day, he would set off for the hobbled camels whilst I packed and stowed away the camp gear. It would be 12 o'clock usually when we stopped for lunch, the camels lying down in their harness and placidly chewing their cud for an hour. Then on again until sunset, when the teams would be freed to wander at will.

While I would be cooking the tea, Bycroft would tether out the two ration sheep. After a few days they would drink water out of a bucket, and gladly accept a ration of chaff. Within a week they became quite tame, eating damper and brownie crusts and potatoes, and would muzzle at our pockets for these dainties.

A week was generally spent at the West Camp; Broken Hill, unloading the wool into motor trucks which trans-shipped it to the railway, and, that completed, bringing out tons of cased rations, and flour and wire and corrugated iron, and tar and paints. All this unloading and loading would be supervised by Bycroft, who took especial care with the loading which is an art acquired only after long practice.

When leaving the Hill we had about six pounds only of salted mutton, and the night we camped at Stevens Creek I mentioned the fact to Bycroft.

"Better kill one of them ration sheep tonight," he said carelessly. "I'll hold the lamp for you, being as it's dark."

He had already tethered the sheep, and they were picking up the last of their ration of chaff when we approached them with the lamp and the killing knives.

"Which one shall it be?" I asked.

"Oh, any one will do. Take this one."

When I went to throw the sheep, it uttered a joyful baa and sprang at me to muzzle my hand for dainties, and for the life of me I could not get on with the job. No, it was impossible. I realised that I was a sappy-hearted sook, and taking the lamp from the most hardened-looking criminal in Australia, I gave him the knives and told him to do the awful work.

It was then I came to know that Lombroso and his school of criminologists were a pack of nit-wits, for George Bycroft looked at me ashamedly, grinned sheepishly, shook his head and confessed that if I offered him fifty pounds he couldn't cut the throat of "that bleedin' trick of a sheep."

"But one of us has to do it," I protested. "We will want mutton the day after tomorrow. Do you mean to tell me you can't kill a sheep - and you an Australian teamster?"

"I could kill all the sheep in the flaming country bar them two." he averred. "Anyway, it ain't my job. You're the cook. It's your job. You get on with it, or it'll be morning before we get to bed."

We argued the matter for half an hour, the sheep bunting us, and both of them yelling for dainties, and we then went back to the wagons and our beds each grumbling at the other's squeamishness.

Fortunately, the next night we camped at a dam at which also was camped a droving outfit, and with the boss drover we exchanged one of our sheep for his, whereupon Bycroft, to show how hard-hearted he was, killed the drover's sheep without a tremor.

George was the king of teamsters. When I got into difficulties, he would halt his team and walk back to lend me a hand, and show me a hundred and one little points of the game. He was one of the few men I have known who never grumbled or lost his temper no matter what the provocation. I have seen him run up and down the long line of camels, his great whip cracking like a machine gun, his roaring voice vying with the roaring camels tugging frantically at their tremendous load.

In a wide creek his wagon became bogged to the axles. When it was seen that his team could not shift it, we yoked my twenty two animals ahead of him. Forty-four camels could not shift that huge, now inert, mass. We were digging the clay from before the wheels when a twenty-six bullock team arrived at the crossing; and, after a conference, the twenty-six bullocks were yoked, ahead of the forty-four camels.

Three drivers and the bullocky's offsider abruptly became yelling, flogging, demented devils. The extraordinary team got down to the strain. The bullocks were magnificent. They pushed into their heavy yokes with bellies almost to ground - and then fell on their noses when the shafts of the great wagon were torn out.

I thought Bycroft would never stop laughing. We were occupied three days making temporary shafts with bush timber, but we got clear of the bog without unloading.

Upfield training a camel; His view from the camel dray.

THREE

Beyond The Mirage

I

Into my young blood insidiously was creeping the wanderlust. After all the money spent on me, money wasted, deliberately I turned my back on my profession, flung away the opportunities of youth, became only too anxious to hear ever more loudly and to see ever more clearly the spirit of Australia and its many alluring voices.

To observe a ridge of sandhills was to wonder what lay beyond them. To watch the shimmering mirage transforming a gibber plain into a dream of fairy islands and spires and minarets floating on a palm-fringed lake was to inflame my imagination to the point of ecstasy. Perhaps it was the sense of freedom both physically and spiritually, the knowledge that should I want to look beyond the sandhills and peer beyond the mirage, there was nothing but my two legs and a water bag to prevent me. Unlike a child bored with too many toys, unlike a man satiated with love, unlike a man lost because he has no more worlds to conquer, the man smitten with the wanderlust can never, never grow bored or satiated or lost by too much travel, too much freedom. And yet, when all is said and done, the wanderer is not free: he is enslaved by the passion to keep moving, enslaved by a mental force as strongly as his body can be enslaved by drugs. Never is he free to settle in a place and enjoy the greatest gift of all - contentment.

The development of the wanderlust in me unfortunately occurred when there did not exist the fear of unemployment. There was always a job waiting on the next station, on a farm and in a city factory. It is unlikely that such conditions ever again will exist; for it was based on a spurious prosperity brought about by almost unlimited cheap money.

As thousands did before me, and as men are still doing in these days, I asked for my cheque instead of orders one bright morning in May, and a week later an eager young man pushed a loaded bicycle out of Wilcannia.

It is surprising how much weight a bicycle will carry. It is surprising how easy it is to push a loaded bicycle. It is even more surprising to feel the joy of travelling beside one of the inland rivers - in May. One's lungs breathe an air that intoxicates; one's eyes are freshened and strengthened by the limitless carpet spread beneath the gums and the box trees, woven by the springing wild carrot, parsnip and buckbush; one's ears are appreciative of the Wild's music - fish jumping in the river, the cries of galah and cockatoo and kookaburra, swan, and pelican and crane. The crows seem to be less malevolent, the smiling bush welcomes instead of watching and waiting to pounce.

And there is ever a gamble on what the next cook will be like. Will he be generous or mean? For every cook who has turned me away with nothing but a snarl, there have been ten who gave me a "fair issue" and about three who offered me as much as I cared to take.

An outstanding character was Rainbow Harry, so named because of his love of highly colouring his dishes. He was a big man with grey eyes and a full beard as white as the moleskin trousers he wore. At our first meeting· he had me at a decided disadvantage.

He was standing on a doorstep, and the effect of this enhancement of his height above me will be understood by any salesman. The cook who can look down on the applicant for tucker is placed as the great man who sits at a table set at the farthest end of a huge room.

By this time, not so foolish as to offer a cook money, I suggested to Rainbow Harry that, perchance, he could give me some flour. The request made him grow one foot taller; made his eyes stand out from his face, and his beard stand out from his chest.

"What! Flour! I can't get enough flour to feed the hands!" he shouted - to add with astonishing softness: "Give us your bag."

When he brought me about twenty lbs. of flour, I suggested that a little tea and sugar would not come amiss.

"Tea! Sugar! Think a station's got nothing else to do but feed tramps?" was the roared question, to be followed by the soft request: "Give us your bags."

Some four pounds of sugar and two pounds of tea duly appeared in my calico ration bags.

I thought of meat, for I was tired of fish.

"Stiffen the crows! D'you think I'm running an abattoirs? Think I can supply every tramp humming on me with meat?" was the shout preceding the whisper: "Give us your bag."

At least thirty pounds of uncooked mutton was handed out, and with a wink and a grin Rainbow Harry wished me adieu. It appeared that his generosity would have bankrupt any station had he not been curbed by the manager; and his loud and indignant denials of what tramps thought him to be was obviously intended for the manager's delight.

Fearing for the frame of the bicycle. I yet managed to get the load to the shearing shed one mile up the river, where in the shearers' kitchen I found the usual assortment of men resting from their labours of wandering about. There was Butch, undoubtedly understudied by Wallace Beery. During the two days I camped here he never wore anything other than trousers and singlet. He had never worn boots for years. There was Musical Treloar who played his violin by the hour - even played it whilst he tramped. There was The Man from Snowy River, who, in appearance, was a greater villain than Butch; a vast man called Pompey George; and a little, dapper, blue-jowled man named Jake the --- but what the something was I did not know till later. It was not included in the introduction.

It was Butch who told me that I need not cook this evening as dinner was ready. It was The Man from Snowy River who inquired if I was "All right" for tobacco. And it was Jake who stepped to within a few feet of me to eye me up and down most offensively. Took his time, too, like a French peasant contemplating the purchase of a cow.

"How much?" inquired Butch unsmilingly.

Jake circled me, his lips pursed, his eyes screwed into pin points.

"Come on!" urged the human gorilla. "How much? A bloke 'ud die of fright waiting for you to make up yer mind."

"Seven feet, two and a half," Jake replied at last, adding decisively: "Yes, I must add that half inch." With that he moved back to the great fire where he had been engaged in grilling a half side of mutton cut into chops and fillets. Butch also retiring, I turned to Pompey George, his measurements were much nearer to Jake's estimate than mine.

"What's he trying to guess - my height?" I demanded irritably. Pompey George was exceedingly attractive when he grinned. He said:

"No. Not your height - your drop." Observing mental sluggishness, he explained: "The little chap is Jake the Hangman. Was hangman once in England. Pulled out when he had to attend to a woman. And he can't break the habit of estimating a man's proper drop."

Here, as elsewhere when bush tramps foregather, Socialism was practised as it is preached. There was none scheming to make a fortune, or even a comfortable living out of the underdog. Despite outward appearances, these men were carefree and in many respects admirable. They made me welcome to the cooked food, as though it was my right, and provided a menu of grilled mutton and baked cod, featherweight damper and strong tea.

When packing up preparatory to pulling out, Pompey George asked if he might accompany me, and, because of his attractive smile and cleanly habits, I agreed. Despite the frosts he bathed in the river morning and night. He carried three shirts, enabling him to put on a clean one every night. I say "night" advisedly, because no self-respecting swagman would carry pyjamas.

Pompey George had one fault - always looking for a fight. Never did a man so love a fight as did he, and never was a man less capable of engineering a situation to produce cause for a fight. I came to see drovers and bullock drivers with iron-bark faces and ironstone fists on their very best behavior in his imposing presence; for a man whose height is six feet three and whose width is about a yard surely does possess an imposing presence, when assisted by yellow hair, violet eyes, and a Rock of Gibraltar chin.

"If there are any likely looking fellers in this shanty we're coming to, never you be backward in coming forward," he said, when we sighted a bush pub between the grey and red trunks of the giant gums forming a two thousand miles long avenue down which ran the river.

There were several hard, poker-faced men in the bar, but nothing happened, and, on our way again, Pompey reproached me. "You might have started something," he complained. "I haven't opened my chest for months and months."

Alternately pushing the weighted bicycle, we camped wherever we pleased. If the weather threatened, in a shearer's hut; if it were fine and cold, then beside a roaring fire on the river bank. The fish we caught and grilled on wire netting. The ducks we bought from ancient fishermen, or traded tobacco for with the blacks. The men we met - how Dickens would have loved them.

We both had plenty of money. We never stayed at an hotel longer than to take two drinks, and, at one hotel, I gave Pompey George his long desired chance. An obnoxious person called me a Pommy with extras.

But before I could get going, I was swept aside by Pompey George, sent flying out through the door. The building proceeded to rock on its foundations, and from doors and windows, and from every crack, poured the yells of men and the dust deposited by countless sandstorms. Men came out of the door one by one as though blown out by an explosion. One issued through a window bringing the frame with him. Some enjoyed it; others appeared disinterested.

Pompey's entertainment cost him three rounds of drinks and two pounds for damages.

For a week he behaved with the irresponsibility of a man

in love, and then, as wonderful day succeeded wonderful day, he gradually became his old self; quietly humorous, even tempered, sometimes pensive. For an hour or more he would gaze into the heart of a fire, without speaking one word. Now and then Latin phrases would escape him, and once he discoursed on a cricket match played in the park of an English country mansion which seemed to indicate that he was not one of the gardeners.

There was quite a number of men in the bar of a wayside hotel between Cunnamulla and Wanaaring when we entered it late one afternoon. Outside were two bullock teams and a drover's outfit. We had been there about half an hour when one of the bullock drivers who was the worse for wear deliberately upset my glass.

Here was a golden opportunity for Pompey George.

I began to discuss the subject of the spilled drink. Began is correct, for I never finished it. An iron-hard fist sent me back against the wall. Oh, Pompey, where art thou? Pompey was outside, and I got the father of a hiding, which was thoroughly deserved.

All the way to Wanaaring George grumbled and growled because I was fool enough not to have been sure he was present. As though I would have started the play if I had not been sure. When we finally parted, I took a scrub-cutting job, and heard no more of him until informed quite recently that he had fallen in Palestine. What a man!

2

I have informally chatted with a foreign royal duke, an earl, two baronets, a Prime Minister and an Attorney-General, and no one of these mighty ones had the picturesque and forcible personality possessed by Father Time.

A quandary at a road junction, a wrong choice, a walk of eight useless miles - then Father Time, in whom was epitomised the sterling qualities of the Australian sundowner. For your sun downer is utterly unlike the uncleanly English tramp and the worse American hobo. He will accept work periodically; he is ever gene rous to his fellows, and very seldom dishonest.

The road I was following led me northward towards Wilcannia, skirting the east side of the Darling, which it touched only at the apex of the greater eastward thrusting bends. The distance from bend to bend might be eight or ten miles, whilst from road into a westward bend might be anything up to six or seven miles.

Pushing the trusty bike - which required no ground feed and demanded no hunting in the morning - I was faced with the problem of choosing one of two roads when reaching a junction. Both roads indicated that an equal amount of traffic passed over them; and, consequently, it was impossible to discern which was the main track and which the subsidiary leading, most likely, to a lonely station homestead.

The surrounding country comprised box-tree flats, and a climb into one of the tallest trees failed to reveal the sweeping line of the much higher gums bordering the river. The junction formed a Y - one track going north-west and the other north-east, and because the westerly one would certainly take me to the river and water, and the easterly one probably across dry and unknown country to a dead end, I chose the former and followed it for four miles to its terminus at a motor and wagon shed on the river bank opposite a selector's homestead.

They have sown wheat in the dry bed of the Darling River and reaped an excellent harvest. They have grown amazing crops of lucerne on the bordering grey flats, but here for the first time I witnessed "The Gutter of Australia" providing dairy pasture. The river was fairly low, and along each side of the slowly-moving stream was a wide border of vivid green water-weed. The selector's cows were feeding on this weed, and now and then they would casually swim backwards and forwards across the river precisely as though they were water buffaloes.

The day was bright and cool; the scene pastoral and peaceful.

Near the house, beyond the river, a petrol engine methodically pumped water to a raised stand from which house and orchard and garden were supplied. There was no hint of poverty there. Why the selector kept his car and truck and wagon on my side of the river was because of the better track to Menindee, and he should have erected a signboard at the junction.

Down the river a flock of black ducks, almost as large and heavier than Indian Runners, were feeding busily among the weed. In the shallows stood several cranes too sleepy to fish, or waiting for the late afternoon when the small fish would become active.

I had boiled the billy, and was eating a lunch of soda bread and cold grilled perch, when round the northern bend came sweeping a large flock of teal ducks. They passed with whirring wings to settle on the water beyond the black ducks. They were the pilot birds to the strangest craft ever I have seen.

There was that about it which recalled an islander's catamaran, a Chinese junk, an outrigger and a Venetian gondola, but presently it resolved into a most ancient river prau. Athwart it, were lashed two long poles, at the extremities of which were fastened a five-gallon airtight oil drum, making the craft uncapsizable and unsinkable. Fore and aft, and on both port and starboard beams were erected short poles which suspended a bag canopy, and attached to the stern was a large wire netting cage partly submerged. In this cage the crew of the ship kept a supply of live fish. The navigator-captain-deck hand reclined beneath the canopy on an indescribable assortment of cargo, and languidly steered with a piece of packing case nailed to a sapling which served as an oar when the current threatened to beach this Dreadnought of the Darling.

My first impression of the crew of this floating home was of glistening snowfields. Observing me and the blue spiral of my camp fire, he waved a hand and began to warp his ship to the bank below me.

The selector, who was labouring with saw and hammer in the shelter of an open shed beside his house, called out:

"Good day-ee, Father Time. How's your whiskers today?" As though he were stone deaf, the mariner stepped ashore and secured his craft to a tree root with an old rusty chain. His every action was deliberate, made without haste or waste of energy, crying out the pride of the ancient in his ship and his home.

"Ain't you talkin' to-day, whiskers?" sang out the carpenter. Continuing to maintain dignified silence, Father Time produced his billycan, and with it filled with river water, and, a gunny sack slung from one broad shoulder, he made the laborious climb up the steep bank.

Arrived, he stretched his powerful body to its full height, and, in a mighty voice, roared:

"Hey, you! You unwashed son of an unwashed ---- " With my pen I can proceed no further, save to state that for fully two minutes Father Time offered his opinions of the carpenter, and the carpenter's ancestors back to the Neolithic Age. He was a master of elocution, for he never repeated himself and never twice used the oaths in his amazing vocabulary. Rare the speaker commanding such diction. He proved himself to be a seaman, an international interpreter, a blackbirder, and a London cab-driver. Then, when a proper climax was reached and the peroration ended, he turned to me with no sign of perturbation or heat in his china blue eyes. The calmness of his soul was unruffled.

One omitted to take much notice of the great naked feet, The soiled moleskin trousers, the tattered grey flannel undervest, and the incongruous brand new jacket. Hatless, the snowy hair swept back from a magnificent forehead, whilst the great snowwhite mane fell to the waist. Stunned, the carpenter offered no further comment.

"Good day," greeted Father Time in surprisingly gentle tones. "Do you mind if I boil my billy on your fire?" When squatting over the fire arranging fresh wood against his billycan, he lifted his head to indicate the selector. "His name's Redditch. He's living in luxury provided by the money his old mother stole from the likes of you and me. She kept a pub beyond Burke, and smoked cigars. When a chequeman got merry on her watered whisky, she would blow cigar smoke into his glass before filling it, and that would knock him right out, and when he came to, he would have nothing in his pockets bar the lining. Two blokes I knew she ruined their minds. When she kicked off, she left eleven thousand pounds to her son, who would have run to the police had I shot one of them ducks, being out of season. If you want to shut the mouth of a jackanapes, make public the sins of his mother - above a whisper."

Blue eyes beamed upon me. The pink skin of this centenarian - he was a hundred by the shortest estimate - matched and toned with the whiteness of his hair and beard. He looked as old and as strong as the bordering gums; as eternal as the river itself. He could have borne no other cognomen than the one given him by the selector. "I know all of 'em who lived on this river since 1845," he went on. "I seen Burke and Wills when they was camped at Menindee. I could have gone with 'em, but I knew that before long I would be arguing with Burke. Explorers! They wasn't explorers' shadows. Coming back to old Mother Redditch - the mail coaches used to stop at her pub for dinner at night, and when the travellers were sitting down at table with her husband and him over there, she would say: 'Will ye be havin' goat, or will ye take a bite of galah?' She always asked her poor husband the same question, and, of course, he always nominated the goat. And always she said: 'Indade ye won't! Ye'll be havin' galah!'"

When he had eaten, Father Time announced his intention of continuing his voyage and making port that night at the Twenty mile Point. I accompanied him down to his ship, and from his larder he pulled out a nice chunky cod, careless of the spines of several cat fish.

A grand old man, his actions were ever slow, but deliberate. The hawser he stowed with meticulous care. Gaining the poop, he settled into his lounge, and, with the oar, gently pushed the craft into the current.

3

I have no exact knowledge regarding Cockney Slater's criminal history, or of the number of his convictions for petty larceny, but I do know that he was a likeable man, a born optimist, unfailingly cheerful, and generous always in deed and thought. He never spoke ill of any man, and I am not now going to write ill of him.

Our first meeting occurred in 1911 on the road from Roma

to Charleville, Southern Queensland, and our last was in 1919 on the outskirts of Cork, Ireland, where I found him established in business as a butcher with a most capable wife to take charge of the cash box. It seems a far cry from an Australian tramp to a captaincy in the Sinn Fein army; and yet, another fellow tramp, one Pompey George, rose to be a major in the Egyptian Camel Corps.

Cockney Slater was undoubtedly a disciple of Henry's gentle grafter. He was without viciousness; he was imbued with a code of honour that dictated giving the sucker a run for his money. Picking pockets, or using other direct methods of getting rich quick, was as abhorrent to Cockney Slater as it is to the average decent citizen.

"If I had five bob I could make some Slater's Permanent Polish," he said one afternoon when we were fishing in a bend of the river a mile above Burke. "That's the stuff that gets 'em, but a man wants quick transport before putting it over."

"A permanent polish. A floor polish."
"Polish anything from a lady's shoe to a gent's bald head. Hey, what's this on my line?"

It was merely a seventeen-pounder chunky cod which quickly gave up the fight and was drawn to the bank as though it were a corn sack filled with rubbish. Of course, the fish's weight was only estimated, and I am inclined to believe our enthusiasm was responsible for at least two pounds.

"We can get sixpence a pound dead weight for this joker at any of the pubs," declared Slater. "That'll be eight and six-pence. We can shove into him another four pounds which will make it up to ten and six. Off with your clobber, and take him across the river."

"What for?" I demanded, thinking of the temperature of the water in August.

"Trade secret. Get ready while I fixes him." By this time the fish was dead. Cockney Slater removed the hook and the sinker, and tied the end of the line to the fish's jaw. The jaws he fixed wide open with a stick.

"You take him across to the other side end let him go when I sings out," were his instructions. Hugging the fish to my chest, I kicked my way across the river, Slater paying out the line. The river was high, the current strong, and the colour of the water warship grey. On the farther side I held the fish pointing to my companion in crime.

Being all set, I let go the fish and Slater ran back from the bank as fast as he could, the fish being dragged through the water quicker than ever it swam. This performance was repeated three times, when Slater judged that several pounds' weight of water had been forced into it.

Leaving me at the camp. he set off for the township with the fish hanging down along his back, reminding me vividly of a famous advertisement.

He reached Bourke about twenty minutes to six o'clock, and sold the fish at the first hotel at which he offered it. They weighed the fish which tipped the scale at 23 and a half lbs, and Slater received 11/9d.

According to his code of honour, he spent none of the money on drink, but he did spend nearly eight shillings on bluestone, shellac, and two powders, the names of which he would not state.

The whole of the following morning we spent in boiling and skimming the liquid these ingredients produced, and early in the afternoon we entered Burke with the stuff in two gallon oil tins. When Slater had purchased two paint brushes, our stock in trade was complete. When he varnished his left boot the effect was startling. There he stood at the kerb, his right boot scored and dusty, his left boot brilliantly polished and brilliantly reflecting the light of the sun.

"Give your shoes a permanent polish, lady," Slater asked a Chinese woman. "Only two shillings the pair, lady. Last for ever."

The lady stopped and gazed at Slater's example on his left foot, fascinated by its wonderful brilliance. She presently walked away wearing shoes that vied in splendour with Cinderella's slippers.

After that we were applying Slater's Permanent Polish to both feminine and masculine footwear, and the shillings came rolling in in a silver flood. Fortune favoured us, for no suspicious police man came to look on at our labours, perhaps to ask pertinent questions. A man parked a car nearby and entered a bank, and, while he was within Slater varnished a narrow strip of the front mudguard. That strip shone out like the sun from between dark clouds. It was not an old car; neither was it brand new. To the owner Slater suggested that we should varnish the whole of the car for two pounds. The two pounds were paid, and no car in a showroom ever appeared so brilliantly spick and span as did that one.

Knowing Cockney Slater, I realized that there was a catch in it somewhere, but just where I could not fathom. The polish certainly was highly successful. It transformed shoes and boots and cars better and almost as quickly as Aladdin's Genii could have done the work. Commercialised it should have made its inventor a millionaire.

Returning to the river, I asked Slater why he did not buy more bluestone and shellac and his mysterious powders, and he said that rapid transport was far more important. Even then I could not discern the "catch" in Slater's Permanent Polish. The dust on his own polished boot had but to be wiped away to reveal that the polish was as brilliant as ever.

Retrieving our swags, we walked ten miles down river to a lonely bend where we camped for the night, equally dividing between us a few shillings over four pounds.

Now Slater was a hard man to get up in the morning; he was a hard man to get to bed at night when recounting his experiences hoboing in America. The next morning, when I was cooking the breakfast as usual, I picked up Slater's polished boot. The polish was all right. The wonderful gloss still remained. But I could, and did, tear the leather to pieces as easily as tissue paper.

As for the car - well, I hate to think about it even now. Providing a subject for psychological study, Cockney Slater was remarkable. Ordinarily, he was scrupulously honest. He exhibited no hesitation in dividing the spoils of that one day's gentle grafting. He did not drink; neither did he steal. He would not work - until he married an Irish colleen and became a Sinn Fein captain and butcher.

Further, he was almost as bashful as I when approaching a station cook for tucker, and yet his brain was ever busy evolving downright swindles which gave the mugs a run - sometimes.

Before I left his entertaining but dangerous company, he related the following experience without a smile.

There was a couple named Trewan who owned a small selection on the Loddon. Mrs. Trewan was twenty-one stone in weight whilst her husband was a little more than seven stone. He was a meek and mild little man, and, after many years of acute suffering, he went and hanged himself on the sheep gallows near the house. Said Slater:

"When old Mrs. Trewan seen him hanging there, she threw a seven for an hour or so, and then she thinks of all the blowflies settling on poor little Trewan. So out she goes to him, and draws up over him a calico meat bag.

"Then me end Spider Kemp come along, and we called at the house asking for meat. The old woman was going on something cruel, and we couldn't get nothing out of her far her wailing and gnashing excepting something about the mail coach what was due at seven o'clock.

"We showed her money and offered to buy some meat, but that didn't have no effect or calm her down any, and off we went feeling sour about it. And then we sights the carcass hanging in the meat bag on the sheep gallows. Says Spider Kemp to me:

"You go back and pitch to the old tart, and I'll soon cut out a coupler pounds of chops."

"Back I goes and engages the old lady in a one-sided conversation till I hears Spider Kemp let out a roar. I seen him tearing off down the track below a cloud of dust. That was eleven years ago, and I've never seen him since."

4

Just fancy going to work by the same train or tram six mornings in every seven, starting work at the screech of a hooter, and working under the watchful eyes of a foreman until the hooter screeches again to knock off! If that has to be done to enjoy the pictures and the beaches in company with a kissable mouth, then such joys will never be for me.

I have mentioned appreciatively the Australian custom of being sacked or leaving a job at a minute's notice. How irksome it must be for both employer and employee to have to wait even a full day before parting company!

No, no! A hooter would send me mad. So would a foreman. Which is not to say that hooters and foremen are not necessary evils, for, without both, many men and women could not work at all. As an inspector on a Government vermin fence once said: "Men can be divided into classes; men who can't work unless the boss is looking at them, and men who can't work if the boss is looking at them."

When he said that, I sat down and did nothing until he had cleared off.

You see, there are so many kinds of work in the bush at which a man must be trusted to do a fair thing. If he is a born slacker, he will not last long, and will be "put on tramp" as he should. And here it is that we come to the second Australian custom I hope never to see die out - the mutual spirit of give and take.

I do not know the station where the Arbitration Court's ruling regarding hours is adhered to. There never was any necessity to give a ruling laying down the number of hours to be worked in one week. In the first place, no station could be run with men starting and stopping work at fixed hours. In the second place, the old custom of give and take was quite satisfactory both to squatter and men.

It is the rule that men living near the homestead gather outside the office at 7.30 a.m. to receive orders for the day. The work set out seldom cannot be performed later than 4 o'clock. I have been set work that has been done well and comfortably in two hours, and had I asked for further orders for that day, I would have been considered a nuisance. Consequently, no man rightly can feel annoyance if he is asked to do urgent work at 7 o'clock in the evening.

There was certainly the practice of give and take at Two Wells in the south-west corner of Queensland, a place then of magnetic attraction to countless animals and birds. Placed in the middle of an unnatural dust heap having a diameter of half a mile, the two wells were sunk within one hundred yards of each other. In one, the water was as salt as that of the sea; in the other, it was almost fresh. A windmill raised the fresh water, and a petrol engine pumped up the salt water. Both wells supplied one set of reservoir tanks that fed a line of troughing in each of the converging three paddocks and, because of the number of stock and wild things watering here, both wells were worked hard.

Nearby was a bush shed, and a windbreak protecting three tents. A humorous, ancient, wild-eyed and wild-haired Irishman acted engineer and cook and sheep skinner. It was the business of two scrub cutters to lay a ribbon of scrub branches across the path of the sheep flocks on their way to and from water; for only at the far ends of the paddocks was there left a little ground feed, the objective of this being to minimise drought-weakened animals travelling eight or nine miles to water, and eight or nine miles back again the next day to feed.

Time, 6 o'clock in the evening of a hot, still January day.

Temperature well above the century.

In the vicinity of the troughs, thousands of strutting galahs and cockatoos; above the troughs a constant whirring of wings and a babel of noise. No emus were present, for they had taken their fill at noon. Here and there in the near distance solitary kangaroos were sitting up, suspiciously regarding the camp and the troughs at which they must drink or perish. Further away little spurts of dust rose to hang motionless above the dust heap, flung upwards by bounding fleas, which presently resolved into swiftly arriving 'roos. Of rabbits there was none. A heat wave with a shade temperature of 119 had killed them all.

"I wish to Gawd it would blow," growled Paddy, observing bow the kangaroos' dust drifted not at all.

"Why they don't put an engine on to that fresh water well beats me. Got to use both wells to maintain a supply, end the mixture about ninety salt and ten fresh. Them poor critters walkin' miles and miles to get a drink of sea water in this heat! The dam mill hasn't gone all day. I had to shin up the mill and turn the fan wheel to get enough water for us."

There was no hint of Ireland in Paddy's voice, but the brogue was strong in Irish Muldoon. In his youth this man of middle height and large girth had studied for the priesthood, and if ever you have been cornered in a bar and compelled to listen for anything up to two hours to light hours and densities, magnitudes and angles and systems, then you have met Irish Muldoon. He had long forgotten all that was known by Sir James Jeans.

"Tanks full?" he asked in that soft, pleasant voice of his, nothing further from his mind than the celestial bodies when he was sober.

"They could be fuller. The mobs are coming in now."

From north of west and from due south, steadily rising brown clouds of dust rose into the red-flecked bronze of the sky, each cloud whirled upward by the close-packed lines of travelling sheep. The vast dust columns marched towards us with the steadiness of tramping giants - to the south mushrooming into a cloud having the precise aspect of a water cloud, snow white, its western face tinged with pink by the westering sun.

Now we could see the dull grey lines leaving the scrub at the foot of those gigantic dust columns. The western one blotted out the sun which, striking upon that to the south, painted the column with ever-moving splashes of crimson. Louder and louder became the sound of eager baaings, faster and faster moved the leaders towards the water which had lured them for so many weary miles. And presently was added the low rumble of thousands of hoofs churning the dust that hid the almost countless followers.

"I suppose we had better get going?" suggested Irish Muldoon.

We set off each to a line of troughing.

Now Paddy had slaved all day attending the engine and the pumps, skinning dead sheep, and cooking for the camp. Save for the midday hours, Irish Muldoon and I had swung an axe against tree branches in the sun which so heated the ground that it would ignite a dropped safety match. Yet there was no suggestion made that this was after working hours; that we were not paid for the task ahead of us; for this was not a matter between the owner of the run - who lived in idleness in England - and ourselves, but between ourselves and poor, helpless, water-famished animals. Your bushman may be rough and hard, he may never grease his hair or manicure his nails; he may always spend his cheque in a pub, or indulge in every city vice when on holiday, but he is a sentimental cuss with animals.

Here at Two Wells, night after night, we each arrived at the water troughs with the sheep. Outward from the troughs spread the flood of wool. More densely rose the now stationary dust columns merged by close proximity into one. A mad, straining, trampling, moaning surge of flesh and bone and wool to get at the water, with here and there mounds of wool heaving above the general level, each mound marking the place where a sheep had fallen and was being trampled to death. Dust-choked and heated, we scrambled from mound to mound to rescue the fallen. Then to the troughs to seize a foolish sheep which had been pushed into it, and was blocking the flow of water.

So it went on. The leaders, having distended their bellies

with brine, forced their way through the streams of arriving sheep to take position several hundreds of yards distant where they waited, stolidly chewing their cud. With the passage of time the weaker sheep arrived, sheep which lurched and staggered, glassy-eyed, gaunt despite their wool, their mouths dry and as hot as fire. They went down in dozens in the scramble, poor beasts that when lifted moved strengthless legs frantically to get them to the water. And having drunk and drunk they laid down with bellies distended close beside the troughs, refusing to get up or to stand up when lifted.

Gradually the dust thinned. Behind the halted leaders massed sheep in their hundreds, heavy with water, tired to the point of exhaustion by that long walk. About the troughs the press of sheep eased to reveal vacant spaces. All about were sheep lying down, muzzles resting on the ground, eyes closed or almost so.

Others lay dead, their last ounce of waning strength used up, expended in effort never to be rewarded.

And now through the hanging dust came the spectres of drought. Strange shapes that moved a little forward, fell, moved again, fell and moved onward yet again, tongues lolling from scorched mouths, some with an eye or both eyes plucked out by the crows. A little rest, and then one more effort; another little rest, and one, oh just one more effort to drink and drink and drink.

There was Irish Muldoon straddling sheep and walking them to his trough. There was Paddy screaming oaths and curses, and carrying water in a tin to pour down the throats of sheep doomed to death. He said he did it to save as many as possible, to lighten the work of skinning the dead ones the next day. The liar!

Evening after evening the western sky was like the wall of

*Upfield and his pets; Out droving, E.V. Whyte on the left.
Upfield would dedicate* Gripped By Drought *to this old mate.*

a slaughter house. Day after day showed the fiery heat of the torturing sun. After the sun had set, the afterglow reddened this field of horror, the standing water-filled flocks, the individual sheep lying down between them and the troughs, and between the troughs out along the path the flocks had taken from the scrub lines. Far and near, black dots moved sluggishly about dun-coloured mounds - crows feasting on the bodies of animals which had failed to come in. Kangaroos were creeping closer on all fours. Others were hopping short distances. Yet others were sitting up waiting, waiting for men to leave the water which they must get or perish.

Faces red with dust, perspiration gluing our clothes to our bodies, we would finally go back to camp and pour water over each other. The dusk was deepening, and flocks were lying down close packed for protection against the foxes. From each flock individual sheep left to drink again, slowly to return.

Over a pannikin of tea Paddy would curse the squatters for breeding sheep to suffer thus, and, in the natural order of things, Irish Muldoon would uphold the squatters. Their voices would rise high in vocal combat.

And when finally we went to bunk, stretchers brought out from the tents, lying on them without covering till long after midnight, the ceaseless cries of the wild came from the water troughs; the warning thrump-thrump of kangaroo tails, the snarl of a dingo, the spitting quex-quexing of quarrelling foxes. The world hidden at long last by the merciful darkness.

5

Have you ever met a man or a woman whose chief occupation is making bullets for someone else to fire? They are to be found in any community, even in many families. One of my brothers was an adept.

Below my father's business house were huge cellars. I can

remember when one of them always contained several hogsheads of beer from which four glass jugs were filled for every meal and placed on the male assistants' table. There was a strict rule that the person who drew the beer had to sing or whistle all the time he was in that cellar. Eventually, the custom of drinking beer was followed by the vice of sipping tea.

In other cellars, my grandfather and my father after him stored stocks of manchester goods and floor coverings, that one under the shop front being lighted by fanlights extending from the pavement to the bottom of the shop windows. They opened inwards, and, standing on a packing case, we boys could look through and across the pavement to the far side of the street.

My brother made a bullet in the suggestion of opening one of the fanlights and, with a catapult, firing duck-shot at the ankles of passing ladies. Not particularly cautious, I saw, however, that such action would be followed by inevitable retribution, and having pointed this out to the ammunition maker, he offered another bullet in the suggestion of making targets of leash-led poodles on the further pavement.

Unfortunately, at this period I prided myself on accurate catapult shooting, and shortly afterwards the first victim yelped and bit at the imaginary wasp sting, then to be picked up by the alarmed lady owner and rushed to the chemist on the next corner. That morning I introduced to the chemist four hideous canine monstrosities. Said the armament maker, offering the third bullet:-

"What about going along to the chemist and asking for a little commission?"

That appearing to be reasonable, I approached the chemist with this business proposition and secured his promise to consider it. On my way home he most unsportingly rang up my father to relate a good joke, and I need add nothing further than to remind you that that generation of fathers knew how to deal with their sons. For much less, a modern boy would be sent to a reformatory and machine-made into an habitual criminal.

Always be wary of bullet makers. Never, however, be so blimey foolish as to make the bullet you are destined to fire, as I was, when in my youth I worked on a station out of Cunnamulla, Queensland.

For something like three months our ration list was minus potatoes. We then were on the usual weekly ten, two and a quarter - otherwise 10 lb. flour, 2 lb. sugar, and 1/4lb. of tea, plus a bottle of sauce and a handful of raisins. When a peculiar form of dust, alleged to be dried potatoes, gave out, the men began to grumble. More than once the manager said that rations were on the way by bullock waggon, but they never seemed to arrive.

In those days, some of the squatters made much money by never ordering rations until the supplies in the station store had almost vanished, so for three, and sometimes five weeks, the hands would be on short commons. It is surprising how many ways there are of killing a crow.

At last, when the bare ten, two, and a quarter was reached, even the cook growled and his inventive genius waned. Every meal time he, Old Humpy, Fly-by-night, Blue Evans, and the others talked about the great strike of '98, and of how the wool sheds were burned to the ground and many of the river wool-boats sunk.

To me it then appeared absurd to growl constantly among ourselves, for, singly or collectively, we had no power to hasten the arrival of fresh supplies. That was entirely the manager's business. In an unguarded moment, I suggested that we go out on strike until the "spuds" did arrive: further, that the strike should take place the following morning after we had eaten heartily of the bread and mutton chops.

It was an idea that came to be regarded by the others as a gem of originality. Yes, that was the idea! Strike till the spuds arrived! Not one would turn out for work after breakfast the next day

"Wot we want boys, is an organizer!" pointed out the cook. "That's so," whined Ply-by night. "We can't go out on strike without organisation. Wot are we gonna do about it?"

"I vote we appoints Hampshire as leader and organizer?" Humpy put forward - and the vote was carried.

Instead of realising I had made the bullet I was to fire, I felt proud in my position of labour leader. I had visions of becoming a great leader of men, the clarion spokesman of the submerged nine-tenths, a great leader of men wielding vast power, dictating to the accursed bosses, finally grasping the Prime Ministership.

"What we will do," I laid down impressively, "is this. After breakfast we will pocket all the cooked food we cannot eat. As usual, we will go along to the office at seven-thirty for orders, but this time I will inform the boss that we will not labour until he gets us spuds from town. The mail coach will be leaving Cunnamulla at 10 tomorrow morning, and he will have time to ring up and arrange the transport of several bags. How's that?"

"Good!" acclaimed the strikers.

That evening I wrote and memorised a 300-word speech which I recited to my excited and approving followers.

"Put a little fire into it, and she'll do," the cook said in final judgment.

Accordingly, the next morning seven men waited for orders outside the station office: and, as usual, the manager came out of the house rubbing his eyes, to walk along to us to give his orders before returning for breakfast He was a short, tubby, red-faced, grey-haired man of about sixty, with piercing dark eyes, a black, bristling moustache, and a mottled complexion. Not an easy antagonist for a new chum strike leader.

The strike leader stepped forward, but the strike leader forgot his lines, and what he said was, in effect:

"We have decided to go on strike till you get us some spuds. The coach leaves town at ten, and you will have plenty of time to see that a couple of bags are put on board. In fact, if you will promise to do that we will, I think, carry on our labours."

The manager's eyes opened wide. His moustache bristled more than ever. His face became suffused with blood. Ignoring me, he addressed the men.

"Oh! So you have, have you?" he said in steely tones. When I turned to them I noted that the cook was not of their number.

"You are not striking, Humpy, surely," the manager said directly to the old man.

"Well, mister, not exactly on strike, but a man must have spuds now and then."

"Well, what about you, Searle?" This to Fly-by-night.

"Oh, I don't want to upset things." whined Fly-by-night, shuffling his feet.

To each of the others the manager craftily put the same direct question, being sufficiently a psychologist to know that he could the more easily deal with men single than collectively under the leadership of one man. Insufficiently experienced, I dumbly permitted this. Still, only Humpy and Fly-by-night and the sneaking-off cook were found wanting. The manager gave his decision.

"The ration teams are due tomorrow night." He said. "I will not have spuds brought out by the coach, so don't make me hurt myself laughing by going on strike for one day."

Obviously he could not concede more than that, and the men accepted their orders. To me he spoke last, saying:

"You can come to the office with me."

Arrived there, he instructed the book-keeper to make up my account and draw my cheque when he had had his breakfast.

"I am putting you off," he said, "not for leading a strike, but for being a fool. No strike succeeds unless the strikers stick together. You would never receive support from men like Old Humpy and Fly-by-night, and Bill, who have been so long on a station that they think they own the top wires on all the fences. Only an idiot pulls chestnuts out of a fire for other people, and only an idiot fires bullets made by other people, too. Let this be a lesson to you. You can start again in the morning."

I did not accept that, the bullet I fired was of my own making, and I did not accept his offer of re-employment. I was too hurt by that man's common sense and my own stupidity. It requires much more than self-confidence to become a Prime Minister.

Some time afterwards I heard that the manager found excuses within a week for sacking the cook, Old Humpy and Fly-by-night.

6

By far the most important person on any station is the cook.

He has it in his power to create for others heaven or hell, for the sky will be bright, and energy at full strength, after a breakfast of well-cooked grilled cutlets and well-made yeast bread; whilst life will be dull and not worth living if the cutlets have been grilled to cinders and the bread is more fitted to putty in window panes.

As a class, all cooks are difficult. Their tempers are uneven, and one never knows the moment when a cook will tear off his apron, dance on it, raise his hands high, and depart, swearing that never again will he feed such low, grousing, lazy crawlers.

There was Ted Ellis. No man ever lived who knew more sea chanties than he. These he sang the livelong day - until someone came along who offered him a "Taste". It was always the taste that did it. Within an hour Ellis was heading for the nearest pub.

There was Crabby Tom. Invariably, when he arrived to take charge of a kitchen, he was on the verge of delirium tremens. I say "on the verge" because he would be too drunk to enjoy them, and only when sobering-up did he see things which did not exist.

I first met Crabby Tom when he arrived at a place named Wombra Lake, meaning in the local aboriginal dialect, Big Lake.

Just where was the lake I never discovered, despite the fact that then I was riding three paddocks totalling in area something like 199 square miles.

My fellow stockman was away on a trip, and for some time I had had to do my own cooking, when the boss rang to say that he was sending out a cook on the truck next day. And during the next day I had visions of beautifully cooked meat and freshly baked, feathery yeast bread. It follows that my interest was aroused when, on sighting Wombra Lake after a long day, I observed a man running round and round the two huts.

Having unsaddled and freed the horse, I was able to give further attention to the sprinter. He was about sixty years old, wore nothing but underpants, and showed remarkable stamina. Now and then he would glance over his naked shoulder, utter a loud yell, and speed up. With the regularity of clockwork he would disappear round the corner of one hut and reappear round the corner of the other, quite oblivious to my presence.

It happened that in the scabbard attached to the saddle I was holding was a 0.32 rifle, and when he again hove in sight, I allowed him to pass me before firing off the gun and pretending to chase an imaginary horror. With that, Crabby Tom pulled up and came about with rasping breath.

"Did you get him?" he wheezed, hair on end, eyes dilated, teeth bared in a terrible grin.

"Wounded him," I admitted sorrowfully. "But he's cleared out. He won't come back any more. Better come in and we'll get some tea."

"Right! But you keep the gun handy: I ain't no shot. I never killed anythink yet, " he said earnestly.

"Leave it to me. Did you bring a drink out with you?" I inquired, desiring to know the amount of the stock, if any.

"No. Old Starlight," meaning the boss, "took a full bottle off me. Blinking shame, and me dyin' for a drink."

The poor wretch sat on a form against the table in the kitchen whilst I got the fire going, and, later, unrolled his swag and made up his bunk. I was in two minds about ringing Old Starlight and giving him my views concerning dumping a madman on me, when Crabby leapt two feet off the ground, vented an ear-piercing shriek, climbed the table, and swung himself up on to one of the roof cross-beams.

"Look out! It's just behind you!" he yelled. "It'll get you! It'll get you!"

Endeavouring to pacify him and allay his terrors, I made tea, and, when he refused to eat or drink, ate a hearty meal, believing that a stormy night lay ahead. And a stormy night it was, too. No doctor handy to give him a shot of morphia; no policeman in the vicinity for whom to yell if Crabby Tom got his hands round my throat thinking he was strangling a green man with blue hair and red eyes. A situation, indeed, to make one exercise what little brain one might have.

"Look out, mate! It's behind you again!" Or - "Shut the door! Can't you see it's trying to get in?" Or it might be in stuttering wails: "Hug! Hug!" and he would frantically brush things off his person, or from the beam supporting him.

With a man in such a mental state, pleading and argument are useless. The only efficient method of dealing with such a person, should morphia not be available, is to club him into unconsciousness with a mulga root; but to this method is attached some slight risk of being charged with the crime of murder, because judgment and finesse are qualities rare in the average peaceable man.

About nine o'clock I gave Crabby Tom half a bottle of pain killer, but to my disgust it had no effect on him. At ten o'clock I was getting "fed up". At eleven, when Crabby was barricading himself into the fowl house in company with twenty squarking hens, I contemplated rolling a swag and going away into the scrub to sleep. After all, I was not being paid the handsome sum of 30/- a week and tucker to nurse a lunatic.

However, there are occasions when one has to do small odd jobs without hope of gain, and about midnight I determined to experiment on Crabby with Dr. Browne's chlorodyne. From five to thirty drops Dr. Browne advised for cases of nervous debility and a hundred other complaints.

Now Dogger Smith once told me without batting an eye-lid that he had drunk two full bottles when he anticipated an attack of D.T.'s, and, allowing a reduction of 75 per cent. to counter exaggeration, I gave Crabby Tom half a bottle. Or it might have been a little more, because in twenty minutes he had regained normality and drank a pannikin of tea, and ten minutes after that he was sleeping in his bunk.

Blessed rest! Exhausted, I lay down to sleep, the two scared cats coming to sleep on my feet as always they did. Peace! Wonderful peace at last! The night so quiet! Aye, a little too quiet. I could hear no sound from Crabby Tom, no snore, not even his breathing.

He was lying on his back. His face was dull grey. His lips were purple. His eyes were shut. There was no movement of his powerful chest. I thought of the looking glass to make sure he was dead. For hours I slapped his face and shook him. For hours I walked him round and round the room. It was full daylight when I collapsed and he was snoring in healthy sleep.

But his D.T.'s were cured, and the trouble and fright he had rendered me were worth it all, for he proved to be the finest cook in my experience.

All cooks have bad feet as well as bad tempers, brought about by standing on hard floors in slippers. A cement floor will cripple a man in no time. Yet, to offset this drawback, there is always a job waiting for a good cook. Cooks, who have to labour seven days in the week, are always scarce; a good cook is as rare as water in the Paroo River.

The day must come when a bushman will have to turn cook, and I found that a knowledge of cooking is no weight to carry, and a trade of value when held in reserve.

My first batch of bread was not a success. There must have been something wrong with the yeast and after forty-eight hours, I baked the dough hoping it would rise in the oven.

Yes, it must have been the yeast. When in disgust, I threw a loaf out of the window, it cracked a cement-hard claypan star fashion.

FOUR

Men and Jobs

I

Today - even today - there is in all Australia but little necessity for an unmarried man to be dependent on others for a bite to eat and a billy of tea. When a young and robust man stops me on the street to tell the old, old story of being short of threepence for the price of a meal, he thoroughly deserves to continue thirsty. In the first place, his story proves him to be quite lacking in originality; and, in the second, his request reveals astounding vanity prompting him to think that all men save himself are fools.

I never did have the slightest acquaintance with the fear of unemployment in the bush, but unemployment in a city was, and ever will be, a nightmare. Once out of a city job I would get out of that city with the speed of an escapee from justice. No other land in the world is so kind to the down and out as is the real Australia. It offers him unlimited firewood, water costs him nothing, and possession of a fishing line and a gin trap assures him of food. But the man with domestic responsibilities is as securely chained to the industrial chariot as are his brothers in the old countries.

I went broke in Melbourne; awoke one morning to find myself possessing capital amounting to seventeen pence, no knowledge of any trade, no knowledge of how to set about competing in the wild rush for casual labouring work, and no friends. I could have wired to One-Spur Dick for financial assistance, but it would have been a repetition.

You see, the week before I had gone broke, too. I then wired to One-Spur Dick urgently requesting the loan of five pounds. He wired the money that same day, but, unfortunately, I did not get it until after the Mildura train had pulled out the next morning. What happened at his end was this:

At three o'clock, when he was unyoking the bullocks, and his offsider was throwing off the load of wood on to the station wood heap, the bookkeeper gave him my telegram. One-Spur Dick read the cry for help from the city wilderness before the bookkeeper left him, and he said:

"Wire him a fiver at once. I'll sign the chit directly I've turned out these colourful hornies."

When they were having dinner that evening, the blacksmith indignantly demanded an answer to -"Wot's the good of sending a measly five pounds to a man in Melbourne? Strike me pink that wouldn't last Jimmy Woodser a day, let alone Hampshire."

This so worried One-Spur Dick that he insisted on signing another chit for five pounds, and he urged the book-keeper to despatch the money first thing the following morning.

Accordingly, at 9 o'clock the next day the second remittance was telephoned and telegraphed some eight hundred miles. At eleven o'clock, when the book-keeper was settling down to his work, there entered his office Tommy Ching

Lung, the station gardener, who laid on the desk five sovereigns. He said:

"You sendum these five pound Hampshire quick. Ten pound no good Hampshire in Melbourne."

So that in the space of four hours I walked from my hotel to the G.P.O. three times to collect a total of fifteen pounds, and, instead of catching the Mildura train the next morning, I lingered among the fleshpots.

With the arrival of the second term of bankruptcy, and realisation of the fool I was, I would, indeed, have been low had I again wired for assistance. I was in a pit of my own digging, and pride dictated the urgency of climbing out of it the best way I could.

How far from Melbourne the Railways Commissioners would have conveyed me for seventeen pence I knew not, but I did know it would not be far beyond where Sunshine now is. Beyond Sunshine lay hundreds of miles of open cocky country where the wintry winds of June are most unkind, and where it always rains, or seems to be always raining. And carrying a swag down Collins Street offered no appeal despite its possible originality in the twentieth century.

Uncle most considerately advanced sixteen shillings on a cigarette case, and with this money I bought a job from a labour bureau and a rail ticket to Neerim. At no time in my life - not even at the war in the winter of 1916-17 - have I felt so cold as I did waiting for the Neerim train on the Warragul station.

I understand that all the country round Neerim is very lovely - during the summer. I would not have thought it, but I am open to conviction. I was there just a month, but I saw little of the country and nothing of the town. At dawn one would step off the veranda into ten inches of mud, and toboggan down the side of a mountain for the thirty cows. The boss and his wife would assist with the milking. That done, one would step out of the ten inches of mud on to the veranda and eat breakfast. How I missed my early morning tea, the night-before-tea in the billy heated to be drunk whilst a cigarette was smoked and one listened for the horse bells!

If it did not rain it sleeted, and if it did not sleet it snowed. To me the real Australia appeared to be on the other side of the world. No wonder that the Kelly Gang got going - they had to do something to keep warm. Bankrupt in Melbourne, I had been like a child blindfolded and turned round and told to walk ten paces. On the bandage being removed, I expected to find my self in Sunny Australia, not at the South Pole. Alas, my blood was as thin as vinegar, and I had no backbone. I called upon my gods to witness the oaths I took never to go broke again in a city.

The boss said:

"I've to go to Melbourne for a week. Finish that ploughing, and if you've got time, get to that sucker bashing in the lower paddock."

That was at the beginning of my fourth week when the rain let up for ten-minute periods. I completed turning the mud with a single-furrow plough, and went to sucker bashing like the local baker went to his ovens - to get warm. But there were the cows to be eternally milked and the separating to be done, and my clothes to be wrung of water, and, when opportunity came, I gave a week's notice to the housewife.

"What's the matter with the place?" she wanted to know. "You foreigners are never satisfied. I can't understand why you don't go back to England if you don't like Australia."

"The place may be all right, but I left England to come to Sunny Australia, not to the Antarctic," was my complaint. "I want to get near to a hundred-square-mile bush fire. I want to see if the sun still rises and sets. The smell of bullocks in a team on a saltbush plain is bearable, but rain-soaked cows in a small shed are beyond my powers of appreciation."

The boss came back the day before I left. I saw him overlooking the ploughing, and strangely enough he found no fault with it. Then we went along to the sucker bashing.

"Hum! Haven't done too bad," he said with evident satisfaction. "How many axe handles did you break?"

"Break? I broke none!"

"Broke none!" he echoed. "Do you mean to tell me you never broke an axe handle?"

"Yes. Why should I break axe handles?"

He regarded me as though I grew wings. Then:

"Well, you're the first man I've had who didn't break axe handles at sucker bashing. Did you use an axe or did you use your teeth? The last man I had broke two a day. The man before him broke on an average four a day, and the man before him broke seven in one morning. Now, what are you leaving for?"

"Feel my clothes," I pleaded. "They haven't been dry for a month. Build me a hut with an open fireplace, and with a hole at the back of it to insert a whole tree trunk, and give me ten pounds a week, and I wouldn't stay."

I was not far off being broke when I returned to Melbourne. I had enough money to get me to Mildura and the woodheap, but I could not go north and face One-Spur Dick and the black-smith and Tommy Ching Lung. They would make nothing of the debt, but I could not stand their grins and well-intentioned gibes. Pride demanded restitution before explanations.

I went disc ploughing with eight horses in the Wimmera. It was in July, and if I was seldom warm, I was at least seldom wet.

Harvest came. I earned £2.10.0 a week and tucker tending sixteen horses - two teams, the first of which I hooked into a harvester at ten o'clock, the second at two o'clock, and the first again at six o'clock. In my spare time I sewed 4,000 bags of wheat for which I received 12/6d a hundred.

Eight weeks that harvest lasted. I mailed the fifteen pounds to the boys up north. To them every Sunday I wrote the same message:

"Seeing you soon."

But never a word about the cows and the axe handles. To them, months afterwards, I swore that the cocky was my uncle who had made me his heir. To myself, morning and night, I swore that never again would I go broke in a city.

2

Should you desire to see flies - you would be an extraordinary person if you did - visit the north-west frontier of New South Wales. If you would experience real dust storms, and would appreciate sunny Australia, by all means take train to Broken Hill, and from there travel some 200 miles by mail car to Yandama or Quinambie Stations any time during January and February. Most certainly you will be tormented by the flies, choked by the dust, and slimmed by the heat; but you will never recall the name of Sturt, Australia's greatest explorer, without "living" with him and his companions every minute after he left Cawndilla Lake, which is beside the Darling at Menindee.

Modern explorers who rush around in motor cars and huge trucks make me smile. When they name pot-holes and ant-heaps as lakes and hills, the mud of the former sucked by a lone prospector, and the elevation of the latter used by a stockman to spy out possible feed for his weary cattle before ever the "explorer" was born, I get that tired feeling. How I would like to have one in my power and say to him: "Here are two camels and equipment and tucker for a month. You can get water at such and such a bore.

The water will be a little salt, but that is neither here nor there. Work along this 22-mile section of dog-proof fence, and don't let me see you for a month. It is unlikely you will see anyone, black or white, but that's nothing as many men live from two to three months without seeing and speaking with anyone. Now get going, my son, and crack hardy."

One can so easily imagine the chuckles and back-thumpings among the old timers of "The Corner".

You face north - it does not matter if you face south, but we will say north - and beyond a narrow flat covered with low bush and widely spaced wind-wracked mulgas you will see a huge wave of sand; here topped with a curling sand-cap, there gouged by a giant scoop. No car ever built could surmount it; it is doubtful if an army tank could make headway up those slopes of fine light-red sand.

Beyond it lies another narrow flat, and beyond that another sand wave, and so on and on for miles and miles, six or seven sand waves to be surmounted with every mile travelled northward. Picture a storm-lashed ocean suddenly petrified, each wave fifty to seventy feet high, each wave miles in length, a land killed by the head of Medusa held aloft by Perseus who refrained to look upon it. Save for a panting eagle perched on the limb of a dead sandalwood tree, and a wide-beaked crow or two, no bird life.

The South Australian Border Fence is an everlasting switch back, a netted barrier six feet in height, topped by barbed wire, which takes a man's ingenuity to scale and which balks any animal. Running north-south, it is opposed to the full force of the westerly hurricanes of wind and sand.

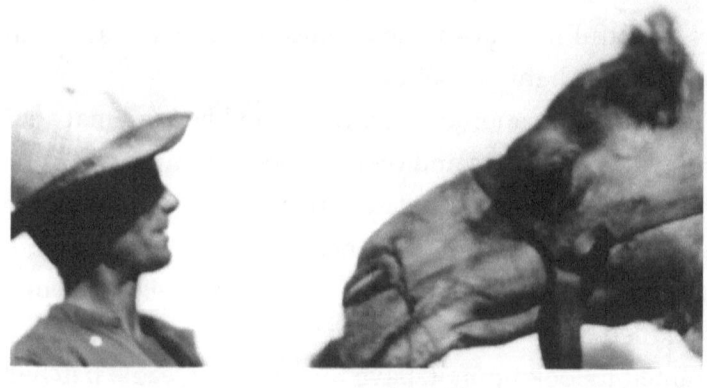

Arthur Upfield and buggy, and with a favourite camel.

"You can have no idea of that region," Sturt wrote to MacLeary in 1845, and, with MacLeary, I had no idea of it until the inspector wrote offering me a job riding twenty-two miles of that fence. I thought.

Twenty-two miles! Why, I could do that on my head, I found that the 22-mile sections were exactly twelve miles too long.

There was Martin, such a staid old gentleman who could not go without a sip of water after two days. Just a sip to wet his cud, or determinedly he would hobble off to the nearest bore. Emily was a gay widow or a placid cow - according to the mood of the moment. When it was really hot, when the ground burned the rubbery soles of their feet, they would go on strike by making for the nearest alleged shade and camp. And I having removed the loads and got a billy going over a fire, they would get up and come to stand over it, their heads steadily thrust into the uprising hot air and smoke in which, in all that land, there were no flies. Between their heads would be mine, and the slab of salt meat and the slab of rock-hard damper, too, because, when not thus protected, it was impossible to convey food to the mouth without flies adhering to it. No butter, of course, and frying fat kept in corked bottles. The flies had a liking for canvas and would blacken the tent used to cover the load on Emily so that it looked like black American cloth. To escape them meant breakfast before dawn and supper after dark. There were evenings when the camels never moved their heads from the hot air of a camp fire or a rubbish fire until darkness vanquished the flies. I used to smear a mixture of axle grease and kerosene round their poor eyes. About my head I wore a woman's veil, but, firing two such veils with cigarette smoking, I gave the flies best and suffered not silently.

The fence job was the most heart-breaking of any I have

attempted. Every little bit of obstruction had to be kept clear of the bottom of the fence to allow the drifting sand to trickle through the netting mesh. Once rubbish was allowed to collect against that barrier, in no time, where there had been a fence there would be a sandhill, over which gambolling dogs and foxes and rabbits could enter New South Wales. With a rake I would remove all such rubbish for a mile or more. The next day a wind storm would sweep from the west millions of football-like, brittle buck-bushes. The whole surface would appear to move, sliding eastward to be halted against the fence, to pile up against it higher and higher, until tons and tons of dead buckbush would steeplechase the fence into New South Wales. Work undone within an hour; work having to be done again and again.

I have found the fence on the summit of a sandhill twenty and thirty feet high, instead of the regulation six feet, swaying in the wind, or it might be lying flat, and all day I have laboured to remove successive "topping" of posts and netting. A storm had blown away the summit of that hill, and the next storm, or the one after, would pile it up again, necessitating rebuilding the fence.

And the wonderful water! How the laundry people would have appreciated it! Arrived at a bore head, the steaming hot water ceaselessly pouring from the angled piping, all that was necessary to wash clothes was to hold them on a stick beneath the gush. No rubbing, no soap required. After the fifth wash you could blow holes through a shirt. Both sides of the bore drain were studded with soda and alkalines, and to obtain drinkable water one had to go half a mile down the drain. Even at that point the water was too brackish to make tea, but with plenty of sugar it was possible to drink coffee made with it.

No wonder that Sturt and his heroic band were dismayed by

this land of sand and wind nearly ninety years ago. If the sun rose like Alaska gold - much more yellow than the Australian mineral - it prophesied a day of roaring wind and stinging, choking sand, in which nothing could be done save to crouch in the lee of a pack-saddle - to face the storm to have one's eyes filled with sand; to turn from it to have one's face a crawling mass of flies sheltering in the windbreak caused by one's head.

The strangest storm I ever experienced swept across this country one afternoon in November. The day was still. Cigarette smoke rose in a straight spiral. The camels crouched in meagre shade. Every time I moved out of that meagre shade I became dizzy. In the nearest station homestead they said it was 119 in the shade - proper shade, of course.

Above the sand-gashed horizon rose a long, low cloud, having a much greater density than the usual sand storm. At a distance it appeared to hover just above the ground, rolling eastward with the irresistible solidity of a sandhill two hundred feet high, stretching from the north to the south. When it drew near at the speed of a trotting horse its aspect was much like a terrific, Medusa-frozen sandhill come alive.

It frightened me. In it there seemed to be no possible chance for a human being to breathe. There was no time to pack up and ride away before it. From black it had changed to dark red, terrifying in its relentless approach, sinister in its silent march. I believe that had there been a rabbit burrow near I would have thrust my head down one of the holes, and at the last instant it was the tent fly beneath which I wormed a way for shelter.

With a gentle hiss it covered up, blotted out the sun, created a darkness known by the Egyptians and the Israelites. The darkness lasted for about two minutes, when the light came back and the sun shone again. Still no wind. Every surface presented by tree branch, the camels, equipment, fence posts, even the fence wires was loaded with sand precisely as such surfaces in a cold country may be so loaded with snow.

It is the land inhabited by the remnants of a tribe of the great Warring Dieri nation, which ousted another in the long ago, and settled all the way up the Barcoo delta from Lake Frome to Lake Eyre; the latter named after the explorer, the former after a Captain Frome, once Surveyor-General of South Australia.

Opportunity came to visit Lake Frome with a Dieri native and a half-caste. When we wanted water they would uncover several roots of a needlewood tree, break them, and place beneath the breaks any tin receptacle with us. Then they would fire the foliage, and the fire would drive into the tins from half a pint to, in some cases, over a pint of drinkable liquid.

When near Lake Frome we fell in with a party of natives who could not, or would not, speak English, but who responded to certain Masonic signs. That mystified Sturt, and it mystifies me to this day. The only explanation appears to be that of coincidence; for the origin of Masonry is comparatively recent compared with that of the sign language of the aborigines.

Anyway, it gained us open sesame, gained for us "official" permission to proceed, without which neither the full-blood nor the half-caste would have gone on.

From the summits of the eastern sandhill on a clear day it is possible to see the summits of the western sandhills across the mud flats, which are designated a lake on all maps. In dry weather wild dogs may cross by rigidly following their own made pads. At all times those flats are death traps to both cattle and horses, whilst, after a heavy rain, there may be stretches of water an inch or so in depth, which last a week or two in winter.

If there be such a place on this fair earth of ours favoured by Satan as his backyard, it is about Lake Frome and the S.A. border fence in summer.

3

It is a singular fact that a particular scent will invariably recall to mind a scene or a person. The scent of carnations will recall to my mind a pair of laughing blue eyes; a snake will always bring out of the past a man known to his friends as the Storm Bird.

He was a man who, most tragically, lived two hundred years too late. Had he lived two hundred years ago, he would not have had to wait for an obscure biographer to bring him forth from obscurity. Had he then lived to rival Captain Kidd, as assuredly he would have done, his "life" would have fallen to the task of every famous historian.

Alas, he lived in those prosaic days before the Great War when, as you know, piracy, and even bushranging, were not considered the pursuits of gentlemen, when the community basked in a doe-like complacency established by an efficient police force. Instead of being the carefree stockman he was, in the reign of Queen Elizabeth, the Storm Bird would have been royally licensed to beard the King of Spain.

"I was camped with a bloke in a hut like this one in o-four," he said, when I was preparing to climb into my bunk for the night. "We 'ad several kittens in that 'ut, and when Alf Stodger got atween the blankets, 'e said: 'Blast you! Get out of it.'

"I said:'Wot's up with you?'

" 'e said: 'Blinded cat bit me toe.'

"I don't take no notice of 'im, being interested in a Garvice where the Dook was about to arst the gardener for 'is dorter's 'and, but after a whiles I'm layin' back smoki'n me bedtime pipe; and it strikes me that for the first night since I 'noo 'im, Alf Stodger wasn't snorin.'

"'Ain't you asleep yet?' I says.

"When 'e don't answer and I can't 'ear 'im breathin', I takes the slush lamp to 'im and finds 'im as cold as a dog's nose. Now that makes me think a bit, and I remember wot 'e said about the cat. So I pulls orf the blankets one be one, and among 'em I finds a saltbush snake about seven inches long. Which is why I always makes me bed afore I gits into it."

Which was why I then made mine for the first time that week. We were in residence among a conglomeration of iron sheets, designated a stockman's hut in all official returns, and situated thirty-seven miles from White Cliffs. The Storm Bird was working on contract, building a set of sheep yards, and he slaved with amazing vigour from dawn till dark piling up a comfortable cheque.

He was imbued with the ambition of visiting New Zealand, but at the time I was unaware that this ambition was of life duration, and that he never got nearer to New Zealand than the first way side hotel. His intentions were always good, but the flesh was always weak.

"I'm gonna work right through this Christmas," he declared. "I'm wantin' another 'alf 'undred to give me a good three months' spell. I'll 'ave enough when I've finished this job."

A day or so later, he said: "It's gonna be a dry Christmas, but it wouldn't be so bad if we 'ad a few bottles out 'ere to wet it, sort of."

Thus it came about that I asked the boss for permission to drive the buckboard into White Cliffs to purchase a tinned Christmas pudding, and thus it was that on Christmas Eve there reposed under my bunk a nailed case containing the Christmas pudding, a box of cigars, two bottles of whisky and a dozen of beer.

We had solemnly sworn not to open the case until eleven o'clock on Christmas morning. At noon, Christmas Eve, we knocked off labour, and, so that Christmas Day should be a real holiday, I set to work cooking tucker enough to last several days, whilst the Storm Bird became busy on the wood heap cutting a pile of firewood. We determined to arise early the next morning and clean out the place before the holiday officially started.

I had two teal ducks roasting in one camp oven, and a damper cooking in another, when my camp mate suddenly ceased singing "The Face on the Bar-room Floor" to utter a yell of anguish. On rushing out, I found him wildly striking at something with the blade of the axe, and the something proved to be a forty-inch speckled snake.

"'E got me 'Ampshire! 'E got me on the 'and!" screamed the Storm Bird, standing up from chopping the snake into small pieces.

"Show it me," I ordered, overwhelmed by my complete lack of toxic knowledge in this crisis.

The snake had bitten his left hand at the edge of the palm.

The punctures were plainly to be seen.

"Suck it! Come inside! We'll have to cut it open!" I cried and ran on to the hut. When he staggered inside, I was sharpening the butcher's killing knife on a steel.

"Cut me 'and orf, quick," besought the Storm Bird.

"You may as well be dead as live with only one hand," was my opinion. "Hold your hand firmly on the table. Shut your eyes."

I sawed into the wound with the blunt knife, but the victim uttered never so much as a whimper. We had no permanganate of potash, so I repeatedly filled my mouth with water and squirted it through our pipe stems into the terrible gash I had cut, having read somewhere that nicotine is a makeshift antiseptic. When a ligature had been fixed, I asked him how he felt, I myself feeling very sick.

"Crook," he wailed. "I can feel the stuff actin'. They say whisky is a good antidote. What about breakin' a bottle?"

I opened up the cellar and gave him a half-pint of raw spirit, took a dose myself, and then rushed away into the night paddock to yard the buckboard horses. Then back into the hut to see if the Storm Bird was dead.

"It's gettin' me orl right," he said, drowsily.

"Walk up and down," I urged. "Have another drink. I'll put in the horses in two ticks."

It might have been five ticks, not longer, when I had the horses harnessed and the buckboard at the door. Inside I rushed to grab the open case and two canvas water bags; the case to put on the driving seat, the water bags to strap to the side rails. In three more ticks I had got the Storm Bird on to the high seat, and, with the case and two pannikins between us, we started on our thirty-seven miles' rush to the nearest doctor like a fire brigade answering a call.

"Don't go to sleep, now," I pleaded. "If you do, you will never again wake."

"It's gettin' me. It's paralysin' me arm," he stated with resignation.

"Take another drink. The poison in the bottle will counter act the venom. Keep awake, now, or I'll have to start pumping you. Take a deep noser this time. You stick to the whisky. Give me a bottle of beer."

Thus he was made busy and his mind kept off the horrible death waiting to pounce on him if I failed to get him to the doctor. His piratical aspect had given place to the solemn appearance of an undertaker who had not shaved for a week and had not washed his neck for a month.

Twelve miles out of White Cliffs we reached a mail coach

change, and luckily the groom had in his yards a dozen fresh horses. An explanation of the urgency of our case produced a rapid exchange of horses, and in less than a minute we were on our way, two half-broken horses tearing along at a gallop.

Now and then the patient would take a half-pint of whisky to keep the venom at bay and dash off the head of a beer bottle against a whirring tyre that I might be refreshed. We had forgotten the ligature, but it had come off and the danger of gangrene was removed.

We entered White Cliffs with the dash of a Marathon-winning four-in-hand, pulling up outside the hospital in a cloud of dust. The Storm Bird was nearly dead. He could not articulate when the doctor asked the reason of our abrupt arrival.

The doctor smiled whilst he washed the wound and stitched it, and then he lectured me on the difference between the bites of poisonous and non-poisonous snakes.

I was a new chum, but the Storm Bird was certainly not a new chum. A long time afterwards he said that he had not reckoned on my surgery, but even that was better than a dry Christmas.

4

If you ride westward from Winton, Queensland, for ninety-four miles you will reach the branch track which will finally take you to Charleville. Beside the junction grew a great bloodwood tree, and nailed to the trunk was the bottom drawer of a once valuable rosewood bedroom chest, then utilised as a letter-box.

It was a year when I was young; when life lay ahead with a promise as glamorous as the mystic land lying beyond the sunset, and I rode a horse and packed another, and camped o'nights beneath trees in the vicinity of dam or bore, and knew not care.

And so, following the south-west track from the junction, I entered the country of Melody Sam.

The reason behind Sam's going bush was never rightly known. One day he arrived, and for seven years he stayed, six of which he lived alone in an iron hut, riding two paddocks and mixing with his fellows only when mustering throughout the shearing. He had never been known to read, or to play cards, and was not a conversationalist, his leisure hours being occupied with playing on his violin. And that, they told me, Melody Sam played with exquisite skill.

By repute he was known for many miles around, and the little iron home came to be called The Musical Hut. It was only by chance that the manager called one day to find its lonely tenant dying.

Melody Sam lies at the foot of a giant gum near the home stead, and his violin hangs on the office wall. It had been there but a week when first I saw it, and The Musical Hut had been vacant ten days when I settled into it and began to ride the paddocks he had known for six sad and lonely years.

It is as well to have a mental picture of The Musical Hut. It was a long, low building of corrugated iron, bordered on the front side by three pepper trees. At the back was the well and windmill and water troughing, and beyond that were the sheep yards. The interior of the hut was divided into a living-room and the "Bunk house"; for, in those days, stockmen and shearers slept in bunks in tiers much like those in the forecastle of a ship. The hut's situation at the end of a track dictated its isolation; and, unless anyone came especially from the homestead, none called to bring news of the world.

It was quite a nice hut as huts went in those days. The

afternoon of my arrival I spent in sweeping and cleaning and browsing among the old books and papers left by the tenant who occupied the place before Melody Sam. At tea time, a ginger cat arrived and entered with such quiet confidence as to proclaim that Melody Sam liked cats. Later, it returned from the bush, and one by one brought in six kittens.

Weary - temporarily, of course - of travelling anywhere, I settled down to the job, working to a routine most days spent in the saddle, every evening occupied with reading or writing. The weeks went by and summer came in with a sudden heat wave which forced me to erect a rough bunk on the narrow verandah.

Havelock Ellis has written much on the psychological effects of solitude on the human mind, and what he has written is convincing enough to compel belief that he experienced it. Others, also, have written on the subject, but they lack the authority of personal experience, and are unable to appreciate the significant fact that, as human minds differ, so the effects of solitude vary with all men who suffer it. Solitude may be personified by a stalking tiger cat which will inevitably claim its victim, and final madness is hastened or delayed by the manner in which the victim exercises his mind.

It was nine o'clock one moonlight night when first I heard Melody Sam playing on his violin when he had been dead nearly three months. Not a zephyr stirred the air or the drooping leaves of the pepper trees. Outside, lying on my bunk, wearing only pyjamas, the topmost blanket folded sideways to be pulled over me only towards daybreak, I smoked and listened to Melody Sam whilst little cold shivers played over my skin.

The music was soft. It was so soft that only when lying quite still could it be heard. At first I thought it came from the bunk house, then from beneath the pepper trees, then up in their branches, then in the living-room. It was impossible to decide at what point it had its origin; it seemed constantly to move about, the low plaintive wail of a violin.

It made me wonder what kind of a man Melody Sam had been. They said he was tall, pale of face, sloping of shoulders. He never smiled. His eyes were dark, almost black, and of great intensity. His hands were finely shaped, and when in the sun he invariably wore gloves.

What had sent him into the bush? Not the quest of adventure which had sent me, I felt sure. Tragedy? It appeared most likely. A broken love affair, perhaps; or possibly the death of one he loved exceeding well. The manager said that when he died he was smiling, and that he whispered a woman's name.

Now, if a man is very unhappy for a long period, during which he has lived in one place, I could find no logical reason why his spirit would want to return to that place to haunt it. There are places which I want never to see again, and yet to others those same places might be the background of happy reverie. But here at this lonely hut where Melody Sam had known agony of mind, he was returned to haunt it with his violin.

I have heard, and even taken part in, arguments concerning the problems of metaphysics, survival of life after death, and time. I have listened, too, to allegedly clever people discoursing on these same problems from public platforms, and never do they get any further "forrarder". They invent extraordinary words to affirm their cleverness, and theorise and argue, but they never prove anything whatever. For ages men have propounded theories and sought to solve these problems, and they would have been better employed making bricks in so far as any results have been secured.

Some ten days after the first haunting of The Musical Hut,

I again listened to Melody Sam's soft playing, so low and so sweet as to be elfin. It was another such night as that first, but moonless.

Eventually, because of the state of the country, further flocks were put into the paddocks I rode, and a man named Dirty Dick was sent to live and work with me. His habits certainly were not dirty, but his language, which lacked artistry, certainly was.

He built himself a bunk beneath one of the pepper trees.

Never once did I mention to him the spiritual activities of Melody Sam, because, firstly, I did not want to be laughed at, and secondly, because I did not want it thought that that Tiger Cat was catching up to me.

Dirty Dick had been with me more than a week when, having dropped off to sleep early one quiet night, I was wakened to see him standing over me.

"Hey!" he whispered. "'E 'as come back.'E is playing on 'is violin. Can't you 'ear 'im? I'm gettin' outer this. I'm not stoppin' 'ere. I never liked 'is eyes when 'e was alive; they must be somethink awful now 'e's bin dead five monse."

And leave he did. He rolled his swag and departed for the homestead at eleven o'clock that night.

The manager rang up the next morning to hear about the haunting. He understood from Dirty Dick that Melody Sam walked round the place, arrayed in his shroud and playing with exceptional verve. Not one of the men would take Dirty Dick's place, and the manager came out, determined to stay until he had laid the ghost.

He had a scientific mind, as was proved once or twice when I considered the weather too hot to ride the paddocks, and he quickly laid the ghost by the heels after we had wandered round with lamps looking for Melody Sam. The tune Melody

Sam played was Tosti's Good Bye, and Tosti's Good Bye was the manager's wife's favourite gramophone record. When the record was played at the homestead, it could be heard at The Musical Hut, but not of sufficient volume to be easily distinguished. Either along the telephone wires, or because of unique acoustic conditions, in certain climatic conditions, the gramophone music was conveyed eleven miles.

5

I have long reached the conclusion that of the money maker and the money getter, the latter is much the better off. Having been both, there is authority for this opinion. The employer has the worry of making money and going bankrupt if he ceases to do so even for a short space of time, whilst the employee has but to wait with patience for the pay days.

Making money is a gift: waiting for a pay envelope is a habit. Habits being more general to the human race than gifts, there will always be many more money getters than money makers.

Joe Foster - one time known by the cognomen of Skylark - was a born money maker. He had that cheerful, buoyant disposition which not only attracted to him money, but friends; but it was not until he was forty-five did there begin to arrive a fine house, a motor car, and boxes of cigars. Before "he took a tumble", he made big cheques sinking dams, and, because he had built up an efficient plant of horses and gear, the Western Lands Board allotted him the leasehold of thirty thousand acres of fine country.

After all, perhaps, it was the woman he married who actually cultivated in him the habit of clinging to the money he made. Anyway, I am quite sure that to her courage and her faith in Australia was due their present Adelaide home and their lives of comparative security after a period of horror through which the weaker sex, sic, again proved its strength.

When the Skylark was granted the leasehold, he had about £400 in cash, and his plant was worth easily another £500. He spent over-much on a house for his bride, and he spent too quickly on improving the property and in stocking it. This, coming at the beginning of a two-year drought, brought him to the verge of Carey-street.

The peculiar thing about an Australian drought is that not only is it difficult to foretell, but it is difficult to realise when it actually has begun. A drought may be likened to a mountain, to reach the top of which one has to climb a succession of lesser ridges, each appearing to the climber to be the real summit. After a six-months' period of dry weather a splendid rainfall will dispel the caution the dry period has engendered in the heart of a squatter. He believes that one good rainfall will be followed by another; when, instead of that, it ushers in a much longer rainless period. He gambles on the probability of rain more than he should do.

Before one May, when two inches of rain fell in three days, it had not rained for seven months. Everyone was joyful, for it seemed certain that the comparatively short drought was over. At this time, I had more than £300 saved, not due to any inherent virtue but to a preference to taking a holiday on tramp than among the fleshpots of a city. The Skylark put to me the proposition of a partnership and paying me a wage of three pounds a week and tucker, and thus it was that I became a bloated capitalist.

With my capital we carried on hopefully. When, after another dry period of five months, sheep went down to 2/- a head, we bought 1,800 ewes, for the dam was still almost full and the drought-defying saltbush in splendid condition.

I am a great believer in divining for water. My partner was an expert, and he selected with a piece of bent wire the site for a well, accurately estimating the water stream to be between fifty and sixty feet below the surface. We found water at that depth, but it was brackish, a little too brackish for the stock to drink without dilution with fresh water.

During the mid-summer months we laboured at the well-sinking. Four thousand sheep on the property was over-stocking at the beginning of a long drought; and, because we did not realise that when it rained two inches in May it was the prelude to a long drought instead of the end of a short one, by the end of the summer the dam was dry and the sheep were forced to live on the brackish water of the well.

We could secure agistment nowhere. No one wanted to buy sheep: all wanted to sell. The price of fat sheep soared, but no one had fat sheep to sell.

How easy it is to be wise after the event. It would have paid us to muster the sheep and slaughter half of them for their skins, giving the remainder a better chance. But what squatter could do that when every squatter eternally hopes that it will rain the next week? When in every little cloud he imagines it to be the forerunner of a mass which will drop water and transform a dust heap into a paradise.

The lambing time came. Because there was no green feed, because the ewes' milk was limited, every ewe with twins abandoned one. These formed little parties of motherless lambs, watched by the eagles and the crows and the foxes, weak little mites which ran bleating towards us like lost and frightened babes in the wood.

For hundreds of miles around, the vermin gathered over this Drought-stricken district to grow fat and slothful. They multiplied amazingly. They ate the lambs alive, and then began their horrible work on the weakest of the sheep. I came to understand how it is that some men, when they catch a crow alive, delight in torturing it.

In a light cart, the Skylark and I drove about skinning the dead sheep and killing and skinning those sheep whose dreadful end was otherwise certain. A cloud in the north-east would cause us to smile until it slowly vanished in the scarlet sky above the setting sun.

"Perhaps it will rain tomorrow!" the Skylark's wife always said when we ate dinner, undimmed hope in her eyes, the horrors of the day in ours carefully kept from her. It was not the slow and inevitable approach of bankruptcy, the wastage of our savings and our labour, dreadful as that was to us in our helplessness, but the vivid never-to-be-forgotten scenes we witnessed every day in the animal kingdom - the cruelty and the heat and the thirst.

"Perhaps it will rain tomorrow!"

"There's a heavy cloud in the north. It might work up into a thunderstorm."

"It's going to rain! I saw the ants carrying their eggs up into a tree!"

But it did not rain.

Frustrated hopes and the horror of the greatest drama Australia produces cowed us to women. Both of us would have given up the battle long before had it not been for the grim determination of a frail woman.

"Perhaps it will rain tomorrow. Let's keep on," she would urge with assumed cheerfulness, undimmed hope in her eyes, faith in the real Australia ever in her heart. The stacks of sheep skins in the cane-grass shed grew in number.

Every lamb perished. Hundreds of sheep dotted the land minus their skins. Sheep died which were not found till long afterwards, and from the rotting carcasses we pulled out the wool and bagged it.

"I'm damned sorry I got you to come in with me," the Skylark often said, and as often I would reply: "What's £300 anyway? Nothing venture, nothing win. There's more to be got where that came from."

There was old MacIntosh. His wife came one day to say he had not returned home the evening before. We found him in his sheepyards, where he had been all night long, slaughtering his mustered sheep and piling them into a mountain of unskinned mutton. He kept on singing The Wild Colonial Boy, and was still singing it when they took him away to Broken Hill. Old Mrs Macintosh found sanctuary with the Skylark's wife.

There was Matthews, owner of a big run. Once he ran race-horses, once he was rich. The mortgagees closed on him and gave him £250 and his car with which to start life afresh. But he was too old to begin again in this life, and with strychnine hastened the start in the next.

"Perhaps it will rain tomorrow!"

Dozens of women were saying that daily, dry-eyed and hopeful when in the presence of their men, haunted with fear of the future when alone in their red-hot homes.

My courage failed me when but 300 of the 4,000 sheep remained to be skinned. Skylark had a buyer for the place at £200 when normally it was worth £5,000, and he wanted to sell and pay me half, but I had no dependants, my old bicycle, and a pair of legs. I deserted the ship like a rat, and so would the Skylark have done but for his wife, who was the real captain.

"Perhaps it will rain tomorrow!"

And when the tomorrow did come and the brave new world arose from the vast dust heap, she and the Skylark rose with it. Today they and old Mrs Macintosh live somewhere in Adelaide.

You see, the real pioneers of the old days, and the real pioneers of these days - are the women.

6

The summer had been long and hot, and the autumn rains delayed in coming. For a year almost I had lived at the edge of a great gibber plain in the far north-east of South Australia, the small hut of iron sheets and its wide verandah roof of cane grass being situated above a lone water-hole in the bed of a creek.

At noon every day there came to the creek a flock of fourteen emus, and at sundown there arrived Iky Mo, Eliza, Dad, the Old Man, Ethel and Flo, and Blue and Brown - otherwise a family of eight kangaroos. It is needless to mention the many birds.

The two dogs and the five cats came to tolerate both the emus and the 'roos which arrived with the regularity of sunrise. Over five months their numbers neither increased nor decreased, the country being in fair condition and offering them no hard ships.

About a fortnight after my friends vanished, there came along a half-caste dog-trapper who told me that down around Broken Hill it had rained about two end a half inches. The south wind had brought northward the smell of rain-soaked earth and the promise of springing green herbage, which proved an irresistible magnet to all things which flew and ran.

Perhaps it was the south wind whispering of cool days and cold nights to come that aroused the migratory instinct within me, for that evening I rang up the manager and asked if the half-caste could take my place immediately.

Thus it came about that with a bank book proving a credit

balance of £88 and a station cheque made in my favour for £30, I met Blue Peter, a stocky little man with red hair and blue eyes, and a winning smile. Together we tramped towards Hergott Springs, each bicycle loaded with a swag end tucker.

For the reason that I liked the sergeant and kissed his daughter, I am not going to mention the name of the township this particular police sergeant controlled. He was an unorthodox policeman who, however, knew his job and his people, and efficiently ran a huge district, the capital of which was a two pub, post office-cum-store, twenty-house town. Beside the police station was erected a one-cell lockup.

Arrived in town, Blue Peter went along to the baker, and I had the station cheque transferred to my bank account which was thereby swelled to £118. That was late in the afternoon, and, whilst waiting for my companion, I sat on the wooden kerbing of the sidewalk outside the store. Then the sergeant strolled to my side.

He was a jovial-looking, white-haired man, with kindly brown eyes and a grim, determined jaw.

"Where you come from?" he asked gruffly.

"Wey down from Swanee River," I replied with unwarrantable flippancy.

"Oh - have you! And where are you going?"

"To my Old Grey Home in the West, sergeant."

"Well, well, well! Many a true word spoken in jest. Now you just take a little walk with me."

And before I knew what was what, I was safely lodged in the one-cell prison, the walls of which were washed grey.

On the hard trestle bed I unrolled my swag and made myself comfortable, for the sergeant told me I would be there all night. Then a trap door in the door proper was slid upwards and a pair of dark-brown solemn eyes regarded me in cool and calm judgment.

"What are you in there for?" asked the sergeant's daughter. "I'm here because I told the sergeant I was making for My Little Grey Home in the West, and he kindly helped me to my destination."

"Oh! Are you hungry?"

"I am."

"What is your name?"

"My friends call me Hampshire."

With that the trap door dropped into place.

Half an hour later, the sergeant's daughter brought me tea and bread and butter and jam on a tray. She unbolted the door and walked in with the provender after she had seriously besought and gained my promise not to escape. It turned out that the sergeant's lady and I originated on either side of Portsmouth harbour, and the sergeant's daughter and I discovered mutual interest in the George Hotel, in which is still the bed Lord Nelson occupied during his last night ashore; and talked of his flagship, the Victory, now in dry dock forever, and of the plaque in the high wall above the spot where the gay Duke of Buckingham was assassinated.

She had left with the tray when I heard outside Blue Peter pleading to be locked up with me. He was pleading not with the sergeant but with the sergeant's daughter, who, without much demur, opened the door to admit him and locked it again upon us both. Having heard of my fate, Blue Peter stored his machine, bought three bottles of beer and a pound of tobacco, and decided to camp with me.

The next morning the sergeant said to him: "What are you doing in here? How did you get in?"

"Well, I was looking for My Little Grey Home in the West, and I reckon I found it last night when your pretty daughter opened the door."

"Well, well, well! Had breakfast yet?"

"Yes, sergeant. Your daughter did not forget to bring it."

The sergeant returned about an hour after that, and hailed us before the "beak". Without visible means of support, was the charge.

"Plead," snapped the "beak".

"Guilty, your honour," replied Blue Peter without hesitation. "Seven days," announced the Court.

I never regained breath until I was back in the cell, and then began to remonstrate with my fellow prisoner. He said: "What are you worrying about? We've got board and lodgings for a full week. We'll get three good meal a day and a real rest."

The sergeant came in to say: " Now, boys, you play the game and we'll get on all right. I want the station whitewashed. Do a fair thing and you'll find I won't be hard. What about it?"

"A little gentle exercise will do me, sergeant," assented Blue Peter, and, because it was useless to kick against the pricks, I concurred with him.

The Law immediately relaxed its vigilance. Blue Peter and I got to work making up the whitewash, and at noon the sergeant's lady announced lunch. She and the sergeant and the sergeant's daughter and the two prisoners sat at a table in the sergeant's kitchen. The sergeant's lady was about fifty years old, and she and I talked Portsmouth till nearly two o'clock, when the interested policeman suggested work. The sergeant's daughter wanted to mutiny, but received no support.

At five o'clock the sergeant instructed me to purchase from one of the hotels two bottles of beer with the four shillings he gave. The work and the bottle of beer gave to us prisoners an excellent appetite, and, after dinner, whilst the sergeant went hunting for the illusive desperate characters, we sat in his par lour with the sergeant's daughter running the gramophone. When he returned without any desperate characters, he locked up for the night the two he did have.

Three excellent meals and a bottle of beer every day for a week. As Blue Peter said: What more could any man desire? The sergeant was delighted with the newly-whitewashed police station, and contemplated charging us with disorderly behaviour in order to retain our services another week to have the front fence repaired.

Our last night I bought four bottles of beer and the largest box of lollies in the store for the sergeant's daughter, whom I had come to know was madly in love with me. When the sergeant, on the following morning, advised us to get employment, I showed him my bank book in proof that I really did have substantial means of support.

"Goodbye, Hampshire. I wish daddy would lock you up again. Come back soon so that he can," cried the sergeant's daughter. Her eyes were very bright, and she wanted to be kissed. She was only twelve.

FIVE

Fog

I

If only all the money and human energy expended on the Great War had been employed in the service of mankind instead of on its destruction, what a paradise we would be enjoying today! If all the stupid mistakes made by generals and politicians - alleged to be intelligent - were committed in the business world the last financial depression would have been as nothing in comparison with the general bankruptcy. Reading the rival autobiographies and volumes of reminiscence by people famous during and after the war causes me to regard my own many mistakes with much less disfavour. The longer I live the more convinced I become that marrying in Egypt, 1915, an Australian army nurse is not to be numbered among my mistakes.

Domestic concerns compelled me to seek discharge from the A.I.F. in London, and I duly signed a paper absolving the Commonwealth Government of all future

Arthur Upfield and his wife, Anne Douglass, a nurse in Alexandria, where they married on November 3 1915.

responsibility concerning my welfare. Then, Time having straightened the tangle, I was obliged to pay my own fare back to Australia in whose army I had served over five years.

It was much easier to adapt myself to military conditions in 1914 than it was to re-adapt myself to civilian conditions early in 1920. In 1914 there was nothing whatsoever wrong with me. In 1920 there certainly was. I was, unknowingly, suffering from neurosis having its genesis on Gallipoli. I was debilitated, unfit to swing an axe all day, erect a fence, perform manual labour longer than half an hour, but I secured a civilian clerkship at the Ordinance Depot, Tidworth, to which I travelled daily from Andover. I had now excellent opportunities, graduating from ledgers to the shorthand-typing branch, and from there becoming the private secretary to the Officer Commanding. There was but one more step to a permanent post in the British Civil Service - War Office Branch - and deliberately I threw away this golden opportunity.

For a little more than ten years I had been out of contact with English people, and this period of time had made me nei-ther superior nor inferior to the status I had occupied when a young man. Without doubt they and their customs and mental outlook had not changed. It was I who had changed. Little snubs we received from people who thought we did not keep strictly to our place in the scheme of life both annoyed and irritated, and we found it boring to have to consider carefully if we were to avoid the snubs.

When I saw a man astride a horse I thought of Australia.

Once I heard a house bell ring for dinner and I was reminded of a belled horse scrambling to its feet early in the dawning. My Australian wife and I talked about Australia for ever longer periods and of our separate lives in Australia before the war. With ever growing clarity I came to see that neither my wife nor I would be happy in England, no matter to what height I might possibly reach. A tree may be transplanted once with benefit.

To transplant it a second time often kills it.

It was really a bottle of eucalyptus which demanded and succeeded in forcing the breakaway at the close of the summer of 1921, the longest and hottest English summer in my experience.

I was then cycling the twelve odd miles to and from Tidworth, and one day returned home feeling unwell. There was ordered an inhalation of eucalyptus dropped into steaming water; and when, having dutifully obeyed orders, I lay with streaming eyes and aching limbs. I suggested our return to Australia.

"But ----," objected my wife. "Well, wad buts?" I snuffled. "What will we do if we go back?"

"Do! Oh, we'll do something."

"Perhaps. But you have a sure billet here and good prospects," she argued, and she allowing me to look into her eyes I saw what I saw.

"Blast the billet and blast the prospects," was my rude observation. "We're still young. I'll get a job easily enough."

"All right, if you think so," she agreed, slowly. "Now why are you getting up?"

"I'm getting up to root out and burn a lot of rubbish to make room in our trunks for things we'll have to take with us," and with snorts and snuffles, despite protests, I arose and girded myself and began the work.

Away back in 1917 I had sold to the Novel Magazine two short stories and to the Daily Mail in 1919 I had sold three articles. Since then I had been an enthusiastic collector of editors' rejection slips pinned to manuscripts, and now the collection contained dozens of MSS totalling in all, I should think, about a million words. I took the lot out into the garden and fired the heap, now and then pouring eucalyptus oil on to the flames in the hope of obtaining one sniff of burning gum leaves when the frost still lay upon the ground.

In course of time we boarded a one-class ship, the old Berrima ship filled to capacity with migrants and ex-A.I.F. men with their families. The long voyage did me a great deal of good, and I was just in time to join in the harvest work on my father-in-law's farm. That, and a couple of visits to Melbourne in search of a job, was the World's beginning in showing me 'where I got off'.

2

I travelled to Melbourne twice to seek a job. It was my duty to secure a billet to finance a home for my wife and small son, and doubtless I could have obtained a pick and shovel job or one which would have kept me slightly below the bread line. There was no influential person to create a vacancy and push me into it. I had been far too long a stranger to my profession ever again to take it up. In any case, women were filling all the offices.

"Go on the land, young man" sounds all right as a phrase, but for a married man to go on the land, unless to his own farm, is quite impossible. He cannot support a wife and family on twenty-five or thirty shillings a week even if the farmer provided a cottage, which Australian farmers do not. The Repatriation people declined to grant me a block of land or the opportunity for vocational training.

Anyway, on my third visit to Melbourne I took a job in a factory. A bell went off in the morning and in we all rushed, to keep rushing about until the bell sounded again when we all rushed out to gobble a lunch and smoke a cigarette. When the bell went off yet again in we all rushed to rush about until it rang for the fourth time and sent us rushing to home or lodging and then, after dinner, rushing to some amusement or other. The most remarkable manifestation seen at this time was the almost fierce desire in the hearts of hundreds earning just a bare living to go on being allowed to earn the bare living. In the mind of every one of them was the fear of unemployment. It was autumn and one evening when walking in a park I happened to walk through a wisp of smoke arising from a little heap of smouldering gum-tree leaves. After that the damned bell could ring till it cracked.

The question has often been asked: what is the use of educating the blackfellow? Even the half-caste will eventually go back to the bush and run semi-wild. Some say that a half-caste is bound to sink to the level of the aboriginal parent. Others point to the half-caste in other countries and say that they always try to assume full white status and always regard the black people as much inferior. I think that this latter statement may also apply to the Australian half-caste, and I am confirmed in the belief that the blackfellow is capable of assimilating education and our civilization.

What is seldom weighed in any discussion of this subject is the influence of the Australian bush on men and animals. It is the reason behind the blacks' walkabout. It is the reason behind the fact of so many old age pensioners living in home-made shacks on the banks of inland rivers. It is the reason behind the migrations of rabbits and kangaroos, rats and mice. It is the reason why hard-headed business men and many others will willingly spare a minute talking about the bush in which they lived as children.

This influence exerted on the mind of a human being by Australia Proper? What is it? It has greater strength and persistence than the primeval longing in man's heart for peace and space and freedom. It is more powerful, even, than the desire to mate, infinitely stronger than the call of the sea to a seaman or the call of the homeland to the exile, it is stronger than love, stronger far than hate.

For nearly five years I dwelt in Australia Proper before spending five years abroad with the A.I.F. I was not born in Australia Proper, or even in an Australian city. My parents had never touched the continent and, therefore, I could not have inherited a receptivity to the lure, the call of Australia Proper. And yet five short years of wandering in it had made me its slave in the company of many other white men as well as all the blacks and the members of the mid-races.

Slaves, that is what we are. Slaves to the spirit of a tract of land. Rebellious slaves we are sometimes, sometimes shouting defiance and running away but in the end surrendering, going back with ears strained to hear the Voice, with nerves quivering to feel the presence of the Goddess, with hastening feet anxious to step into Her radiance.

Should you scoff in disbelief of this influence try to answer this question. Why will aborigines abruptly and without apparent reason pack up and leave a permanent water-hole, to which come a plentitude of game and in the vicinity of which are yam beds, to walk away across the semi-desert just to see a hillock or a dry canegrass swamp or the site of a battle with another tribe, and leave behind several of their old men and women to die like true aborigines, themselves to return gaunt and tired and nigh starved unto death? Or answer this one. Why do men, having worked all their lives in Australia Proper until they are old, refuse to live in a city and enjoy the delights of trams and pictures and pubs, preferring to build for themselves a humpy on the bank of a river within walking distance of a small township?

The blacks cannot tell you why they must go on walkabout or sit down and die. The old white men probably cannot explain in words why they will not live their declining years in a city, but you will see why if you will but look into their eyes, serene and fearless. Have no pity for the blacks, and have none for the whites. You need it all for yourselves, you chasers after wealth and power and sensation.

It was February 27th when I last heard the factory bell, and when I arrived at Wentworth I possessed the sum of five pounds to the penny. The objective was Wilcannia; for somewhere in that vast district were One-Spur Dick, Irish Muldoon, George Bycroft and others I had known who, if still alive, would surely kill a rabbit if not a fat calf. But Wilcannia was three hundred miles up the Darling and the fare was four pounds only to Menindee. An uncle in Adelaide was my sole relative in Australia and uncles are born to be stung. To him I wired for the loan of ten pounds to be telegraphed to me at Menindee. Menindee was reached late the night of the day I left Wentworth, my wad shrunken to four shillings - two for the bed at one of the hotels, and two for the breakfast the following morning. My uncle wired:

"Much regret unable to send money. Am up against it."

So that was indeed that. Controlled by a pensive mood, I strolled along the sandy sidewalk back past the hotel and then, turning left, down across the sand-filled space to reach the river bank above the road-cutting leading to the ferry.

The river was middling, the water like blue-grey marble on which leaf and branch were etched in black. The giant redgums drowsed in heat - somewhere about the century in the shade in which I sat. Two cars appeared at the top of the far bank cutting and one driver shouted for the punt. The captain of the punt appeared, blinked his eyes, straightened his lank body. The second car driver yelled for the punt. The punt man expanded his chest and roared nine words proving that brevity is the soul of wit and that nine words only are neces-sary to describe a man and his parents and his ancestors back to the time of William the Conqueror. The crushing load of despondency was made a fraction lighter.

Cars here at Menindee! Ten years before that day I had sat in the shade cast by this same red-gum and then no motor cars appeared to be ferried across the river. A truck halted behind the waiting cars. A truck! I had travelled to Menindee on a speedy mail motor car from Wentworth in the space of twelve hours. Forty hours had been approximately the time taken by the horses.

Cobb & Co's coaches had vanished. The four-horse buck-boards had vanished. That truck! Perhaps the bullock teams, the horse and the camel and the mule teams, had been wiped off the tracks, too.

This unthought-of change in the bush occupied my mind only for a second or two, failing in its attack on my other and much more pressing problem, my absolute lack of money and/or credit. It was as nothing to be 'broke' in the bush, but this time the matter was more than ordinarily complicated by the non-possession of essential gear with which to face the track.

A morning coat, striped trousers, spats and a topper are raiment not suitable for the task of mixing cement. Cement workers would consider such apparel in working hours as excessively bad form. I was almost in the position of going to work mixing cement in the garments outlined; for I was wearing a tailored lounge suit, a collar and tie, and thin-soled black shoes. To go on tramp in such clothes would be the height of bad form among swagmen.

Up at the hotel was my suitcase containing underwear, shaving and hair gear, silk pyjamas and figured socks, an alarm clock and a pair of slippers. Other than the underwear it was all useless to me in this situation. I could tramp in the shoes but I couldn't carry the suitcase. I hadn't a billycan but I could pick up and use a two-pound fruit tin. I hadn't a water-bag but I could pick up a glass bottle and use that.

But no swag! What the devil would I do without a swag? And tucker! To be on tramp in the summer without a billycan or a water-bag was bad enough, but to be on tramp without a swag, winter or summer, was, well, just too bad. Life was about as tough as it can be.

Although I hated it like hell I went back to the hotel and sought the proprietor's wife to whom I outlined the position and offered to exchange the suitcase for a sheet from a single bed and two lengths of rope for strappings. She was relieved that I did not ask her for money and readily consented to the exchange. (She sent the case and the things I left in it up to the station where I got my first job). Laying the sheet out upon the floor of the bedroom, I placed on it my travelling rug and those articles of clothing I thought necessary, and then, folding in the sides of the sheet, I rolled the swag and secured it with the rope. The two strappings I connected with the towel to form the loop for suspension from the shoulder. And then the proprietor's wife entered and presented me with a real gift - a 70-lbs. sugar bag for a gunny sack containing a cooked leg of mutton, a loaf of bread, and quantities of flour, tea and sugar and salt.

It was now noon, and the temperature on the hotel veranda was 102 degrees when I stepped off it and slunk out of

Menindee by a back track, picking up a fruit tin and a beer bottle before clearing the town. My lounge coat was in the swag. The creases down the legs of the trousers occasioned me a little misgiving but I met no one. The shoes 'looked' peculiar in conjunction with the cigarette swag, but they could not be helped. They were better than no footwear.

For a mile or two I walked over shadeless claypan country skirting red sand-dunes, and then the river and its bordering red-gums came westward to meet me and the track. Off the road I made temporary camp beneath one of the welcome trees, and, after scouring out the fruit tin, I made a fire and boiled water for tea. And, sipping this and smoking a cigarette, I concluded that Life's punch on the jaw was wearing off.

3

The scene was sylvan. The stately trees with their red and grey trunks, the far bank of the river, steep and warship grey, the water calm and cool and inviting, the whispering of the dwellers along the river, the far distant call of a cow in search of its strayed calf, all were enchanting to me who felt like a mariner having gained port after a long and wearying voyage. A small flock of galahs came on whistling wings to settle on the branches above me and, after a few preliminary screeches, began their soft mutterings. Attracted by the smoke of my fire, a crow came to investigate and finally perched in a tree beyond the river and yelled for its mates.

Quite abruptly depression and worry were swept out of my mind to give entry to happiness born of security and peace.

An hour or more slipped by without notice when the galahs awoke and began to screech. Their activity was not due to any movement made by me, for I seldom moved, content with this life I had but regained an hour or more since that I could not be bothered even to look about to ascertain the cause of the galahs' uneasiness. From behind the trunk, against which I lay back, a twig cracked but of it I took no notice. But I sat up quickly when I heard a low, wingeing whimper, and stared when I saw a lean, red dog of nondescript breeding crouched half a dozen yards from me, its jowl resting on its fore-paws, its eyes dust-rimmed and dulled.

Standing up. I looked back at the road expecting to see the animal's owner and seeing no one. There was not a house in sight. Like me, the dog wore no collar. It was famished, the condition of its coat indicating a long course of involuntary fasting. When I called it approached me with chest hugging the ground.

Five years we've tramped through wind and weather
And slept outdoors when nights were cold,
And ate and drank and starved together.

I must have read those lines somewhere and for a moment or two, whilst I stared at the wretched dog and it at me, my mind was exercised to recall where and by whom they had been written. Strange how the mind so crammed with odds and ends is yet so often empty.

Empty! By the look of him that dog was empty. He continued to implore me to be friendly, wingeing softly and wagging his ragged tail. The rims of his bloodshot eyes were as hard as leather, and at the corners were badly cracked. The condition of his tummy reminded me of my own, and so, from the leg of mutton having cut a number of thick slices, I offered the meat-covered bone to the visitor and he, like a gentleman, stood up, came proudly forward and took the meal without haste.

Having dined we rested for another space, the dog lying

with the polished bone but three inches from his nose whilst he never ceased to watch me with his sore cracked eyes. Thus we stayed whilst the red hot sun slid down the inverted bronze bowl of the sky to the horizon. It was now nearly time to push on, but before the tramp I stripped and ran down to the water and plunged in and swam towards the far side. Behind me the dog yelped. I heard the splash of his body and looking round saw him coming after me. From the far side I swam back again, and the dog kept pace yelping now and then and obviously uneasy, but his joy was unmistakeable when finally his new friend and his brand new bone came into close juxtaposition to receive his attention in equal measure.

He offered no smallest objection to my treating his eye-rims with mutton fat as I had with me no other ointment. His bone he wanted to take with us, and as I had no string with which to tie it to his neck, it needs must be wrapped in a piece of newspaper and carried in my gunny sack. It was still a perfectly good bone and there was the probability that we would starve together. I expected that he would suddenly leave me and make off for a hidden camp, but he trotted behind me for mile after mile as the sun went down in a field of blood, promising another hot day on the morrow, and the full moon came up over the tops of the distant river trees at that place several miles to the east in one of the river's mighty bends.

We tramped till the moon was directly overhead, and then camped on a cement-hard claypan in order not to be troubled by the ants and wandering scorpions.

At dawn I awoke refreshed mentally and physically. The dog was still with me. With him I divided the remainder of the meat and the water from the beer bottle - knowing that we would come to the river before the sun became fierce.

"I will call you Hool-Em-Up," I said, as I treated his eyes.

"I hope you will prove to have more toe than that other Hool-Em Up I owned away back in the old days, otherwise we'll starve together for sure."

And away we went to climb over the horizon.

4

That there had been something very much wrong with me I came to understand ever more clearly as day by day the dog and I walked leisurely up river. I felt like a man who, having for long been confined to a sick room, was taking his first short walk in his garden.

The unmade road, winding here through box timber, now crossing grey flats covered with herbal rubbish, now skirting red sand dunes flowing in from the west, was familiar because all outback river tracks are much alike; but the tracks on this road were not those of the old days, and to me were entirely out of place. The ruts were less deep and more broad. Here and there they revealed the clear imprints of rubber tyres. Rubber tyres! The steel tyre of wagon and coach and buckboard had been obliterated by these rubber tyres on car and truck.

Not only was there something wrong with me: there was decidedly something wrong with Australia Proper. There came rushing towards me a giant truck carrying about a third the load of wool One-Spur Dick and I used to shift down to Broken Hill. By me it sped to disappear in the dust it left to choke me. No stopping. No kindly 'Good day-ee!' No indirect questions concerning the condition of the track farther on. No seeking of local news items: No "Ah well, see you again some-time. Now then, you loafing blighters! Away O!" The friendly meetings of travellers had been banished by a rush of hot air and a cloud of dust.

Later, when approaching a gate, I saw a man standing before a bush letter box from which he was taking mail matter. He was, I observed, a youngish man, clean shaven and well set up. He wore a smart narrow-brimmed hat, a silk shirt, riding breeches and military riding boots. By the shade of Henry Lawson! Top boots and riding breeches And the horse! It was a fine upstanding hack that was well groomed and probably recently rubbed down with a kerosened rag. A horse groomed! Perhaps they feed bush horses on oats nowadays. Flatten the damper!

"Good day-ee!" cried I.

Turning, he eyed me without smiling. The quiet and spontaneous greeting I looked for did not come. "Good day!" he said, indifferently, and went on with his examination of the mail. Puzzled, I walked on.

After sundown I came upon a mob of sheep herded for the night within a calico yard. A little way off the track the drovers were lounging on their swags and eating dinner. Another man, the cook, hovered about a roomy buckboard and the fire.

Their dogs came to meet my dog and my dog stood his ground. "Good day-ee!" one of the drovers called out. "Come over and have a drink of tea."

Ah this sounded more like Australia Proper. So every bit of it hadn't vanished during the war years. Four pairs of eyes regarded me as I approached the camp, noting my city shoes, my cigarette swag, the fruit-tin billy. A little fat man pointed to the cook.

"Dish out a feed, Fred," he ordered.

I was given a pannikin of tea, a plate heaped high with stew, and a slice of damper.

"Making up river?" inquired the little fat man.

"Yes - Wilcannia."

"What's the feed like down around Menindee?"

"Not good near the river, but there's whips of buckbush away back of the sand-dunes. Where you takin' 'em?"

"Down to the Hill."

A long silence followed. I enjoyed the stew and my dog enjoyed the short rib bones and the tit-bits I tossed to him.

"Dog any good at sheepwork?" asked a tall, lanky youth whose face was nut brown, whose eyes were deep blue, and whose teeth flashed when he spoke. On the first finger of each hand was a diamond ring. Like those on the others, his moleskin trousers were tough and of good quality. Like his companions he wore a waistcoat, open, and which flapped every time he moved.

"I don't know," was my reply. "He joined me when a couple of miles out from Menindee and he stays put - according to him." Then to them all, I said: "Do you happen to know where I'd find a man known as One Spur Dick?"

The little fat man glanced at the youth. The others obviously waited for this young man to answer my question.

"Too right!" he said. "Ole One Spur Dick is living on the river other side of Wilcannia. He's sort of retired like. You wantin' to see him?"

I nodded.

"Yes. He's a friend of mine. Or he was before the war."

"That so! You musta one time been workin' in the Wilcannia district. Ole One Spur's never been out of it since he come over from Tasmania when a kid."

"Yes, I used to work on Momba and Grimpa. In fact, 'way back in 1910 I was offsiding for One Spur Dick."

The blue eyes contracted. A frown gathered above the bridge of the long nose.

"Ah? Come to think of it," the young man slowly said, "I

was thinkin' I'd seen you afore. Long time ago, though. Ole One Spur Dick's me ole man."

This made me look harder and I knew him.

"You're Young Harry," I told him. "You were just a hool-em-up rip when we struck for spuds on Momba."

The blue eyes now became big and the weather-seasoned face expanded.

"I get you now," he asserted. "You're Hampshire. Now where the blue hell have you bin all these years?"

I had not met the others before, but they knew men I had known. This manager had retired, so and so had gone down a well to look to a pump and the foul air had blotted out his life, that camelman had been last heard of fighting in Palestine, and Fencer Bill had gone to the war and had come home minus one leg and was driving a lift down in Sydney. Night fell, and still we talked with the firelight revealing faces before the black wall of the bush. No one offered remark about my shoes, nor was anything said when I unrolled my cigarette swag. The others turned in and Young Harry brought his swag and unrolled it beside mine.

"The ole man will be glad to see you," he said softly. "Too ruddy right he will. He ain't altered much, but he's had a thin time of it since he went blind."

"Blind!"

"Yep. His eyes went bung on 'im back in nineteen sixteen. Me and Alf fixed him up with a humpy on the river bank among the old age pensioners. He gets the invalid pension, and I hands 'im out a quid or two now and then."

Blind! Poor old One Spur Dick!

"He'll be glad ter see you, as I said, 'Ampshire," went on the soft voice. "If you camps with 'im a night or two and reads 'im a coupler blood and thunders it'll keep his mind occupied for months. And look here, what about taking a fiver off'n me?"

A Commonwealth Bank note was held forward.

"It's mighty good of you, Young Harry," I countered warmly. "But I can't take it. I've yet to get a job, and the way I'm feeling I mightn't take one for a long time."

"Take the note," he insisted. "You c'n pay me any ole time. You see, the ole man's bound to paw you a bit. It's a bad 'abit he's got into. He might paw your fruit-tin billy and things and that would worry him. You know what he is. He's always bin used to being lash with his money, and he don't take it too kindly now he's got to make a shilling go where once a quid went. Any'ow, what-in-'ell's a fiver?"

Young Harry slept before I did. I lay awake while the thinning moon came up to give the bush a ghostly illumination The silence was accompanied by the music of distant horse bells. From the river came the low quackings of busy ducks. After all, Australia, Proper had not changed. It was still the same under the new veneer.

5

I had seen no important difference in the state or condition of Menindee, due probably to the fact that I had not known this township intimately before the war, but there was to be seen by me an extraordinary alteration to Wilcannia. With a feeling not remote from alarm I beheld this new Wilcannia; for, instead of the famous Queen City of the West, I looked upon its ghost.

It was late in the afternoon of Saturday when I reached Wilcannia. In the main street were four cars and two trucks. A few people were walking: a lesser number were lounging in shop and hotel doorways. Pub after pub was shut, or turned into what might be boarding houses. The Court House on the corner was deserted. I took a short walk down that road leading to the track to Broken Hill, and saw here vacant land where once had stood comfortable residences. Again in the main street, I stared with wondering eyes at its emptiness, its dusty dreariness.

There had been Saturdays, in my time, too, when at this hour the sidewalks were so crowded with people that two could not keep abreast for longer than a quarter of a minute, when the curbs were lined by buggies and buckboards, when outside every pub horses were fastened to the hitching rails, when all was bustle and noise and life, when further along the street a Cobb & Co's coach, newly arrived from Broken Hill, stood outside the Post Office unloading the mails, and another Cobb & Co's coach waited to take on the mails and passengers to Cobar. What in the name of Paddy's nearside leader had happened to the place?

I entered a store where once one had to wait ten minutes to half an hour to be served. This day there were no customers. A man came from the rear to walk along behind the counter towards me. He seemed surprised to see me, thinking probably that I was there to cadge rations. I bought a pair of elastic sided boots, a pair of drill slacks, a waterproof sheet, a billy can and canvas water-bag, tobacco and matches, tinned meat, flour, tea and sugar, pepper and salt, and two yards of calico, needles and cotton with which to make ration bags. There were some fly-spotted reprints of thrillers and I purchased three.

With the goods under my arm and with my cigarette swag up behind, I emerged into the street once more. I never saw a policeman. I could not see anyone remotely resembling a chequeman. The silence was terrible - for Wilcannia, not for the remnant of ornamental trees along the river front, the rotting wharfs, the splendid bridge, I could not have believed I was in Wilcannia.

The new township, or rather the remains of the old, ended abruptly to give place to allotments from the ground of which still stuck upward the foundation posts of buildings taken away piecemeal or removed to other places. Here and there a few pepper trees, still flourishing, appeared utterly lonely and dismal at having been left behind by the house removers. Still farther out sand semi-buried paling fences and old posts from which the wires had been withdrawn, and the tumbled goat and cow sheds all so plainly told of those activities assisting in the running of a prosperous town. I looked westward across the common, saw the faint tracks leading to Mount Brown, White Cliffs and Wanaaring, half expecting to see the dust clouds of coach and team coming in to Wilcannia. Almost gladly did I leave this ghost of a once splendid township.

Out of sight down in a sand gutter which carried rain water into the river, I changed into the new things I had brought and re-rolled the swag in the waterproof sheet. With drift wood I made a fire, and on it placed the filled new billy thoroughly to blacken and blister it in case One Spur Dick should touch it.

The small tin pannikin I deliberately dented and then scoured with sand to remove its new smoothness. I performed the same operation with the uppers of the new boots, especially around the toes, and then, after a drink of tea and a smoke, I began the half mile walk up river to the old age pensioners' camp.

Small neat little dwellings were built in the open between the river gums, built with fence palings, stretched hessian protected by wheat sacks sewn together. One was built entirely of sheet iron, and one was built entirely of opened petrol tins soldered together and nailed to a wood frame. Even the chimney stack was built of petrol tins joined end to end. This was the house occupied by One Spur Dick.

I approached it from the back, the west, the front evidently facing the river, the edge of the sloping bank being but ten yards from it. A wall-eyed brindle dog came round the corner and at once sparred up to Hool-Em-Up. Neither giving way they decided to be neutral. My old mentor and friend was seated in a bush chair outside the door of his dwelling. He was better dressed than in days of old. He wore tweed trousers, a white shirt beneath the usual open waistcoat, and elastic-sided boots. His hair was almost white and overlong. His moustache was grey and wanted trimming. O there was no mistaking him, for at the heel of his right boot was a spur and at the other there was no spur.

He knew that someone stood before him and when I did not speak, he said:

"Good day-ee! You're not one of me neighbours." Disguising my voice, I said:

"Bet you a quid you don't know me."

"Quid is a quid these days," he countered. With my normal voice, I said:

"Well, I'll bet you a zac you don't know me."

The poor sightless eyes stared upward in my direction, and his expression became strained.

"I'll take your bet," he said quietly. "Too right, I know you. Wait a minute. I'll place you for sure. You're young Jack Eldridge. No - he was said to be killed in France. Wait. Don't tell me. Speak again."

"I met Young Harry down the track near Menindee. He told me where to find you."

"By the Paroo Burglar! I've got you now," he said with quiet triumph, to add with sudden warmth: "You're Hampshire. Strike me purple with yellow spots, you're Hampshire."

Now on his feet he stood with both hands out-thrust to take mine in a grip which thrilled me.

"You old geaser," I cried. "You haven't altered a bit."

"Me altered! Course not," he shouted. "If I could see I could still drive a team. Here, lemme get me whip and I'll show you I can."

As volcanic as ever. With unfaltering action he went to his house, brought out a packing case, placed it against the end wall and stood upon the case. Then, like a man drawing a splinter from a horse's hock, he drew out from beneath the roof a young sapling at the end of which were yards and yards of a leather whip. As he uncoiled it I saw how the leather had been scrupulously kept in condition, and that at the end of the thong was a long cracker of horse hair.

"Mind yer eye!" he yelled, hair already dishevelled, moustache ends slightly up tipped. His dog came and crouched behind me with Hool-Em-Up who, too, evidently knew a little about bullock whips or stockwhips. One Spur Dick walked a little beyond the house to the westward and away from the river. His one loose spur clanked softly and made the so well remembered mark on the ground with every step. The sapling now lay over his right shoulder and the long whip dangled to the ground where it made the so well remembered trail like a snake's track.

Slowly his blind eyes gazed back and then slowly he 'looked' forward and I knew he 'saw' a team of bullocks working two by two along their heavy draw chair and beneath their heavier yokes. He began to talk, softly, gently, confidingly.

"Whey whoh-back! Come here, Lion. Come 'ere, Blackie!"

His voice rose. "Blackie, you cross-eyed blank of a blanky blankard, come 'ere!" Up rose the whip handle and out went the long snaking leather to describe the arc of a full circle. "Come here, Blackie," and with the name the whip cracked like a gun over the place where his sightless eyes plainly told me poor Blackie was bucking into his yoke.

"Get into it, you loafers," roared One Spur Dick. "you're gonna stop en use the wagon's in a bit of sand? Think Baldy! Leopard! Ringer! Come 'ere, Lion! Stiffen the crows - come 'ere, Blackie!"

Now up and down the imagined line of heaving, grunting bullocks, One Spur Dick trotted, the while the tree sapling swayed around and above his head and the leather sang through the air in full and half circles and uttered its ear-splitting reports. All the oaths of Afghans, Chinamen and Australians poured from his lips as he dashed now to the leaders and now back to the polers and then up again to the mid-body where he attended to a chronic loafer named Mr Murray, after the manager of the station. Mister Murray came in for a torrid time, the mister being accentuated at top volume.

"'Ampshire, you loafin' Parcels Post son of a Pommy," yelled One Spur Dick. "What in 'ell do you think you're doing of sitting up there on the load? Come down off it, and attach yerself to a shovel handle and get to these unprintable imitation bullocks on the offside. Come on, now, lamm into 'em! Think they're gonna. stick me up in a pannikin full of sand! I'll lamm 'em."

The sapling waved like a guardsman's sabre. The leather shrieked through the air and the cracker snapped like a machine gun. I flung down my swag, which 1 had had no time to remove, and seeing a long handle shovel over against the open fireplace, I rushed to it and returned with it to the off-side of the team. There was an empty bag lying on the ground and I used it to take the blows from the flat of the shovel as I shouted the names of the bullocks or rather the ghosts of those we used to drive.

Back it all came to me. I remembered every name of the twentytwo. I could see every animal of the team, and out of the air emerged the outlines of the huge table-top wagon bearing the mountain of baled wool.

"Stick to 'em, 'Ampshire," shouted One Spur Dick, who was rushing up and down the long line and never once missing giving each straining animal a smack either on the near or the off side to bring it into dead straight and thus get the maximum effort on the draw-bar chain. "Look at that there Bluey! Can't you see he's doin' nothing? By Cripes! Let me get at him! Sulk, would you, Bluey?"

With a final burst of terrific energy he flayed the bullocks along the near side whilst I lammed at them along the offside.

The ghosts had materialized. The entire team of twenty-two, from leaders to polers, was straining and heaving to keep moving the mountain of wool. Then ---

"Wh-hoo, you beauties!" sang out the teamster. "Let 'er stand on the clay-pan,'Ampshire," he added as he grounded the end of the sapling and allowed the long whip to dangle on the ground at the back of him. I knew what he had 'seen', and why he had gone into the frenzy of energy. In his imagination the wagon had reached a bar of soft sand into which the wide-tyred wheels were sinking, when to allow the team to stop would have meant terrific labour.

"Never let 'em ease up when the going's hard, 'Ampshire," he shouted. "Once they stops, getting the wagon on the move again takes more out of 'em than ten miles of travel."

Then the years came crowding back upon him and he

wilted ever so slightly. The ghost team vanished and I saw him listening to ascertain my whereabouts. I spoke, and he came across to me, the solitary spur clanking, the long whip trailing.

"I told you I could still drive a team, didn't I?" he said. "I can still use me whip to some order, and I can still perform when the hornies gets into a jam. But I got to get me team away from the river bank afore I starts, cos once I 'ad 'em too near the bank and over I goes down into the water, whip and all. Anyhow, it does me good to think I'm larnin''em how to pull long, strong and steady. And now, lad, on with the billy whiles I gets the fire going."

He waited for me to lead the way to the house, and I had sense enough not to offer to guide him. Immediately he touched his house he never faltered, and later I was to see him show me how he could cross to the bank and follow a path down it to the river where he filled the two petrol tin buckets and returned with them.

His house consisted of two rooms, the inner providing a bedroom, the outer the living room containing a spotless table, two cases for chairs, shelves and a meat safe, with the cooking utensils hanging on either side of the open fireplace.

"You've got a nice and comfortable joint, Dick," I said, wondering at what I saw. His face became re-lit by the undaunted spirit.

"Too right, lad," he agreed. "Young Harry and Alf put 'er up for me inside a fortnight after the tins were collected and busted open. Young Harry's been real good to me. So was Alf afore he went up to Queensland since when we ain't had no word from him. Things was a bit awkward at first for me. I burned meself a coupler times and skinned me shins a good many times, but now I sorta got used to being blind and I don't carry on like I used to. The parson wanted me to go inter a old mans' home down in Adelaide. Coo I'd sooner walk inter the river and drown meself. If I can't see I can hear mighty well. I can hear the birds and the talk of the old river.

"Get going now. No loafing. You'll find the damper in the oven under the table. Get 'er out and the plates and things. I've got a fine perch in the safe. Caught him last night and cooked him this morning. Cripes, I'm glad ter see you, 'Ampshire. Lemme see, but it don't matter. Someone or other told me you 'ad gone off to the war. I've thought a lot about you, lad. We got on well together, didn't we? No arguments, no troubles tween us. Old George Bycroft will be glad to see you. He drew a block in the land lottery and is about gettin' on his feet. You didn't get wounded, did you?"

When the billy was coming to the boil we went outside and washed at the bench. My swag was leaning against the wall and he touched it with a boot. Down went his hands in no rude curiosity, and I was made glad that Young Harry had enabled me to make it a real one when my host remarked:

"New, eh? You ain't bin on the track long, then?"

"No. Only a week or two. I've only just got back to Australia."

"Well, you'll camp here with me for a week or two, a month or two if you like. Cripes, I'm glad to see you. 'Ampshire. It's a bit lonely being blind and all, but one of me neighbours comes in sometimes, and sometimes I go over to one of them for a chinwag. I'm not complaining. I never did and I'm not gonna start now. I gets me bit of pension regularly, and parson comes out sometimes and leaves something his wife sent, but times ain't what they uster be. A bloke has to go very careful. Stiffen the crows! Why, in the old days, 'Ampshire, we jingled golden sovereigns in the pockets of our dungaree pants, didn't we? Remember that night we sat in to a game of poker with a droving crowd at Tilpa Hotel and cleaned 'em all out? Them were the days, lad: them were the days."

Ah me! Yes, indeed they were the days to remember. After eating, and having attended to the wants of the two dogs, we sat outside and yarned far into the night. I had bought a half-bottle of rum, and we drank a stiffener in a pannikin of tea before turning in like we used to do on the road to and from Broken Hill.

And like I used to do, every night thereafter I read to him till one and two o'clock in the morning, lying on a woolpack wogga with my head to the firelight, he seated beside me and living in the novelists' created scenes. And then, whilst we drank our nightcap, he would recall books I had read during those halcyon days on the track, and talk of the characters as though they had played their parts in a book I had just concluded.

We would fish early in the evening when the gums were aflame with the sun's afterglow, and the birds would be chattering and screeching whilst they watered. That was his time for scandal.

How Mrs Blank ran away with a butcher: how Bell's third girl went wrong: how Jack the Groveller was caught with so and so's wife by so and so, and how they fought it out for an hour and twenty minutes without a breather. That must have been some fight, for an hour and twenty minutes is a longish spell. How Ted the Dogger became a major in the Egyptian Camel Corps Transport, and how he came home after the war and slew his wife because she had had more children than he had kept count of. And all the while One Spur Dick would chuckle, and end up with shocking details of other people's loves and lives.

I spent a week with him and in return for my attempts to

entertain him was given by him a firmer 'holt' on myself than I had managed to do for years.

"No, I don't know where you would drop into a job, lad," he said one evening as we walked homeward carrying the evening's catch. "You go up and call in on George Bycroft. He might know something. Times have changed so. The war and Kidman's Blight have about done for the Wilcannia district, and there's no sale for opal so no-one's doing any gouging over at the Cliffs. When me and you was workin' on Momba there was from forty to fifty men employed there. Now there's a white boss in charge of half a dozen nigs. It's like that up the Paroo, station after station done for by the Blight. All the teams have gone bar one here and there. There's no improvement work going on. Still, there is the lamb marking in a month or two and the shearing to follow that. And why the blue hell you want to leave me for, I don't know. You'll come again,'Amp-shire, won't you? Promise me you'll come again."

Always a fine man on the open roads, he was a truly great man in his world of darkness. As I tramped up-river I felt that the fog was swiftly lifting.

Camel train at Albermarle Station 1920 (photograph by E.V. Whyte); Upfield's mates near Wheeler's Well 1928.

SIX

A Phase Of Life

I

Life in Australia Proper as life elsewhere, is much like one of those Chinese nests of bowls in which each fits snugly into another. The surface of life in Inner Australia appears to be pastorally simple to the newchum and to the visiting student, many of whom desire to write a book about it and are satisfied to observe it from a squatter's homestead veranda and his six hundred pounds sedan. Life lived by a squatter is vastly different from that lived by the stockman whose life, in turn, is vastly different from that of the swagman and the sundowner.

When I tramped from Menindee to Wilcannia I had an objective and a destination, but after visiting George Bycroft I had neither the one nor the other. Possessed of an objective and a destination I had kept to the road which maintains a more or less straight line from river bend to river bend. For every mile of road the river runs three miles in its twists and turns, often making an abrupt angle to complete a gigantic and almost full circle to come again to within a stone's throw of itself before turning yet once more. Some of the bends are but a mile or two from point to point touched by the road: others there are which are ten and twenty miles from point to point and ten, twelve, fifteen miles from the road to the centre of the bow. Within these bends the land is lower than that across which runs the road: in time of flood submerged by water; normally dry as dust and deep with a fine cement-hard rubble. Billabongs and water gutters criss-cross in all directions. There are vast lantana swamp areas, patches of box trees, and a sea of bush as brittle as straw and not nearly as useful for stock.

All this tangle of tree and bush and herbal rubbish had been produced by flood water which, having started life, receded to leave life to take its chance and provide evidence of the kind of jungle which would cover Inner Australia were the rainfall two hundred inches instead of ten.

Many strange things have happened along the Darling, more especially within its deep and lonely bends which provide 'grand places for a murder'. There yet awaits the future Edgar Allan Poe of Australia, a mine of material for tales of horror. There is hidden in these bends a phase of life unknown by the casual swagman, perhaps because, seeing them from the road, one is repelled by their dark mystery, their appearance of powder dryness and grey death.

2

I stood on high ground which turned the river at a sharp angle. A short distance back from the everlasting redgums which line the river's course grew a climbable box tree, and up this tree climbed I to view the scenery whilst Hool-Em-Up barked at its foot. From the look-out the brighter and higher foliage of the red-gums could be seen stretching eastward and then north eastward finally to become merged with the general bush. About three or four miles to the northward the road could be seen rising to pass over a low land swell, and as nowhere near this part of the road could the tops of the red-gums be seen it was evident that not till many miles beyond that land swell did road and river again meet.

Time having no value, with no objective and no destination, I decided to quit following the road and to follow the river for a change no matter if the river led me for thirty or forty miles till again I came to the road.

The interlude with One Spur Dick had deepened the mental depression born of the knowledge that I was a failure in that I had been unable to make a home in or near a city for my wife and small son. Added to this was an uneasy conviction that I could have tried harder to find a situation which would have provided that home. I had accepted failure too easily. I had not stoutly resisted the call of Australia Proper. The life road I was now travelling wasn't going to take me upward into the light of prosperity and happiness and content. I had lost more on the swings than I had gained on the roundabouts; and, because I could not put this knowledge from me, I was not happy when, without the knowledge, my present circumstances would have provided a fountain of joy.

Even had I not sauntered – this is the right word - progress along the verge of the river would have been slow. It was constantly necessary to leave the river bank to skirt a deep water gutter or a stubby creek or a billabong filled with water from the river. Still, there were intervals when it was possible to walk the bank for half an hour without being forced to make a detour, when to walk in the shade of the gums was delightful and to observe the life about and on the river was both instructive and amusing.

Hool-Em-Up had a splendid time. He chased iguanas into trees. He chased rabbits and actually caught one. At the end of every chase he entered the river and swam about whilst constantly yelping his happiness. By now his eye-rims were in a healthy condition and the state of his coat indicated an improved physical condition.

The rabbit I cooked one evening a la Australia Proper by smearing the carcase, fur and all, in wet river clay and burying the mass in the hot embers of a fire. When removed the clay was as hard as a brick and on being broken up neatly into two-sections withdrew all the fur and skin and offered a meal fit for any tramp.

From George Bycroft I had cadged a fishing line and with this one could command a supply of fish. From one hole at a minor bend I caught a codfish weighing at least ten pounds within ten seconds of casting in the baited hook. I caught another, slightly larger, within a minute of the second cast and threw it back as unwanted. I believe I could have loaded a truck with fish for the Broken Hill market from that one secluded hole. And having obtained a square of wire netting from an old fence with which to fashion a griller, there was no danger of starving to death. Never in my life have I lived to pamper a stomach I yet can state with confidence that a fish caught and immediately bled and then grilled over hot wood coals is a dish to make the stomach cultivate or so write whole books about it.

The harmony of the succeeding days and nights was unbroken till the early afternoon of the fifth day after leaving the road when we approached a camp comprising a tent erected beneath a bough roof. It was situated on relatively high ground distant from the river's bank some fifty yards and therefore not to be seen by anyone travelling up or down the river or from its far bank which was much lower. Beneath the bough roof, and in front of the tent's opening, stood a green table beside which a man sat on a chair. I saw before we drew near that he was watching us, and noted with astonishment that he was wearing bright yellow pyjamas with black facings. His raiment made a splash of colour against the general green toning.

I was not in a visiting mood but it was impossible to avoid the camp. The sunlight was reflected by many bottles lying helter skelter between the camp and the river. Then I saw a bottle and a glass on the table beside which sat the camper.

Throughout the period of my approach he never once moved, and this was an oddity where the flies were many. Then, although he was seated in the shade, the sheen of the pyjamas informed me that they were made of silk or a material as costly. My interest was aroused.

In the first place, I did not expect to see a camp because on neither side of the river was there a road. In the second place, this was not the camp of river fishermen. It was too tidy and the quality of the tent under the neat bough roof was too good for fishermen. Thirdly, the man's attire was decidedly not that of a fisherman or a stockman. Whilst yet many yards separated us I decided that the camper was an artist, a writer, or a naturalist, taking his ease.

Now I saw him watching me with a fixity of gaze which, allied with his immobility, was to say the least unusual. I came to see that his hair and beard were red, that he was a very big man weighing in the vicinity of fourteen stone and standing would, I estimated, reach the six feet mark in the canvas shoes he was wearing.

I pretended to pass by, expecting to hear his greeting,

and then turned towards the tent front and so came to stand immediately under the edge of the bough roof. Still he did not speak, or move. His eyes were terrible to look into, being a washed blue. The whites were stained with red as the eyes of a jaundice case are stained yellow. I already wished I had not stopped. Then I said: "Good day!"

The eyes seldom blinked. Not a single little movement was made. Did I not see life in his eyes he might have been dead, seated in the wicker-work armchair. The situation rapidly became unbearable. I could not inquire of him the distance to any place because I was not bound for any place. I could not ask the time because such a question would have been absurd. It was almost with relief that I watched his lips part to frame the word: "Drink."

There was no expression on his face, none in his eyes, and there was no inflection, no expression in his pronounciation of 'Drink'. There was no hint of interrogation in it, or of contempt, or of demand. It might have come from the sentence of 'Drink this tea' for all the sense it made as he pronounced it. He spoke again, and this time the words made sense although they were entirely void of inflection.

"Only the one glass," he said. "Use your tin pannikin."

Clearly it was an invitation to help myself from the bottle on the table. The day was still hot and the timber permitted no lightest waft of air to circulate. An ice-cold bottle of beer would have been a gift from the gods themselves. My attention in the man became transferred to the bottle, and to my relief I saw that it contained neither whisky nor gin, which I abominate, but brandy. This I saw was good brandy and, therefore, should be treated with respect. To drink good brandy from a tin pannikin was sheer callous murder, but needs must when the devil lurked in those blue eyes regarding me so fixedly.

Into the battered tin pannikin I poured a generous two fingers and then glanced about for water with which to make it a 'long' drink. Having travelled along the river's bank my water-bag was empty.

"River," suggested the camper like a child naming a blue line on a map.

Down to the river went I with my billy, and on my return to the camp found the camper still seated in his chair but three full bottles of brandy in addition to the one on the table. There was, too, on the opposite side of the table a wood case set down for my occupancy. I seated myself on it, made the 'long' drink, raised the pannikin and looked above it to my host.

"Luck!" he said as though making a statement of fact.

"Good luck!" I returned and, when he reached for the bottle, waited for him. He half filled his glass, his stomach winced, and then he drained it of the raw spirit. I took a drink from the pannikin, set it down, and fell to rolling a cigarette. He poured himself another stiffener, set the bottle down midway between us, and said:

"Drink."

The meaning of the word had now become something stronger than a suggestion. I should have complied with all speed. I should have thought, what a lucky chance I came this way. A man might tramp a hundred thousand miles and not meet with such a liquid entertainment as this. Yet I was uneasy, made so by the man's strange eyes, his bizarre appearance in this sylvan setting, his condition of being neither drunk nor sober. Having completed the making of the cigarette I determinedly lit it before again raising the pannikin to my lips. Over it I looked into his eyes - and wished I was well away from them.

"What's a drunken man like, fool?" he stated.

"Eh?" was my somewhat blank reply.

"You heard what I said. Shakespeare coined the question and he gives the answer. It is: 'Like a drowned man, a fool, and a madman.' It's a wrong answer because I'm no fool, or a drowned man, or a madman - yet. Drink."

Lacking enthusiasm I complied with the invitation. He poured himself another stiffener. We drank. I should by now have experienced a sense of exhilaration. I experienced only a sense of great uneasiness. His placing on the table three more bottles of brandy during my absence at the river indicated an intention of making our meeting the excuse for a drinking orgy: but his mood, his manner and his bearing indicated no warmth in the invitation to such a party. Had he shown evidence of being well soused, had he been hilarious, the invitation would have been natural. As it was there seemed to me to be some ulterior motive dictating the invitation to drink, some objective to be gained which was not conducive to my continued well being.

I had never seen a drunken man if this man was drunk. Yet his face and his eyes plainly indicated prolonged intoxication. But only his face and his eyes. There was no sign of intoxication in his hands, his feet, his body, his voice. Then I thought I understood. I had watched men drink and become almost incapable of standing, to go on drinking and become outwardly, sober again. The process is described as drinking oneself sober. The flanking array of dead marines hinted that this probably was what had happened to my host. Here was he, set down alone in the lonely bush, a modern Jimmy Woods. The dead marines, the bottles on the table, spoke of a still well-stocked cellar - probably under his bunk inside the tent. I now could visualize his end. If the stock did not go dry on him, he would fall into the river and be drowned in a desperate effort to escape the little blue gentlemen. Only with an effort did I keep the unease in my mind out of my voice.

"Seems to be a better method of committing suicide than cutting the throat," I observed.

"Takes longer but is not so messy," he replied, making it the statement of a problem he had worked out satisfactorily.

"How long has your method been in operation?"

"Two weeks, perhaps three, perhaps a month. I shall continue with it till it accomplishes the desired end. It is what I live for here for. Drink."

The brandy was banishing discretion. We drank.

"Been properly drunk yet?" I inquired conversationally.

"It was some time ago. I have got beyond that stage. I am not sober, mind you. I dare not let myself become sober. It is my intention to commit suicide. This is my way of doing so. I fear a bullet or poison as much as I fear becoming sober. If I shot myself, or drowned myself, or poisoned myself the world would say I was a coward. By drinking myself to death the world will say I was an unfortunate fool,"

"So you care for what the stupid world would say?"

"Yes. I have my people to think of."

"You are considerate."

"To them, yes. To myself or to others, no. Drink."

Having helped himself, he pushed the newly opened bottle towards me. I shook my head.

"Drink," he repeated, still without vocal inflection.

"No thanks. I've had quite enough. I must be getting on my way."

"Drink," he said, for the third time. At this third utterance of the word I fancied I detected a threat. I saw the pupils of his ghastly eyes grow big, watched them become still bigger.

In them for the first time I saw expression. I felt as a fly probably feels when first enmeshed in a web, and knew that his insistence on my drinking was based on an ulterior motive. What?

Despite the heat of the late afternoon I experienced a kind of numbing cold and a sensation of tingling at the soles of my feet. The eyes of the man before he had become points of blue steel surrounded by a sea of blood. Drunk? He wasn't drunk. He was mad.

"Drink."

Finding it difficult to disengage my eyes from his, I realized that to do so would require effort. It was this, I think, which deepened my unease into positive fear. He was telling me to drink, not to be generous, to show hospitality, to profit by conversation, but for some other reason, some horrible reason. A trembling began all through my body and could not be mastered. I heard the sound of the pannikin against my teeth but was barely conscious to drinking. To avert my gaze from his eyes was a feat of will power of which I had never suspected myself capable, and whilst my fumbling fingers rolled a cigarette I heard him say:

"You have never been as drunk as I am. I know I am drunk because I can't hear the watch in my brain ticking, ticking, everlastingly ticking. The ticking began when I regained consciousness after a fall from a bucking horse. I discovered that the only thing to stop the ticking was hard drink, and that every time I became sober it began again. It's like a cancer. As time goes on it requires ever more booze to stop it. So I had myself transported to this place by boat, and here I am employed in keeping the damned watch from ticking me into an asylum."

The cigarette was badly made. I refused to look up into his eyes. I succeeded in evading them whilst I lit the cigarette.

I was thinking how I could escape, and the doubt of

being able to escape assailed me. He sat with his back to the tent entrance.

I sat with mine to the river bank. A foot or two behind me lay my swag, with the water-bag and gunny sack tied to the straps.

Then again came the word which had become terrible. "Drink."

If I obeyed what was after all a command I would become drunk and at his mercy. To the centre of the table I directed my gaze and found myself struggling to maintain it there. To look up into the points of steel surrounded by the red seas would mean my finish. He was hypnotizing me. And he was a maniac. Of this I was sure. And I was sure, too, that he had no need to hypnotize me, for he was twice my size and weight and had but to lay a hand upon me to make me his helpless victim.

"Drink," he said again.

Then I saw his hands held an inch or so above the table beside the bottle. There was long red hair on the back of each of his fingers which were gently flexing and unflexing. The table was one of those cheap card affairs to be purchased in almost every store. Those hands could reach me without his standing up.

Like a spring the tension snapped. As I leapt to my feet I heard my own yelling sounding like that from another man. With all my strength I pushed the table away from me and against him. I made a flying dive for my swag, snatched it up and, while still moving, flung it over my shoulder and then ran. Never before was fear so uncontrolled.

As I ran I looked backward and what I saw made me stop. The maniac was standing beside the fallen table and before him crouched Hool-Em-Up, hackles stiff and teeth bared. It was necessary to fight for self command before whistling. The dog heard the call. He began slowly to move backward, his smouldering eyes still staring upward at the huge red man, until, widening the distance between them to several yards, he turned in a flash and came racing after me.

And I turned again and again ran. Men with watches in their brains were not pleasant people to know.

3

Passed the days and the weeks in travelling northward towards Bourke, distant by river some six hundred miles from Wilcannia.

The still autumn days were interrupted by heavy rain, and the third day after the rain I noticed a green tinge here and there which swiftly spread to join in one vast carpet within the week.

Sometimes I camped with other tramps at a shearing shed where I met men named Bill the Blackguard, Shaver Harris, Tom Thumb - a man weighing seventeen or eighteen stone and standing six feet four inches in his naked feet - Fedler Joe and Alf the Liar. A tome could be compiled of Australian swagmen whose like are nowhere found outside this country.

Sometimes I travelled with a fellow swagman who in nearly every instance had his pet theory of life. One believed devoutly in Communism; another in the fiery hell of the Calvinists; yet another was a hot admirer of Mr W.M. Hughes; and another suffered from a brain malaise prompting him to recite poetry. One damned the Protestants and another cursed the Roman Catholics.

I fell in with aborigines all of whom tried to cadge the makings. A fat lubra showed me how and where to find and to dig after the honey ants, and a thin lad showed me how he could cross the Darling by walking over its bed with nothing more than a length of hollow lantana cane one end of which he held in his mouth, the other being maintained above the surface, and thus he was able to breathe.

I was asked by four squatters within a space of five weeks if I could cook and would cook. I replied that I could not cook and would not if I could. I saw one squatter on a Sunday morning issue from his house in the full regalia of a Colonel with medals and all, including the sword. I was told that he did this every Sunday morning. Why, I could not ascertain. I arrived at one station when a game of cricket was about to begin. One side was short of a man. In I went in my turn and by a remarkable fluke I scored fourteen not out. I happened to be playing for the boss's side and he wanted me to take a job gardening. I met a man and a woman in a car. The man was driving the machine all out. It had passed me some twenty odd minutes when there appeared a man on a horse. The horse was lath-ered with foam and sweat and the man held the reins in his left hand and gripped a double barrelled shotgun in the right. He was trailing the man in the car who was bolting with his wife.

There was never a shortage of tucker. The majority of station cooks were generous, while at many stations the old practice of giving to travellers a hand out of flour, tea and sugar, and a little meat was still in vogue. It is a practice that has its origin in the early days of squatting when the squatters, in order to avoid going to a distant town for men, encouraged men to tramp from place to place by giving them rations so that when a man or men were wanted there were always men on hand.

The surface knowledge of Australia Proper acquired during the pre-War years was now being rapidly deepened. I observed the phases of cloud formation and movement in conjunction with the wind, the activities of the ants, the habits of the birds. At this time I had no faintest inkling of the career

I was to carve for myself, and yet was preparing myself for it.

Summer returned for a short spell in the first week in June. I had boiled the billy for tea one noonday and was eating a meal when seated on the swag and resting my back against the trunk of a box tree. A few feet distant to my right lay the trunk of another tree which yet was unattacked by the termites. From a place beyond my vision there travelled an army of little black ants along their own made road to a crevice in the fallen tree trunk.

What I knew about the ants was not obtained through books and, consequently, I am ignorant of the Latin names of ants ranging from the ferocious bull-ant to the tiny red one no larger than a cheese mite. I doubt if such knowledge would have increased my interest in them.

The ants I watched this noonday as I ate damper and salted fish and drank milkless tea were, as I have stated, small black ants known as sugar ants by many and named piss ants by our early writers. In relation to size they are the strongest of all the ants, and this day the workers were engaged in transporting merchandise from the old nest to the newly selected one in the recently wind-wrecked tree. Some were carrying the small elongated eggs, others carried items of food three and four times bigger than themselves. One came along with the entire wing of a small moth. It could be seen that here and there along the road travelled ants that were not workers. There was no visible difference between them and the carriers, and it be unclear that they were performing none other than the duties of traffic policemen. They assisted anycarrier ant in difficulty with its load. They conversed with ants returning to the old nest. I watched one order several carriers to drop their loads and buck to in removing a fallen leaf off the road; and, having done so, return to and take up their loads again and continue towards a new nest.

Then I saw some ten or twelve feet distant from me, and several feet from the ant road, a member of the oldest ant family on earth, a bull-ant. It was supporting its long body on its hind legs, standing straight up and working its mandibles as it stared at me. Stared is correct. It saw me, not smelled me or heard me. Just where the position of its nest was I knew not, but was certain it was not nearby because I had, as habit dictated, made sure the immediate locality was free of bull-ants before selecting, the place as a temporary camp.

It was a fine looking fellow with a plum-coloured body and black head. That it was a scout was evidenced by the absence of its fellows. That it was mastered by curiosity and not the desire to attack became evident, too. It came down on all its legs and without haste came toward me – and thus came close to the road occupied by the scurrying black ants. As though in obedience to a command the black traffic policemen ceased their road duties and gathered together into little parties around which the burdened carriers struggled with their goods and chattels. There came an end to the procession of loaded carriers, and the reason why the policemen were drawn into conference was without doubt that which ordered the stoppage of the transport of goods.

The bull-ant continued to advance towards me, and thus drew nearer still to the ant road. It halted when about three feet from my boots, when I lifted one and thumped the ground. Thereupon it rose up on its stern and became supported by its hind legs to stare at me and gnash its mandibles as though by making faces at me I would move again and betray my identity. It appeared to have no sense of its danger from the black ants, but they were aware of its close proximity to them and their road and were preparing to give battle.

The rearmost of the carrier ants entered the crevice leading to the new nest before the traffic policemen led the returning carriers from off the road and towards the bull-ant. It was still standing end up and now its two antennae were waving above its terrible head and constantly clashing together. If it was not thus sending out signals to its fellows to come along and support the attack on me, if air waves were not set up to be received by the antennae of other bull-ants, then it must have been winking at a passing queen moth.

With no slackening of speed, no hesitation, the first of the little black fellows dashed at one of the plum-coloured legs and bit. Even before the bull-ant came to earth it had plucked the attacker from its legs and had tossed aside the pieces. There is no fear in the insect world. There appears to be the one emotion only, that of anger. The massed vanguard of the black ants now arrived and the bull-ant killed and killed and killed, but he could not kill fast enough. It was clearly a victory of ant-power over armaments. One by one the plum-coloured legs were severed. Steadily the plum-coloured body was covered with black ants until nothing could be seen of the bull-ant beneath the heaving attackers.

Then I saw the coming of the supports and counted five of the giants advancing with the deliberateness of army tanks. At a dozen points of the road the black ants were deploying to meet and attack them. From the old nest they came pouring in a massed formation along their road. One by one the giants were over-whelmed and taken to pieces and carried back to the road and along it to the new nest.

Engrossed in this battle I failed to note the approach of a swagman until Hool-Em-Up barked and ran forward to greet him. He was of medium height and walked well despite a heavy swag. He was, I could see before he neared me, a half-caste. The diversion of my attention to him was momentary. I pointed to the battle and waved a hand to indicate that I desired him to make a detour and so come up behind me. Reinforcements of both sides were arriving and the general battle was joined. Hundreds of black ants were slain. One after another the tanks were destroyed piecemeal.

There was no mercy, no success here, retirement there. The fight proceeded with the inevitability of life and death. Before me there now were dozens of heaving black masses obliterating plum-coloured bodies.

Australia Proper has in store an exhaustless supply of surprises, and it presented me with one when I heard a voice from behind me, a voice which was soft and liquid and finely modulated.

"There is not a great difference between the behaviour of men and that of the ants," remarked the voice. "Neither the Ant nor Man could maintain the social structure without the application of laws and the blind obedience to them. Man, being less perfect than the Ant, more often breaks the law and is much less heavily punished for breaking it. To the Ant is meted out only one punishment for law breaking - death."

These observations, coupled with the pleasing voice, caused me quickly to twist around to look upward into a dark-brown face having sharp Nordic features and the blue eyes of the Nordic which at the moment were beaming.

"Might I boil my billy on your fire?" he asked.

"Certainly," I agreed. "If you're not very thirsty you may save yourself the trouble by helping yourself to mine which is still hot and fresh."

"Thank you. Although time is of no consequence to waste any of it is a sin. Pardon me for the paradox."

He was wearing clean khaki trousers of drill and a shirt

of the same colour and material. On his feet were the usual elastic sided boots. He was hatless, and I saw no hat attached to his swag. His hair was short and fine and straight. For a half-caste he was remarkably free of self-consciousness and entirely free of shyness.

"The ants always remind me of the Roman Empire under the Caesars," he stated whilst he poured tea into a tin pannikin. "Obedience to the State and an iron discipline in the army made the Roman Empire what it was. It crashed only when the termites of licence and luxury worked upon the central authority. Did some power destroy the central authority governing that community of black ants not one of the bull-ants would have been beaten in the fight."

"What is that authority? Where and with what is it invested?" asked I, wondering. His speech was pedantic and yet wholly natural. There was no striving after effect, no endeavour to impress me, no evidence of conceit. He ate and drank more politely than did I. His smile was ever ready and spontaneous. With quickened interest I tried my best to rise to the conversational level set by him.

"All the old Imperial Empires were established by iron discipline, don't you think?" I said. "Babylonia, Egypt, that created by Kubla Khan. In the main there seems to me no difference between the ideology forming the foundation of those Empires and that on which is based the new brand under the leadership of Lenin. In fact, Lenin and his Bolshevics are very much like the ant policemen I have been observing as they directed the workers."

"I have not given much time to the study of Communism," he said, gravely. "It appears to me that the form of government does not matter. We all must, I suppose, be governed else human society would not endure. What matters to the worker what uniform the policemen wear?

There is nothing new in Communism. It means merely to render to the current Caesar those things stated by the current Caesar to be his. In a democratic state like ours Communism has been especially evolved for the comfort of suckers and the profit of publicity seekers."

"I doubt that our condition would be improved by a change to Communism," I contributed. "We would still have to pay taxes--"

The quick smile broke over the sharp features of my noon companion and he laughed. Knowing at what he laughed, I joined him. Here we were, two unemployable tramps discussing forms of government and the payment of taxes. It had been his charm of personality and singular manner of speaking that had caused me to forget it.

"What is your destination?" he asked with just the right shade of hesitancy in the circumstances. "The next camp fire. And yours?" Smilingly, he replied:

"The next camp fire. Do you object to travelling in company?" What a companion was that half-caste! To me, a quite ordinary man, his erudition was delightful and never at any time forced on one. His mind was a storehouse of knowledge of the kind obtained by wide reading as well as through observation. He showed me to what height of efficiency a human could rise in the art of tracking:and the wiles that could be used to fault the keenest tracker. He opened my eyes - which I had thought were wide open - to gaze at worlds beyond the mundane, the worlds of the insect, the bird, the animal and the reptile.

At odd moments he permitted me to see into his heart and regard the picture therein of the eternal warfare between the influences of his black and his white parents.

The companionship endured for a month and then he said he would have to end his walkabout and rejoin his old moth-

A pair of camels I recently broke in for an inspector on the Number two fence to drive in a heavy buggy with a half-caste offsider. We had quite a lot of sport. So did the camels.

Upfield and camels on the Number 2 Fence, with his notation to reverse.

er's tribe. That going back to the tribe was an anti-climax; and from the vantage point of today I am convinced that the white man's crime against the blacks was not and is not their wholesale reduction in numbers but his refusal to give them a chance of competing for a civilized livelihood and life's prizes. The crime is all the greater against the half-castes.

4

The cool days of June gave place to the still colder days and nights of July when I would wake up mornings to find frost on my bed coverings and on the tips of Hool-Em-Up's hair: when the smoke of a camp fire is never more blue and never smells sweeter: when to be alive is fine and to be on tramp in Australia Proper is great.

For five weeks I worked in a shearing shed as a rouseabout and with my cheque I bought a stout bike into the frame of which I built a canvas bag for rations. Having removed the pedals it could with ease and comfort be pushed while I walked, and made to carry besides the swag plenty of rations, fishing lines, a gun and cartridges, and a fry-pan.

We were camped, the dog and I, on a wide bar of sand which rolled westward across the flats to stab the flank of the Warrego River. There were no flies these days and no inconve-nience to be caused by ants and scorpions: hence the selection of soft sand for a mattress. The damper was baked for the morrow and I smoked cigarettes while, aided by the firelight, entering into a diary the small events of the day.

Beyond the narrow radius of the firelight the wall of black night reared to the glittering stars. The stillness of the wild was disturbed only by the leaping flames. Not a sound from all the encompassing world of space reached my material ears.

Yet there was a sound to be heard by the dog. He sniffed suspiciously, then curled himself into a ball near the fire.

Then again he stirred, raised his head and sniffed, raised first one ear and then the other. Once he whinged. Slowly the hackles stood up along his back.

Moments passed whilst I, too, listened. The dog's unease continued. The sound which had awakened the dog, and which eventually I heard, appeared to originate from a long way off. I failed to name its cause: yet it was not a normal night sound.

A minute must have passed the while I watched the dog and strained my hearing. At last Hool-Em-Up decided from what direction the sound was reaching us. He stood still, stiff and still, with hackles raised, his nose pointing northward along the track which passed at the foot of the sand-dune.

Presently I fancied I heard music, organ music, the organ being played in a church down in a peaceful valley late on a summer's evening. Surely I was not hearing heavenly music: surely I had not reached that milestone of the sundowner's life! Yet music it was: most certainly it was. The notes rose and fell in rhythm and in perfect time. The timing seemed familiar, or was it the slow intoning of a grand hymn?

To the best of my knowledge there was neither habitation nor human being within eleven miles, and never yet have I known a swagman to travel on a dark winter's night singing hymns or playing hymn tunes on a mouth organ. Gradually the music became more distinct. There was now no doubt that someone, out there in the blackness of the cold night, was not singing or playing an instrument, but was humming in a high pitch. But the tune hummed! Surely I could recognize the tune? Ah, I caught it at last. How often had it been played during the war years, that hymn of praise, that hymn of grief. that most wonderful hymn of triumph.

Yes, this was the tune without a shadow of doubt: nor could there be any doubt that the hummer was mentally unbalanced, in these circumstances one bushman does not play a practical joke on another. Had not the dog been with me I would have been inclined to doubt my own sanity. In such a situation a dog can be relied on to prove whether a man's mind is balanced or not.

Beyond the radius of firelight there was nothing to be seen by me. The hummer now was drawing close, had probably left the road and was walking up the dune to my fire, yet it was quite a time before there appeared a tall figure emerging from the pervading blackness, not dissimilar from an image appearing on a developing photographic film. My suspicions of the hummer's sanity were confirmed when I made him out to be approaching with slow measured steps.

Continuing its humming, the figure drew near. First I saw that he was a very tall fellow, then that he was gaunt, and, finally, that his hair and eyes were dark as well as his trimmed beard and moustache. In striking contrast, his face was a dead white - the putty white of a corpse. "Boom! Boom! Boom!" At each 'Boom' down came a foot without sound on the soft sand.

The fellow's face was tilted slightly upward. His hands waved as he kept his own timing. He carried no swag, neither billy-can nor water-bag.

Without a halt in the tune he hummed, he came to the fire and stared down at us from its far side. The lines of his face were now plain, lines which drew down the mouth and puckered the forehead into a vision of despair. Standing there, he hummed the tune to its end whilst with wide black eyes he regarded the dog and me.

"Good night " I said cheerfully, or as cheerfully as I could force my voice to indicate.

He answered in a somewhat unconventional manner, the while his face retained the fixed expression of grief. He said, much as a child repeating a lesson:

"I'm dead - dead. I'm dead."

Having it in mind to assure him on the point, I invited him to a drink of tea and a slice of brownie and reached for the sugar bag. The offer, however, made no more impression on him than it would have made on a gum tree. Although Hool-Em-Up growled and I was obliged to grip him in restraint, I think that the hummer was even less aware of him than he was of me. Again came the statement:

"I'm dead - dead - dead."

Half turning he raised high his left foot and, when he brought it to the ground, hummed the first booming note of the March. Slowly, with funeral steps, he passed from sight, leaving me with an amazed sense of unreality. Softer and softer did distance tone the tune of death and life, until at last my straining ears could register it no more. The visit appeared a hallucination induced by a damper wrecked digestion. I was really assured of the condition of my mentality only when examining the fellow's tracks on the far side of the fire.

An hour later the dog sprang up and barked vigorously. This time a figure emerged from the black well of night without a sound. It was much shorter than the other had been, and it bore two swags and several billy-cans fitted one into another. Hool-Em-Up greeted this second man with evident friendliness: whereupon the visitor shouted before actually reaching the camp:

"Good night! Have ya seen me mate? Tall bloke. Name of Dead March Harry. We was camped about five miles up river, and I left him to cook the tea while I went to looksee the fish lines. Gone when I got back. Gone without his swag, without me. I knoo then he's got one of 'is 'ummin' turns. He's been a lot of trouble to me in 'is time 'e 'as. But he's 'armless, mate, quite 'armless. Well, so long. I'll soon catch up to him, for he don't do more'n a mile per when he's hummin' that there funeral song. Good night!"

After he, too, had disappeared, I pondered on the ability of a man to bear affection for another. Mateship! And there was Hool-Em-Up lying full length on his chest, with his head resting on his fore-paws and his gaze fixed on me.

SEVEN

Embarassing Moments

I

Australia has suffered more than is thought by the lack of a historical background of romance and adventure. There was nothing cleanly adventurous about the penal system which tarred official and convict with the same brush of frightful bru-tality; and Australia was unfortunate in the particular brand of bushranger that infested it for a period, the bushrangers being a dowdy lot, very slow on the draw and very poor shots even when they had unlimbered their quite unsuitable ironmongery.

The extraordinary influx of people to North America during the latter half of the last century was due much less to the real and imaginary get-rich-quick opportunities than to the love of adventure which throughout the ages has burned steadily in the hearts of young men and women. Australian history offers no such stirring tales as those provided by the Texas Rangers and the Two-gun Alecs, the Buffalo B ills and the Canadian Mounted Police. Never has Australia produced such heroes like Wild Bill Hickok and others who, it has been alleged, killed twelve men with twelve bullets in twelve sec-onds with two six-guns, our own desperadoes were never suf-ficiently artistic to equal that.

Then, too, Australia's native population was numerically small, destitute of wealth and peacefully disposed if treated as human beings. Rider Haggard could not possibly have staged his stories in Australia. Our allegedly anthropoidal aborigines have ever been too independent to carry the lordly white man's goods and chattels a la African natives. They have always objected to cleaning the white man's boots and protecting him when he went big game shooting at wild dogs, buffaloes and kangaroos, regarding with contempt any man who cannot go hunting without a huge escort. We are unfortunate in that our aboriginals do not make a show with their witch doctoring and magic accompanied by the beating of tom-toms and the slit-ting of throats, although in their shy manner their magic and witch doctoring make the Africans look like innocent children.

Notwithstanding Australia's lack of Wild Men and a servile black population, it can as it has ever done provide adventure and romance. The adventure is here but the romantic back-ground has never been here - to our great disadvantage from the point of view of an adequate population. Were I the manu-facturer and distributor of the immigration literature in Great Britain I would not so incessantly harp on the opportunities in Australia for work. No one wants to work, certainly not the youth of any country. The young man and woman like to dream dreams in which he or she is the central romantic figure. They are simply not interested in the annual rainfall of Sydney, by pictures of the poor devils working harvester machines, others chopping down trees, and others digging irrigation ditches. Their interest and their ardour to emulate would be fired by pictures of a buffalo shooter in action, a man patrolling a section of fence on his camels, even a swagman eating his supper beneath a red gum on the Darling River. Show pictures of a Queensland cattle camp engaged in calf branding, a buck-jumping show with a background of a saltbush plain, and a tarpaulined bullock wagon stuck in a sand-drift with a One Spur Dick and a Hampshire at work persuading the hornies to get a move on, and there would never be any difficulty about securing immigrants of exactly the class desired. Even to hint at work is fatal.

There is more real adventure in Australia to-day than in any other Dominion - adventure with the lid off but adventure without a romantic background.

2

On the first Sunday of every month I went to the homestead of a certain well known station for rations and the mail. For a station homestead this one was lonely, being situated at the end of a road and some three hundred miles out of Broken Hill. There were no travellers to pass through this station, no swagmen, and, since the advent of motor transport, no half-yearly delivery of stores by chains of camels driven by Afghans.

At the homestead dwelt the squatter and his wife and children, a married couple - the man cooking for both hands and 'government house' and the woman housemaiding at 'government house' - a young Birmingham fellow who milked the cows and was generally useful, a few aboriginal stockmen and one half-caste camel driver. Nearby lived a portion of an aboriginal tribe.

It so happened that during one Saturday night prior to the

Sunday I was to visit the station homestead one of my camels broke a hobble strap and led the others on a twenty-mile ramble. By the time I got them back to camp it was too late to set off on the seventeen mile journey to the homestead, and I was obliged to defer the trip till the following day.

It was near noon on the Monday when we surmounted a sand range and saw the cluster of red-roofed buildings skirted by two windmills and partly surrounded by pepper trees, and as was my custom I rode to a patch of wind-tortured mulgas behind the blacksmith's shop and there neck-roped each animal to a tree and unpacked.

With my outward mail and the empty ration bags I walked round the blacksmith's shop, passed the harness shed and the stockyards, then skirted the men's quarters and so arrived at the office store building immediately behind the squatter's house.

There was something strange about the place this day. It is as easy at a station homestead to distinguish a Sunday as it is in any city. This day the homestead had a super Sunday atmosphere of quiet and peace although the day was a Monday. When there should have been cows and goats and horses and people engaged in their everyday employment. This day not even one goat was in view. The place was as deserted as an empty house at midnight. Even the crows were absent.

The office I found locked. Passing across the back of the main building I reached that containing the men's dining room, the kitchen, and the married couple's rooms. The kitchen door was shut, and when I tried to open it I discovered that the door was barred. Astonished, I went on to the verandah and looked in at the fastened window - to encounter the cook's white face and staring eyes.

In a moment he was holding it ajar and peering out to greet me with infinite relief depicted on his face and in his eyes.

"What the devil's wrong, Joe?"

"Come in – quick," he urged.

Having slipped inside, he at once shut and barred the door.

Before turning to question him, my gaze was drawn to the table and held by an array of chunky billets of firewood and three bright-bladed butcher's killing knives. The cook came round me to stand and look into my eyes with fear in his own.

"Did you see Dingo?" he whispered.

Now Dingo was the half-caste employed by the station for many years, he being a handy fellow at building a stockyard, mustering cattle, as well as driving the camel team. Despite the loss of an eye and his six and a half feet of bone and muscle he was fairly well liked for his cheerful disposition and a readiness to laugh.

The cook related a tale both interesting and curious despite its disjointedness. On the preceding Wednesday, the boss and his wife and children had left in the car for Adelaide, the cook undertaking to issue the necessary rations and deal with the mail. Here was presented a grand opportunity to Dingo to spend money on that which the station rules as well as the law forbade. Riding thirty odd miles to a selector's homestead he telephoned a wayside hotel and persuaded the licensee to send him a case of whisky by the mail driver on Sunday.

The whisky being duly delivered Dingo carried it to the men's quarters, broached the case and invited all hands to take a drink unmeasured. The mail driver left when affairs were quickening, but nothing of note occurred until about eleven that night when Dingo stretched his mighty arms and announced his intention of chasing the girls.

He had, of course, first to find the quarry. However, the

owners of all the local girls, being acquainted with Dingo when in his romantic mood, by this time had hidden their gins and the lubras with the cook's wife in the cellar beneath the squatter's house. Discovering no girls to chase in the manner of his paternal forebears Dingo had it out with the bucks in their camp down along the creek. They united in winning the day - or rather the night - and Dingo returned to the men's quarters to lick his wounds and soften their pain with more whisky.

His only companion at this time in the men's quarters was Fred, the lad just out from Birmingham: and, being a peaceful citizen, Fred made the mistake of trying to calm the drunken maniac with words instead of with a billet of wood. The more whisky Fred drank the more peaceful did he become. He insisted upon being allowed to sing about roses clustering to a doorpost and evinced no interest whatever in Dingo's grand idea of chasing the girls.

Shortly after day broke Fred had become a lamb and Dingo a lion. A bleating lamb fled from the hut with a roaring lion in pursuit, and before the horrified cook, standing at his kitchen door, the lion captured the lamb and smote it to the ground with one paw. Gleefully, Dingo picked up Fred and tossed him high into the air, then jumped aside and watched the body return to earth 'with a sickening thud'. The cook said that Fred went up about ten feet, an altitude with which Dingo was not satisfied, for he now began to break his own records and succeeded in tossing Fred up to about twenty feet when the cook could no longer look on and yelled admonishments.

Observing the cook Dingo rushed at him, to be met with a slammed and barred door. Whilst hammering on the door he detailed at length what he would do once he got his paws on the cook. He continued these details when outside the window which he refrained from smashing open when he saw the cook inside with a butcher's killing knife in each hand. Quite abruptly he remembered the girls and set off to find them, obviously thinking that their owners had taken them away among the surrounding sand-dunes.

He had disappeared among the sand-dunes but ten minutes later when Fred regained consciousness, staggered to the hut, fortified himself with more whisky - according to the cook who noted the time he was within - and then appeared with Dingo's bicycle on which he had fled along the Broken Hill track.

To me it appeared that the case of whisky was like the Serpent that invaded the Garden, or the ferret that invaded a warren inhabited by peaceful rabbits. Although two hundred miles from the nearest policemen, the people living at this homestead were law-abiding and peaceful until the arrival of an innocuous case of whisky. Result: a new chum riding like the devil in the direction of Broken Hill, a cook on the verge of collapse, ten or a dozen women cowering in a cellar, a party of blacks planning murder in their camp, a maniac rushing over the sand-dunes, and a fence man wondering what on earth to do about it.

It seemed that the first step to take in order to restore normality was to remove to a safe place the cause of the upheaval – if any of it was left to remove to a safe place. To make this first step would require care and great caution because, although taller, I was no heavier than Fred and did not regard with favour the prospect of being tossed to a height of twenty feet. Still, if the cause could be removed it would be but a matter of time before Dingo and the other members of this community would be settled into the ordinary routine and conditions of life.

In the men's quarters I found two full bottles of whisky and a couple of fingers of the spirit in the other. Requiring courage

I sank the two fingers straight from the bottle and carried the full ones to the cud-chewing camels where I 'planted' them in one of the pack bags. The next step was to withdraw from the scene and to allow time to complete Dingo's reformation.

This, however, was not to be. The pack loading had been roped and the animals brought to their feet when, with shouts of joy, Dingo appeared from round the blacksmith's shop to charge towards us. His appearance was not pleasing. Usually neatly if flashily dressed, he now wore only the garment in which he was born. Even whilst I shrank from the prospect of being seized in his mighty arms I could but admire his splendid physique. His eyes were like black opal, and his black, straight hair stood out from his head like canegrass. On his not unhandsome face was an expression of exultation, and in the working of his hands was indicated the lust to hurt. For me there was no time to escape. This all happened not in Texas or in Rider Haggard's Land, or even in Sydney, but close to the junction of South Australia with Queensland and New South Wales and, as I have said, two hundred miles from the nearest policeman, where men keep the laws and where the transgressor is apprehended with astonishing speed and conveyed to Broken Hill and a judge and jury, or at the least a magistrate. The consequences of a man killing another to avoid bodily injury, even death, are not pleasant. It means a loss of wages over a long period, expenditure of savings on maintenance and the employment of legal assistance, besides a deal of worry. Up to a point, therefore, bodily injury is preferable to preventing such injury by the employment of a lethal weapon: or in other words the same idea can be expressed - shooting a man is worse than being dumped into unconsciousness and perhaps to death.

This thesis flashed through my mind even as Dingo rushed

upon me and I turned and reached upward for the .44 Winchester repeater rifle slung from one side of the riding saddle. Armed with any weapon less effective than a rifle, and a repeating rifle at that, I would be no match for Dingo.

It was necessary only to cock the trigger for it was customary to carry the rifle with a cartridge in the breach for quick snap-shooting at a chance-met wild dog or a kangaroo that would provide fresh meat as a change from the eternal salt beef.

It was at this critical moment beyond my power to produce a yell or a shout of warning from my mouth which was open. I was like a stage struck singer, vocally, but an automaton in movement.

Aiming at Dingo's legs I pulled the trigger and instantly ejected the spent cartridge and pumped another into the breech.

I was obsessed by the idea of preventing the half-caste from reaching me and yet escaping the charge of manslaughter. In actual fact I could not have done better than aim at Dingo's shins; for, like the full blood, the shins of a half-caste are the most tender portions of his carcase.

The heavy bullet sped between Dingo's twinkling legs to kick upward a spurt of dust just behind him and then, most fortunately, to ricochet and cause a high-pitched scream. Dingo fell almost on his face so violent was the effort to stop his rush, then he turned away to the north and ran yelling towards the mirage. As he retreated I sped bullets to chop upwards spurts of dust on his right and left, merely as an inducement to increase his speed.

Three cigarettes and a stiff dose of the lately acquired medicine were necessary to banish the effects of reaction, and three hours later Dingo returned to the homestead a reasoning human being but one doomed to suffer a splitting headache for twenty hours.

3

Since early morning the heat had been so severe that the flies had taken refuge in the meagre shade cast by the mulgas, and the hundred and one species of ants had remained deep within their nests.

In the more pronounced shadow given by a small grove of cabbage trees my three camels watched me at work with such lofty indifference as to make me feel foolish, labouring as I was in the sun when the temperature within the black shadow of the bloodwood tree at the nearest homestead was hovering about at the 119 degrees mark. To be sure, that registration of heat away up in the north of South Australia, with its remarkable lack of humidity, is much less trying than is 100 degrees in Sydney.

I was labouring to clear a section of dog-proof fence, a six feet high wire netted and barbed topped affair, of winddriven dead buckbush which gathers the sand so fast that within a week or two where once was a fence there is a sand-dune. It was about three o'clock when the bull put in his appearance, while I was waiting at the camp fire for the billy to boil. The camp was situated beneath a stout leopard-wood tree - so called because its trunk is spotted green and white. Here, where the camels had been unloaded the evening before, were the iron riding and straw stuffed pack saddles. Close to the tree was the canvas stretcher bed, on one end of which was the tucker box and on the other my current cat, red mouth gaping, flanks working like bellows. Round about lay the iron water drums, the rolled tent which was never erected save when it rained - on an average about four times a year - and odds and ends of necessary gear. From the branches of the tree hung the meat bag, the flour bag, and the leather saddle bags containing the rations so attractive to the ants.

The scenery of sand-ranges and stunted trees elevated to Jack's bean stalks by the mirage might be thought not idyllic but was most decidedly peaceful. I found nothing displeasing about it.

I was rolling a cigarette whilst seated on the stretcher, and feeling pity for poor Tum-Tum drinking lukewarm water from the billy lid at my feet, when, with unnerving abruptness, the Intelligent Bull snorted loudly from a position directly behind me. There, at a distance of a mere twenty yards, he stood, a tawny picture of nine hundred pounds of malignant fury, his head held so low that his snorting breath raised the dust, his forefeet snapping upwards from the knees and tossing sand high above his back. Without doubt he had called on business. And when a bull of the sand ranges means business - well, he means it.

A camel can unlimber into a gallop from a standing position in about three yards. The bull accelerated to top speed in about three feet, and it was then that I made the mistake which was to prove so costly. Instead of snatching the blanket off the stretcher to meet the charge like a gallant screen star, I shinned up the leopard-wood tree hard behind the cat, and when the bull flashed by I was inelegantly lying along a bough twelve feet above the arena.

When I had obtained a more comfortable seat where the bough joined the trunk, and when Tum-Tum was on my shoulder and spitting defiance at the bull, the opportunity of viewing the situation was presented. The bull now stood face about, giving himself another sand bath - and then with incredible swiftness he launched himself into another charge.

Physically he was in excellent condition, but the hollows punched into his flanks indicated his want of water. Doubtless he had lingered too long at a dried-up water-hole when the other cattle had moved on to a bore: and now he was mad with thirst, his mind governed by panic as a man's mind can be so governed by the ever watching and patient spirit of the bush.

I at first thought he meant to charge the tree, but he sped past the tree end made for the alarmed camels, and they, despite their hobbled feet, lounged away in three directions roaring with terror. They left in great haste, but the bull was faster than they and assuredly would have done a lot of damage had they remained together.

Here was my chance. Placing Tum-Tum on the branch behind me, I slid to the ground and rushed to the riding saddle. It was when I was bending over and fumbling with the straps to release the Winchester repeater that the Intelligent Bull spun round in his own length and came charging back. Without the weapon I rejoined the cat.

The bull now began to earn his sobriquet. From beneath the tree he regarded us with displeasure gleaming in his wicked eyes. When he tested the tree hopefully with his head I expected him to back and then to deform his brain in attempt to butt down the trunk. But not so. Instead, he walked round the trunk and tested the tree's stability from several angles. Then, to demonstrate his annoyance, he tossed over the stretcher and walked on it to examine the contents of the wrecked tucker box.

Then he nuzzled the water drums and tramped on them and kicked them until the seams burst and the precious water leaked away into the hot and thirsty sand. Then he dug his hoofs into the rolled tent and proceeded to toss the pack saddles until most of their straw packing was scattered.

Having thus demolished the camp he took up a stand about a dozen yards from the tree, there to glare at us and to throw up over himself further showers of sand, apparently knowing full well that the moment would surely come when I would drop to the ground alive or dead. The heat would first madden and then kill me long before he went to ground for the last time.

I was becoming desperately parched when the sun neared its crimson setting. The colour of the evening sky increased the bull's ardour for a killing. For me the situation was fast becoming serious, for, even at night in that country, and at that time of the year, one must drink. The water drums were smashed and empty but the canvas waterbag, containing about a gallon of water, was hanging from a hook on the fence where I had been working, and the water in the billy on the almost dead fire was not upset; but I was more than a few difficult yards from these supplies and twenty odd miles from the nearest source at a station homestead. And to yell for someone to come and drive the bull away would have been the first sign of madness.

Hope suddenly flared brightly, however, when the bull walked away, as though tired at long last of this cat and mouse game.

Yet, when I attempted to reach the ground and the rifle, back he came at a gallop. Immediately he saw me again in safety, he again sauntered away, now and then bellowing loudly and appearing to stare in all and every direction save back at me up in the tree.

This time I gave him a hundred yards. On he went. Instead of slipping down the trunk of the tree I dropped to the ground and rushed to the riding saddle and the rifle. Back came the bull, head down, tail up, a cloud of dust behind him. Back up the blessed tree I clawed my way to reach the friendly bough and the interested cat. Oh - if only rifles grew on tree branches.

The sun vanished in a sea of blood, promising another hot

and windless day on the morrow. The bull wandered away, pretended to forget us, but he neither wandered far enough nor ceased to watch us. A willy wagtail fluttered down from a higher branch to alight on the iron saddle and dance his evening jig. The next instant, Tum-Tum jumped to my shoulder, then to the trunk and proceeded to slide down it stern first. Aghast, I could do nothing. She reached the ground and began to stalk the dancing bird.

The bull just as interestedly watched the stalking of the wagtail, possibly laying odds on the bird. He permitted the cat to make her fruitless spring before coming once more into violent action, and when she had recovered from her disappointment he was only ten yards from her and arriving fast. And, perched like an ancient and featherless galah, I was unable to render her any assistance when in wild panic, instead of running for my tree, she ran for safety to the distant cabbage trees with the bull hard upon her tail and snorting like Saint George's dragon - a little furry fugitive pursued by a terrific Juggernaut.

Such was my haste that I fell out of the tree to land on all fours on the sandy ground which came up and struck me like a ton of bricks. I had only just unstrapped the rifle when the furious bull was well on his way back. Made heroic by thirst, a worm turned at long last, I rushed to the protection of the tree, and from round its trunk I brought the rifle into action.

Some twenty thousand cartridges fired in practice were not wasted. Malignant to the very last, the Intelligent Bull pulled up short, staggered towards the stretcher - and deliberately laid down on it with the bullet in his brain.

It was impossible to drag from beneath nine hundred pounds of beef either the ruined stretcher or the blankets. It was impossible, too, to sleep on the bare ground of ant-infested country, even had water been abundant.

Having made and drunk tea, having watered Tum-Tum and promised her a dozen tins of milk, I raised her to ride on a shoulder and trudged the long long miles to the station homestead for a new camping outfit prior to a search for the three camels. To me it seemed that the bull must have had a thoroughly enjoyable afternoon, even to his crowning death-bed joke. Of course, I had the last laugh, but the laugh was laughed long before the last of the weary miles was covered.

4

When Hereford the Wake left his job to rush to the magnet at Wilcannia - Mrs Goonery's Hotel - I was set to his work until another groom could be engaged.

For the station groom the day began by riding out after the horses at half past six in the morning, in order to have them in the yards by seven-thirty, the time they would be required by the stockmen. The horse paddock was four by four miles in area; the mornings were solid with frost; and the leader of the horses was a vicious, man-killing outlaw named Tiger.

Long before the sun rose beyond a distant line of box trees marking the course of a winding creek, I would be stalking the groom's horse in the small night paddock. For half his life Toby had been a groom's horse, and for the other half, the first half, he had been a stock horse with cattle on the tracks of Western Queensland. He knew his job from the top down. His legs were short, his dark-brown body was like a barrel, and his shoulders were so massive as almost to present a deformity.

In the dawning of a winter's day it was unwise to slap a

saddle on him, and then at once to slap oneself into the saddle. Such haste was productive of circus stunts at a time when legs and hands were numbed with cold. One placed the saddle on him gently, and one tightened the girth-strap against his expanded chest gently, too. Then one walked him across to the yards to make sure the gate was efficiently propped open. If it was exceptionally cold one walked him past 'government house', and then, before he had time to expand his chest again, one took up the girth-strap another two holes.

The homestead and the stockyards were situated in a corner of the horse paddock, and outward from the corner lay a mile-wide stretch of open claypan country almost as clear as the famous Daytona Beach and as hard as cement. At the far side of this open stretch a line of box trees marked the edge of a vast land depression which held water for a year or two every thirty odd years.

At this time it was covered with herbal rubbish among which grew wild carrot and spinach. The lake's surface was composed of hard clay rubble, and it was scarred with wide and deep leg-breaking cracks. Here and there the stock had tramped narrow winding pads which avoided the larger cracks, and all these pads appeared to lead from the shore to an island about the middle of the dry lake, which also was edged with timber and thus provided a fine wind-break throughout winter nights. Sheltered within this ring of trees would be the forty odd horses from which the day's workers were selected. They were always found there, replete with spinach and wild carrot, but a few yards out from the island would be standing Tiger, a chestnut beauty with white hooks and a white star on his forehead.

He was one of the few super-beautiful horses I have thrilled to see. His heavy mane and long tail were as yellow as gold against the gleaming colour of him. As I have mentioned, the lake's surface was terrible: only along a horse-made pad was it safe to ride. Off the pads, the horses would suspiciously 'nose' every step they took, and even when following a pad they would not dare to canter or gallop.

In the vicinity of the island were none of the leg-breaking cracks, and Toby would make to one side or the other of the island, watched by Tiger and his following, as well as by the two buckboard greys that always tried to hide themselves behind trees. It was ever necessary to ride close to them before they realized that their cunning had failed, and then Tiger would squeal, fling up his heels, trumpet with contemptuous defiance, and lead the way across the lake at a smart trot towards the homestead and the yards, following, of course, one of the beaten pads.

This procedure never varied during the five weeks I was station groom. I came to understand that it was an equine game played every morning by Tiger and his mates, the two greys, and Toby. The rules were explained by Toby, who offered violent objection were one broken.

Thus was the game played:- Off stream the horses, winding like a monstrous snake as they trot in single file along one of the pads. They are hidden from us by the fine grey dust rising to hang motionless in the brittle air. No amount of cajolery will induce Toby to hurry. That would not be playing the game.

Presently we reach the harder surface near the lake's shore, where we find the horses waiting for us, with Tiger standing a few yards beyond them. He is like a bronze statue whilst we yet are travelling the dangerous ground: but, on our reaching the harder ground, he is off, running beneath the border of trees to gain the open claypan country, beyond which the risen sun is varnishing the red roofs of the homestead. After him run the others. There begins a cavalry charge, a thundering assault upon the horse-yards. Leading the assault runs the magnificent Tiger, mane and tail all smoking gold. No longer has Toby a mouth. Rein pressure has but little effect on his iron jaw. He draws close to the heels of Nugget, the light dray horse, who is the finest charger of the lot and does his bit with enthusiasm.

With stockwhip cracking, and the icy air slip-streaming by face and ears which no longer register feeling; with the thunder of hooves exciting to madness a passing flock of galahs; the regiment of horse sweep past 'government house' which is saluted by Tiger with a scream of hate.

There live there those whom he has fought and vanquished, poor simps who thought they could rope him again after slapping a saddle on him and thrusting a dirty bit between his white teeth and then springing on to his back as though he was a gelding. Let them try it again and he would throw them and crush them and stamp on them and tear them to pieces.

There is no pulling Toby back before the yards are reached. In we go with the mob, I to fall off him and rush to shut the gate before Tiger can fight his way out of the press and lead his followers back to the lake.

There was never anything so glorious as that whirlwind rush across the claypans to the stockyards on a crystal-clear, frosty morning. Tiger loved it no less. Even Nugget was rejuvenated. As for Toby, well, he appreciated the permission to show off. The regular groom used to use a snaffle bit on him, a thing which should be outlawed by the law.

And then the boss had visitors: a banker and his wife and two daughters. Such daughters. It was my duty to carry their luggage from car to rooms, and when I winked at the daughters they smiled and winked in return. The day after their arrival, the boss said:"Tomorrow morning I want you to bring in the horses with extra smartness. My guests are American, and I want to show them how we begin the day. I'll have them out on the veranda to watch you bring them to the yards."

Now I was not so old that I could frown upon the opportunity of showing off before two such lovely girls as those with whom I had exchanged winks. And then the boss laying slight stress on the 'extra' when be said he wanted the mokes brought in smartly, as though the horses had in the past been brought in like chargers practising for a funeral.

We set out the next morning with a new silk cracker on the best stockwhip owned by the hands, and in our hearts was determination to show how things are done in Australia. In due course, Tiger and his followers waited for us at the lake's shore.

When all was set for this 'extra smartness' act, I uttered a yell. Tiger glared his surprise before answering me with a scream of fury, and we got off the mark in very promising fashion. The whip cracked and Tiger lifted his heels to the sky. The mob laid well down to it, and Toby travelled well. He sensed the great importance of this morning, and forty odd, bush-fed, real gallopers streaked for the homestead yards.

And then I committed the unpardonable sin of touching Toby with the whip, an act of sheer carelessness. Clamping his jaws on the bit, he determined to prove just what he could do.

We passed Nugget as though he were harnessed to his dray. Then we passed the greys - and they were not loafing. Then we were in among the mob and edging up behind Tiger. With Tiger we raced neck to neck, and Tiger's vile temper flared up at the impertinence. His ears dropped flat, the pupils of his eyes became mere pin-points of fire on a white background. His teeth were bared and he swooped to crunch my near-side leg. I slapped the whip-cracker against his shoulder and he screamed his rage and mortification.

Then he was falling behind. It was astonishing. Tiger shrieked like a demon. With undignified effort I tried to haul Toby back, but a winch could not have hauled him back to his rightful place at the rear.

Tiger continued to squeal and scream but he lost no more toe. We were in the lead, and he was a mere placed horse, when we passed the main building and the dressing-gowned figures on the veranda. I worked hard on the whip and yelled. We were easily the first into the yards and, because I could not reach the gate for the mob, Tiger got out and led them back to the lake.

It took us all the morning to get the horses again into the yards, and the boss had to explain to his guests that in this country where water runs up hill and the trees shed their bark and not their leaves, the station groom always leads the working horses to the yards early in the morning.

Aboriginal workers' camp at Albermarle, 1922

5

Since early morning the heat had been so severe that the flies had taken refuge in the meagre shade cast by the mulgas, and the hundred and one species of ants had remained deep within their nests.

Then there was that meeting with the Yandama Dragon. I had heard many stories of the Yandama Dragon who roamed the country in the far north-west of New South Wales and across the border of South Australia. He was a bull camel that had been abandoned by his Afghan owner, and in course of time he became a tiger, a lion, and then a dragon, charging here and there and smashing down fences, killing fence rider's camels, sending horses mad with fright, chasing stockmen and the few aborigines, and keeping women and children in their camps and houses.

On five occasions rifles had been brought into action against the dragon, but he was impervious to bullets, even when directed by experts. He was reported to be at places 100 miles apart in the one week. He was fearless, audacious, as cunning as a crow. The local Saint Georges fell down on the job of slaying him, and it was they who assiduously built up his reputation to cover their own failures.

Consequently this fearsome creature was more legendary than real at the time I took over three camels and the requisite gear, and began the patrol of twenty-one miles of the South Australian New South Wales Border Fence - well in the country of the Yandama Dragon.

The inspector assured me that the Yandama Dragon had been neither seen nor tracked for three or four months, and that it was generally thought it had gone through into South Australia when a brainless traveller had left open one of the few gates in the famous netted and barbed topped barrier.

The three Government-owned camels I took over and signed for were quiet and reasonable. The riding camel was a bullock of uncertain age, while the two pack animals were females long past the kittenish phase of life. Having been on this section of the fence for many years, they were all good and contented campers and so, save for the bi-weekly sandstorm and the sodafilled bore water, life was pleasant enough for a common working man.

I had been on the section for three weeks when I met the first human being since taking over, and he was the inspector. Fortunately, I had done a little work - clearing wind-driven buckbush off the fence for a mile or two and burning it, slicing away the tops of several sandhills which threatened to bury the fence, and topping the fence with an extra layer of netting and wire and posts when the sand had buried the fence - when over a northern sandhill a short camel train appeared bringing down the inspector. He said, regarding me steadily: "I get two kinds of men here: the man who won't work unless I am looking at him; and the man who won't work when I am looking at him."

At that I promptly sat down until he went on his weary way. Some weeks afterwards I met Good King Wenceslaus, an ancient aboriginal chief who wore suspended from his neck a brass plate on which were inscribed his name, alleged age, rank, tribe, totem, and vices. He rode a mule and was escorted by two young gins, one of whom wore a pair of old dungaree trousers.

In thus making the one suit cover two wives the king proved to be a real, and not a theoretical, economist.

Like an emperor flanked by his guards, Good King Wenceslaus surveyed me for nearly a minute before he consented to speak, when he announced that the purpose of the expedition was to locate wild dogs. I pointed out dog tracks that a breakfast plate would barely cover, and, further that I had myself set traps along this fence section to earn a spare pound or two. He became thoughtful only after he had cadged a half-plug of tobacco. Then he made a pronouncement.

"Looks like ole Yandama Dragon feller he come back into Noo South," he said slowly and with such finality as to bar argument. "You see them track? Them tracks made by wild feller dog wot walkabout with Yandama Dragon. Yandama Dragon he kill camel sometime, sometime he narked and he kill steer, and that there wild dog feller he stand by and eatem up. You see that feller Yandama Dragon you run like hell for tree quick. Him eyes beeg as so so -" and he held his hands about a foot apart - "and him have tree four firesticks down his mouth. Bad feller him. You no shoot Yandama Dragon, and you no trap Yandama Dragon's wild dog. Them's too cunnin'."

After this visitation I enjoyed three weeks of restful peace, the quality of peace precluding the necessity of agreeing six times every day that the weather was nice and warm and that we wanted rain to freshen the lawns and things. Came then the evening when I camped among a bunch of mulgas at the edge of a large dry lake. The fence crossed this depression in under two miles, and on it at this time were patches of green pigweed for which camels have a passion. Immediately on being freed in hobbles my companions at once set off for this pigweed and I knew they would not be far away the next dawning.

As is to be expected in December, the night was clear and silent and hot, and, never erecting a tent unless it threatened rain, the camp stretcher was set up beside the stacked saddles. For several hours the bell suspended from the riding camel's neck sent from the invisible lake its musical note which gave one a sense of company, keeping at bay the forbidden knowledge that the nearest habitation was twenty-three miles distant. During the night I was awakened by the snapping of dry sticks close to the camp. The camels were lying down and the absence of the bell's notes intensified the solitude. For the breaking of the dry sticks I charged a feeding steer or a cow, and went to sleep. But again the cracking of sticks near the camp awoke me, and this uneasiness prevented sleep. I added wood to the fire and sat on the stretcher with the fully loaded Winchester repeater across my legs, watching for the flame which would reveal the position of the dragon's mouth, and trying to decide which of the poor trees would be the quickest to climb.

The new day revealed the camels feeding away out on the lake.

I visually searched its many acres, as well as the curving line of scrub bordering its shore, but the Yandama Dragon was either asleep or gone on a long journey for I could not spot him.

I did, however, quickly examine the tracks of the animal that had skirted the camp and trod repeatedly on dry sticks. It had been that enormous dog. His tracks were all round the camp and never before or since have I known a dingo or a wild dog to tread on dead sticks. The brute evidently feared nothing.

Having eaten breakfast, and packed and set out the loads handy to the saddles, I took the noselines and left camp for the mokes. It should be understood that a camel's noseline is a length of light rope, to one end of which is attached a loop of twine to slip round the wooden plug drawn through the animal's nostril.

With the noselines looped over an arm, I approached my beasts, who came to stand motionless and to gaze at me with singular fixity. I was midway between them and the lake shore, and a full thousand yards from the fence, when from behind I heard the bellowing roar of the Yandama Dragon.

An enraged bull can move fast. An angry stallion can move even faster. Both bull and horse are mere beasts controlled by instinct. The camel stands on a plane higher than either. He can move faster than either and he can think and reason. When dealing with a bull one has to deal with so much animated weight. When dealing with a stallion one had to add nervous excitability to so much animated weight. With a bull camel, however, one has to deal with a reasoning beast that when roused is the devil.

There was this dragon charging at forty miles an hour, his four legs splayed like those of a beetle, white foam being flecked back to his shoulders and hump, his red mouth bladder blown with wind and as large as a soccer ball. There was not even a rabbit burrow offering escape.

To run was useless. I would have been caught and trampled to a jelly long before I could reach the fence. My three camels set up whimpering mumbles of fear. I could see fire in the dragon's eyes, while the distended mouth-bladder looked like a flame and the foam from his mouth was like a steam.

Now came a remarkable exhibition of the subconscious mind taking control of the conscious mind. It compelled me to stand quite still and shout without cease the language of the bullock driver which, as everyone knows, contains many Afghan words.

The Yandama Dragon duly arrived. The spasm of fear had

been replaced by a cold curiosity. I was unconscious of feeling, even of myself. It was as though I lived within a steel ball and gazed upon a scene outside it. The dragon thrust into my face his great and noble head, and, when he sidled round and round, my subconscious ego forced me to turn round, too. He blew clouds of 'steam' into my face and I could have lit a cigarette at one of his terrible eyes. He bellowed and roared, and he danced on his rear legs, using his fore-feet to keep the flies off me.

More than once his scarlet mouth-bladder touched me. His eyes expressed awful triumph. I saw that through his left nostril still was drawn the wooden plug affixed there by his one-time Afghan master. All this I saw between clouds of 'steam' and, controlled still by my unconscious ego, the fingers of my left hand parted the loop of twine at the end of one of the noselines, and my right hand flashed upward and gripped the dragon by the snout.

The next instant he was noselined.

Sound stopped. Steam was cut off. We regarded each other with dumb astonishment, wondering which of us looked the more stupid. From a dragon the beast was become a gentle lamb. I took him with the others back to the camp, and there I put on him one of the cows' saddles and loaded him with gear, he grunted with satisfaction and determinedly chewing his cud.

All that the Yandama Dragon wanted was a little human attention. He was tired of being neglected. Subsequently he did prove to be a little frisky when he was not noselined, but he was harmless enough even for a new chum like me. His reputation, after all, was one vile slander.

6

I am faintly amused when explorers and others complain of the solitude they have endured when surrounded by the attentive service of a retinue of natives, or when voluntarily marooned and yet maintain human contact through radio. They know not the complete solitude experienced by fence riders who live for weeks without seeing a human being, and then enjoy human contact only for a few hours before begin-ning another period of solitude.

To withstand successfully an insidious attack on the mind made by long terms of solitude the mind must be kept employed with reading and constant observation of natural phenomena - study of the ants, study of the tracks made by all living things, the movement of clouds. To use a hackneyed phrase: man is a gregarious animal. He is seldom happy when alone and always mentally comfortable when he is a unit of a crowd, for then he is not conscious of his own littleness and of his futile life. Man's fear is not so much of extraneous things but of himself. He hates to think, for thinking encloses him with a barrier within which he stands and sees himself 'a nothing but a nothing'.

There are men I have known who have lived in solitude for years, men who have endured periods of four, five and six weeks when they have not seen even at a distance a single human being, periods separated by only a few hours of human contact at a homestead. They are remarkable for mental stability, emotional control, and a well hidden humility.

Of course, I do not claim to be one of them. A year of solitude is about as much as I can stand, and a year is no mean achievement. A term of solitude will benefit any man, as will a term of fasting. Solitude will bring a man to face reality, prove to him that he is not so important to the welfare of the universe as he has always thought, sharpen his sense of humour to the extent of making him laugh at his own conceits and chuckle at the conceits of others, make him see clearly the futility of striving after wealth and fame. Man lives, or should do, to prepare himself for death. To live for anything else is to waste that fraction of a second which is life. Once I wrote a novel based on the effect of solitude on the mind. Financially it was foredoomed to failure because no one could understand it.

No less than the body the mind must be nourished. If it is not fed it will feed upon itself until it becomes exhausted and tumbles into madness. The difficulty is to prevent the mind thus destroying itself when its normal nourishment obtained from human contact in pubs and drawing-rooms, theatres and streets, radio and newspapers is cut off. If it is not employed by the study of natural phenomena at hand, then it must feed upon itself for there is no other food for it.

Yet no matter how the mind is employed, a man in solitude will soon begin to talk with and at himself just for the sake of hearing a human voice. There is only one thing that can go part of the way to make up for the lack of human compan-ionship and that is a dog, but a fence patrol cannot take a dog with him because along a vermin fence are set many traps and much poison is laid for the destruction of wild dogs.

In six months I have reached the point of taking opposed sides in an argument, and the peculiar aspect of this mental condition is the facility of thought and speech attained. Here is a sign of danger, for the mind becomes abnormally excited and trembles on its wonderfully adjusted balance.

I heard of a man who, in the light of his camp-fire, would play cribbage with his own ghost. Having first played his own hand he would move across to take the ghost's place and play its hand. Invariably a dispute would arise and the poor devil would constantly move into the two positions to maintain the argument. He could, he said, actually see the ghost, and then, when he was the ghost, he could actually see himself.

He is a wise man who knows his own limits.

When I discover that I have set out two pannikins, two knives and two forks, and two plates for dinner for one, I at once pack and leave the job for another less mentally dangerous.

Arthur Upfield, 1925.

EIGHT
Ambition

1

It required several years for me to work back to normal mentality after the war. The process was gradual, imperceptible. It was as though my mind, far from being halted in growth by the war, had been thrown back, wilted like a plant in dire need of water.

The post-war years of wandering about Australia Proper provided benefecient rains which revived the growth of my mind and slowly set my feet on the right track called ambition. That was what had been wrong with me - lack of ambition.

Having made the fatal mistake of writing impossible novels when I should have been interesting myself in my profession, and then following this by committing the mistake of throwing up a career leading to the civil service in order to answer the call of Australia Proper, I may perhaps be excused for making lesser mistakes. I still make them. I have a kink for making mistakes; and having been born in September and thereby being doomed to ill luck suffered by all Virgo people, nothing can be done about it.

Actually, of course, bad luck is the result of mistakes: good luck is the result of coincidence. Mary - I am not going to give her married name - was before the war the wife of a man who owned a selection north of Broken Hill. After the war she was a widow and the owner of the selection. When first I met her I was offsiding for One Spur Dick.

Her husband was a really fine looking man, a born bushman, tolerant and generous. If he had a fault it was his disinterest in all subjects save those of wool and sheep, bullocks and the meat market. Mary went up from Adelaide as his wife to manage what was really a small station, and I think that soon she became starved of interests and sought relief from sheep and wool and bullocks and the meat market by interesting herself in other people - including me.

At that time she was round about forty whilst I was a mere twenty. She was tall and stately and still handsome, and renowned for her unfailing kindness. Arriving at a certain Government Tank on the main road, we would free the bullocks, or the mules, spruce ourselves and walk the two miles across the open saltbush plain to the selection homestead where dinner was certain sure to be waiting.

Mary's husband and One Spur Dick held a lot in common. They were of the same generation. They knew the same people. They liked to talk about sheep and wool, bullocks and markets, and after dinner they would go out to sit on the veranda and talk and talk and talk.

Now a skewbald bullock that once had been owned by So and So and now was running in Such and Such's paddock held but little interest for me after having heard the tale. Once was sufficient for me, but One Spur Dick and Mary's husband regarded that bullock as a personal friend. I was never a man who liked taking his bullocks to dinner with him, and then to bed with him. Having unyoked them at sundown I wanted to forget them until the following dawning.

Mary generally had a lubra or two to assist with the house work, and after dinner she would leave the clearing for them to do whilst she would lure me to another veranda, make me comfortable, and 'steer' me into telling her about England. Thus it was that she became conversant with my early novel writing, those unpublishable works of art which gave me so much pleasure in the writing.

In the second or third year of the war her husband drove out to the run one day in a horse-drawn buckboard. The horses brought home the vehicle but the driver was absent. They found him with his neck broken, and how he came to fall, or to be thrown, to the ground could not be ascertained. Did Mary crumple beneath the blow and retire to a city to take in boarders or breed cats? No, sir! She undertook to interest herself in the subjects of wool and sheep, bullocks and the meat market that she might keep her young son at college in Adelaide and later on pay for his medical training. When she could not afford to hire a man to repair her fences, she took the lubras with her and did the work. While her husband lived she was always too nervous to ride a horse: after he died she rode a horse when the sheep required mustering.

In the early summer of 1923 I had put in a second spell on the South Australian Border Fence, and on returning to Broken Hill by the Quinambie mail coach after eight o'clock I missed dinner at the Masonic Hotel where I always put up. Having obtained a room, shaved and showered, downed a drink or two with a couple of long-time friends, I walked down Argent Street in search of a restaurant. And in Argent

Street I met Mary. Her walk was as stately as always but her complexion had been vanquished by the sun - imitation and subterfuge had never met with her approval - while her well-kept hands of the past now were browned and coarsened by real work. Her hair was silver grey, adding mightily to her attractiveness, so that what she had lost on the roundabout she had gained on the swings.

She consented to drink a cup of tea while I ate. She was not satisfied with what I managed to tell her of myself between bites, and insisted that I accompany her to her hotel where we sat in the lounge yarning to a late hour. She had done well with the selection. The boy was in his final medical year. Every-thing was right with her and with her son, but everything was not right with me and this vexed her. She was that kind of woman - bless her.

"Will you come to see me in the morning? Say at eleven?" she asked when I was about to leave.

The bright lights of the lounge appeared to be reflected in her big grey eyes. She was a woman who seldom smiled but she was smiling now. I had the feeling of a schoolboy who knows he is to be blamed for one delinquency of several, and wonders which one. The request was an order.

Coincidence! Life would be a tame affair without them. It was pure coincidence that I met Mary in Argent Street, and it was coincidence that among my mail I collected at the Post Office the following morning was a letter from the Editor of The Wide World Magazine.

A few months before I had sent him two articles, one on dingoes and the other on trapping for fur, and here he wrote accepting both for publication and asking me to write for him a 10,000 word article on the opportunities awaiting migrants in Australia.

Mary I found waiting for me when I called at her hotel at the hour she had named. Completely comfortable in any setting, she had selected a shady corner of the balcony where she had arranged chairs and a table; and, on seeing me, rang for the service of morning tea. At once I sensed that something in the nature of a storm was brewing. The setting indicated it. I was not wrong, for after the tea had arrived, she said:

"I am going to talk to you straight."

It was less the words than the upturned corners of her mouth which foretold the breaking of the storm. "How old are you?"

"Thirty-five or six."

"Are you that old? Well, I'm getting close to sixty. Age permits me to speak plainly to my friends, and you are old enough to hear plain speaking. What in the world are you doing here, and have been doing for several years, when you have a wife and small boy to care for? When you told me last night that you were married, you gave me quite a shock."

I felt about two feet high.

"Here you are, a man arrived at the prime of life, just wandering about from track to track and from odd job to odd job. Despite the passage of fifteen or sixteen years, you are no better off today than you were when offsiding to One Spur Dick. You haven't gone back during that period, I am thankful to say, but you have not gone forward. Even the fact of marriage and responsibility hasn't shaken you out of the devil-may-care nature of yours. Have you ever thought much of the startling change in the outback brought about by the motor engine?"

I breathed more freely at this apparent shift of subject, and admitted that I had observed the other change.

"I'm glad to hear that," she said, and her lips became compressed and the corners of her mouth again turned slightly upward. "You knew the bush before the motors came: the kind of transport we used, the kind of men and women who made the outback what it was. You know the outback of today, what the motor has made it, and how the motor has not changed the people. You have looked long at the picture of the outback which time has destroyed. You are looking at a new picture of it, and time will, in 25 years, destroy this new picture to make another. Can't you see the opportunity offered you?"

"I'm sorry, but I am feeling dense this morning."

She made a little clicking noise of impatience with her tongue. "You remember the story in the Bible of the prince who gave talents to his servants before going on a far journey?"

"Yes. I know you are pushing me into a corner, but these scones are delightful, and cream in my tea is dream come true."

"Somewhere at home is a thick wad of foolscap covered with your handwriting. You remember it?"

I smiled, saying: "You should have burned it. No one likes to come face to face with the follies of his youth."

She refused to be non-serious.

"Do you know the chief fault in that novel?"

"Yes, the spelling."

"The spelling is awful, I'll admit, but its chief fault is that the writer was lacking entirely experience of life. But you've got the experience of life now. I should think you have got sufficient experience for half a dozen men. You've got that one talent, and if only you would use it! Why don't you?"

"Because the talent has never been trained."

"Fiddlesticks and flapdoodle. Talents have not to be trained. They have to be practised. Oh, don't you see it? You have already gathered together a shearing-shed full of bush experiences. You could write of all you have seen and done out here in the outback. Take up the writing again. Aim to be a Ralph Connor or a Rider Haggard or a Henry Lawson. Don't you see that this would be your road of escape - from the dusty, profitless tracks leading out of Broken Hill - to that home on a mountain top you visualized in your early book?"

"I'm afraid I'm too old now to begin to tread a road much harder than any out back track."

"That's right, defeat yourself before you attempt it," she cried bitingly. "How like a man! Here is the outback offering material enough for a hundred novelists, and so far I have only read the work of one writer who really knew it as well as you must know it. And there you sit calmly drinking tea and smoking cigarettes and looking bored and probably wishing that the devil would fly away with me."

My attitude was, I thought, beginning to hurt her and that would never do. Without speaking I opened and placed before her the letter from the Wide World editor. She regarded me curiously before she began to read, and then, as she read, her body slowly drew upright. Returning the letter, she said: "How like a man!"

"That is the second time you have used the phrase. Why this time?"

She sighed, but her eyes were bright. "To let a woman beat herself against a rock for nothing", she replied, and fell silent end just looked at me.

"For some time," I began in explanation. "I have been thinking along the lines you have been urging. Only too clearly have I realized the kind of fool I've been, but I have lately arrived at the understanding of how I might turn my foolishness to profit. That causes me to think that I'm not utterly hopeless. I am not at all swelled headed from the success of selling those two articles to the Wide World and being commissioned to write a third, because past experience in the writing game has taught me what to expect in the future. Up to now I have been like a man who has learned to play the piano by ear. This won't do if I am to become a professional writer, one who earns a living with a typewriter. The row I've got to hoe is long, so long that the end can't be seen, but I can see the opportunity all right, and I am going to take it. Why? Because, as you just said, it offers me the only road of escape to that house on the mountain top."

"That is splendid, Hampshire, really it is," she cried softly, and proceeded to talk about her station and the trials and tribulations of the owner-manageress of it.

Three women have exerted pressure on my life: my mother, my wife, and Mary. Of all the people I have known in Australia Proper, two are outstanding in their influence on me. A man and a woman, both courageous and both true. They stood up like tall lighthouses to encourage me with their examples, well as with their friendship - Mary and One Spur Dick. A man is, indeed, fortunate to have known one or the other: I am doubly fortunate by having known both.

2

With the resurrection of ambition came purpose of living. The phase of not caring where I slept and where I went or what I did during the day peculiarly enough did not swamp interest in the men I met and the insects and the birds I watched. It was a period of negative living actually beginning on Gallipoli and only ending in this year 1925, some six months prior to meeting Mary in the hotel lounge and hearing her speak her mind.

How much or how little does a man do in the shaping of his life? I have come to believe in an exterior power taking a

The family of station owner, James Hole, at Wheeler's Well, photograph by Upfield's off-sider E.V. Whyte.

hand in the direction of the individual towards his destiny, a power not always successful but, notwithstanding, a reality. A very old woman once said to me: "At nine o'clock at night let your mind relax so that it can fall into a state of receptivity. Act on the ideas your mind receives when in this state and you will be bound to go on and up." I have seldom done this, but it is good advice. I do not believe in luck, the mere, blind working of chance.

When I left Broken Hill, after my meeting with Mary, I was bound for a job of stock-riding west of Wilcannia. On arriving at the homestead I was met by a new manager who said he had already filled the vacant job. And so I tramped down river, along its east bank this time, and the next job I was offered could not better have served my needs and ambition if I had searched for it for twenty years.

What I wanted was a place in which to write, and bushmen will know how few and how far between are the jobs offering a working man the privacy to be obtained in a bed-sitting room in a city. And I was offered the job at a place where I could have opportunity to write in quiet and privacy.

The boss said: "I want a man to go out to Wheeler's Well, cooking. The overseer will be going to Victoria Lake in the morning. What about it?"

Knowing this Wheeler's Well, I did not hesitate but rejoiced. It is situated midway on the run named Albemarle, 26 miles out from the river homestead and 26 miles from the out station of Victoria Lake. A man named Wheeler sunk the well in the days when Henry Lawson first tramped the Paroo, and after the well was put down there was put up what is called a whim to which a horse was harnessed and worked so that it pulled up a full bucket of water and let another down, empty. With the advent of windmills the whim was no longer used, but it still stood a monument to the shifts resorted to by that vanished generation.

Near the well were two huts, pine walled, iron roofed, built so close together that an energetic stockman had built a canegrass roof connecting them and thus obtaining a cool sun shelter. The whole place was set in the middle of a 'vast open space' bordered along the north end the west by low sand-dunes, to the east by a great land depression, and to the west by a canegrass swamp backed by a maze of sand hummocks. When the westerlies blew there was sand in the air! When the heat danced over the swamp and distorted the sand-dunes there was comparative coolness beneath the canegrass roof connecting the two huts. There were wide cracks between the laid pine logs forming the walls, the roof iron rattled in the wind and creaked and clanked in the changing temperatures of silent days and still mere silent nights. When I first arrived there was no stove, just the open log-burning fireplace.

The shearing was over and the sheep had been mustered into their summer paddocks. It was November and the Spring dust storms were but an evil memory. There were usually stationed at Wheeler's Well two stockmen, but one had gone off on six months' leave and the other had been transferred to the bullock wagon for a period.

At home to receive me were Paddy, the pet sheep, two galahs which had never known a cage, an old ginger cat, four dogs and about a dozen ancient hens.

Before leaving the main river homestead, the boss had said: "I'll be sending out a couple of riders tomorrow."

It was his invariable custom to ring Wheeler's Well at seven in the evening, and again he said he would be sending two men out on the morrow.

By this time I was settled in. The smaller of the two huts housed the stockmen and the larger was devoted to kitchen-dining room, with the cook's bunk in one corner. I swept the earth floor, tidied the place, heaved outside old tins and cut the wood. Paddy insisted on a meal of potatoes and, being dissatisfied with two, tried his hardest to bunt me. I began on him early and was not afterwards ever caught bending. The dogs had their run and then were fed. The galahs yelled and screamed and flapped their wings in venting disapproval of the old bread crumbs I gave them, but after issuing each a handful of wheat from the hens' supply, they insisted on climbing to my shoulders whilst I ate my dinner of bread and meat, and there murmured sweet insults into my ears.

With the cool night come, the dogs chained to their humpies, the cackling hens silent and shut into their yard, and the two galahs perched on a rafter of the kitchen, I mixed a batter for yeast bread and decided that life was 'not too dusty'. In the morning I was awakened by the cockbird crowing in the yard, a dog barking, and then the mutterings of two hungry galahs. Presently they fell off their cross beam with low screechings, then to cross to my bunk, climb with claw and beak up a draggled blanket to waddle about on my body and begin again their sweet insults.

When the old ginger cat jumped up, too, they yelled defiance at her and there was no more peace.

The bread turned out not badly, and late in the afternoon I put mutton to roast in the camp oven and potatoes with it, thence often to walk outside to see if the stockmen were coming into sight across the sand hummocks. The sun sank to the mulgas backing the western sand-dunes and no stockmen came riding my way. At seven o'clock he had to put them to other work but that they would be arriving on the morrow. They did not come for seven weeks.

On an average twice a week someone would call and be offered a meal. It might be the boss in his car, or the overseer on his truck, or a very occasional swagman who would stay the night. Once the musterers came, stayed two days and nights, and then departed.

Lonely! Oh no, I wasn't lonely. My life was more crowded than it could be in a city. The horses would come in night and morning for a drink, and every fifth day or so I would catch one and put it into a gig and drive out with the dogs after a ration sheep. I noted that where the square iron squatter's tank leaked the rye grass grew mightily, and where grass would grow with this well water so, too, would vegetables. Why therefore perish for the want of vegetables, or rely on the erratic supply from the garden lorded over by old Tommy Ching Lung at the river homestead? I put it to the boss for wire netting and out it came by the bullock wagon. The temporary bullocky was instructed to cart me firewood and I went out with him to help load and cut posts for the garden fence. I had the garden going within the month, and vegetables on the table within two months. The tomato plants lived and bore for three years.

Then, when the sun was going down, I would bath and don pyjamas and canvas shoes, and set off on an evening stroll. The dogs would race ahead and Paddy would lumber on behind. The old ginger cat would refuse to be left at home, and in due time would complain of fatigue and have to be carried. The two galahs would insist on coming, and they would soon be fatigued and yell for a lift. I used to 'park' them on Paddy. Thus would the circus stroll away to wander among the sand-dunes. I would sit on the top of a sand tower - so fashioned by the wind - and gaze across the 'vast empty space' marvelling at the colours the aftermath of the flaming sun would lay over a far timber rise, paint a sand-ridge in the middle distance, stain the sky. Thus at ease the dogs would lie panting from exertion. Paddy would nibble at tussock grass, the cat would mirril and want to go home, and the birds would take delight to shriek defiance at a passing crow. In the stupendous silence of approaching night we would fall in again and, in procession, return to that place we all called home. And then, surrounded by my silent friends, I would get to work with my writing.

Oh no, I wasn't lonely. Had it not been for my waiting wife, had I been single and free of responsibility, I would have been supremely happy.

I came to feel gravely suspicious of the old ginger cat. She at first always disappeared shortly after sundown and would not be home when the sun rose. Ah, these women! Then she gave up the nightly wanderings and would lie on the table, whilst I wrote, and alternately doze and regard me with violet eyes reflecting the yellow oil light. After supper of coffee and brownie-powdered milk sweetened with sugar for her - she would follow me out to the short veranda where I had my summer sleeping quarters, and 'park' herself on the foot of my stretcher.

Time went on and the happy event drew nearer and nearer. Not on my stretcher, my dear, I would say and think, not on my stretcher. I watched her with ever closer attention. I prepared a nice comfy nest in a box for her, but she would not accept it. Every morning when I woke I would hastily raise my head and look to see if anything had happened.

Even so, she beat me. With her five babies I found her on my stretcher one afternoon when I came in from tending the garden. Each was black and white. I went out and returned with an old petrol tin bucket half-filled with water. I told the mother she could retain one of the babies, and selected the most beautiful of the beautiful litter. The four I removed from the stretcher and took to the bucket. The old cat mewed and came and rubbed herself against a leg. It was no use. I gave her back her kittens.

They grew to just lovely cats. The pranks they played and the chuckles they brought from me. Every night mother and children would all arrange themselves at the foot of my stretcher, and, during the night, every time I moved they would unite in a chorus of purring. As time went on they grew bigger and heavier. When I put knife to steel preparatory to walking down to the killing pen - for a ration sheep, the youngsters would gambol, and the old girl would purr, the chained dogs would bark with frenzied energy and the galahs would yell and flap their wings. All hands bar Paddy would accompany me to the killing: All hands would race with me back to the huts where the dogs would be fed with offal and the cats fed with chopped liver and heart.

The five kittens grew and grew. They became heavier and heavier. When I pushed one off my stretcher with a foot it would determinedly return. With five hefty cats sprawling where my feet were entitled to rest it was the cats who won. And when I went to Broken Hill for a spell they all went bush and did not return till after several weeks following my own return.

Aboriginal workers at Albermarle Station in Upfield's time there; Upfield (left) helping out with lamb marking at Brummies near Victoria Lake (both photos by E.V. Whyte).

3

There came one evening to Wheeler's Well two gentlemen of Australia. One, was the chief representative of the Darling tribe, a fat and jovial aborigine who, to use the parlance of a past age, knew his onions. In his veins flowed royal blood, but there was no tobacco ever reposing in the pockets of his dungaree suit. Far and wide both his name and his renown as a gentle grafter were well established. He shall introduce himself.

An old family connected with Menindee are the Maidens. They own station property and the first hotel. Being pioneering folk they command respect. Across the river one afternoon rode Pluto, king of the blacks. His business was urgent, but there was other business to be transacted with Mr William Maiden which could wait, and to a man standing on the hotel veranda, Pluto shouted:

"If you see Billy Maiden about tell him that Mister Pluto wants to see him."

Mr Pluto, as I have stated, arrived with a companion at Wheeler's Well. The companion's name I have forgotten, but as he was wearing a grey suit I will name him Mr Grey. He was of Mr Pluto's age, build and temperament. Travelling on an old and overloaded sulky, drawn by an ancient horse in wickedly poor condition, they were on their way to the river.

"Good day-ee, Hampshire!" greeted Mr Pluto. "Can me and my mate camp here tonight?"

Two pairs of big black eyes anxiously regarded me. Pluto's voice was pleasing to the ear. I was aware that they had camped but four miles to the east and had carefully timed their arrival to accept permission to camp the night. When giving them a horse feed I told them to come in for dinner in half an hour. The black eyes beamed, and the grey whiskers on black faces parted each from the company of others when the skin was stretched in a satisfied grin. Artful old Pluto! Many a traveller's horse had he planted deep within a river bend and waited then for the traveller to offer a reward for its tracking and recovery. It was Pluto who decided when the young men should go seek a station job, who afterwards ordered an educated half-caste girl to write letters which they would have read to them. These letters would run thus:

"Dear Albie - How are you? I hope you are well. Old Mary Ponting has got a bad cold and she ought to have plenty of painkiller. Elsie's got another baby, a boy this time. Joe is away on Henley. Dear Albie, we all send you our love. Please send us a cheque sometime."

The 'dear Albie' or 'dear Joe' would ask for a station cheque on account of wages, and send it to a member of the tribe from whom Pluto would get it and cash it and then deal out the money at the same ratio as the captain, officers and crew of a ship receiving salvage money.

Mr Pluto and Mr Grey came in for dinner after I had made sure they had given their horse a measure of chaff and when they had made camp under the swaying wreckage of the well whim. They sat down to cold roast mutton and potatoes, bread and brownie, and a large peach pie, and when they had eaten everything within range, I did not wait to be asked but gave them tobacco and then proceeded to lead the conversation.

Remarked Mr Pluto: "This old Grey feller, he's a cunning feller all right." Mr Grey chuckled and poked the end of a thumb into the fat armouring Mr Pluto's ribs.

"Too right!" he agreed.

"Me and him's been out to Victoria Lake and up to Tintinallogy looking for a horse or two."

"Ah! Did you find any to suit you?"

"Yes. Plenty. But the --- squatters wants too much for 'em. Horses ain't worth much these days, Hampshire. Four or five quid is enough for any horse, but the ---- squatters wants ten and twelve quid for animals what's ten and twelve year old."

"Too right!" agreed Mr Grey, and they turned inward to face each other and beam mutual approval.

To Mr Grey, I said: "I haven't seen you before along the river."

"Oh - no," Mr Pluto replied for his companion in villainy.

"Old Grey he live mostly out Ivanhoe way. Y'see he's a Victoria Lake blackfeller."

"Ah!"

Midway between Victoria Lake and Wheeler's Well is a vast land depression named Ratcatcher Lake which, before the Darling was snagged to permit flood water to slide swiftly to waste into the sea, was, with Victoria Lake and others in a long chain, almost permanently covered with water. Today the remains of huge heaps of mussel shells mark the sites of ancient camps along the depression's one-time shore. At the western end of Ratcatcher Lake are still to be found human skulls and bones at a place where took place a fearful battle between the ancestors of Mr Pluto on the one side and those of Mr Grey on the other. And now, in 1926, these two representatives of once powerful and numerous aboriginal tribes were joined in friendship on a horse buying expedition. I mentioned the battle of Ratcatcher Lake.

"It was a big fight," Mr Pluto said, by no means saddened by the subject. "Long before my time, of course."

"How did it come about?"

"Well, it was like this here, Hampshire." Black hands swiftly arranged the pie dish, pannikins and plates to mark geographical positions with true accuracy relative to points of the compass. "It happened when my father was a young feller. Too right, it did. The river had come down in a big flood and filled bung up all the lakes out here." The pie dish marked the position of the lakes. "The next year the river stopped runnin'. No rain come that year or the next, and the year after the water in the bend holes went salt or went bad with drownded emus and kangaroos.

"My father's father got to hear that there was still water out at Ratcatcher Lake, plenty of fish and plenty of mussels, and plenty of nardoo on the plains about. Him and the mob all left the river and went on walkabout out to Ratcatcher where they was stopped by the Victoria Lake blacks. The river blacks had to fight for water or perish. There was no getting back to the river without water.

"She was a great fight, Hampshire. Hundreds of millions of blacks was killed, more'n was killed in the Great War. My father's father was killed, too, and them what was wounded was killed as well."

"And all that was before your time?" Mr Pluto nodded his head, cheerfully.

"Have you ever seen a real blackfellers' battle?"

"Too right!" he replied, heartily. "I was only a little fella when the lakes went dry and the Victoria Lake blacks come to the river for water where they was met by the river blacks. Me, I was old Saddler's horseboy" - Saddler was the manager of Albemarle - "and one day me and old Saddler was out in the buggy up near Black Gate. We heard the row a long time fore we got to it. They was on a flat. Spears and wommeras was going hard. Me and old Saddler stopped the horses and watched. I wanted to get down and join in. My father was there. I seen him fightin'. I wanted to get down and join in, but old Saddler he says I was too young and he tied me to the seat with a hobble. There was lots killed that day. I seen them being killed."

"Who won?"

"We did." The fat face expanded, and Mr Grey added his assurance both by word and grin. Mr Pluto continued in his cheerful manner: "My father that time got his legs broken and he wasn't no good anymore. The blacks was bad in them days."

"Were they? How did they get on with the white men?"

"Pretty good," he replied, to add with abruptly troubled eyes: "There was bits of fights now and then over the white man taking the land what belonged to us and the blackfellers taking a sheep or two what belonged to the white men. More blacks was killed by blacks than by whites, Hampshire. Then me and Grey was brought up by the white men. Me and Grey could eat the white man's tucker, but them blacks growed up on kangaroo and emu and fish and yabbi and nardoo when they took on damper and things it bound 'em up like too much cabbage tree does the sheep. Tucker, that's what killed a lot of blackfellers. Too much tucker. Wild blackfeller he eat and eat, and then he go on walkabout and starve a bit. When he got plenty of white man's tucker he didn't do no more starving in between, like."

"Well, neither of you look to have done any starving in between, like," I observed, and this brought prolonged roars of laughter and much mutual rib digging.

And so Mr Pluto discoursed on history with the clarity not achieved by many white men, using the white man's aspirates in their proper place, and speaking with a full and throaty voice without the accent either of Pott's Point or Woolloomooloo. Now and then Mr Grey would interject with a 'too right!' Not as talkative as his companion, he was slightly awed by the presence of royalty. Nevertheless, he was an intelligent listener.

It is certain that Mr. Pluto would not have spoken to such length and with such fluency had I not invited them to dinner and treated them as equals. To an anthropologist, dressed in white duck and supported by a camera, he would have answered evasively any question put to him, as does every one of his race. Sensitive to an extraordinary degree, any exhibition of superiority makes them don the armour of mental density. Accept them on an equal plane, treat them with human kindness, and there stands the true gentleman, the man whose mind has never matured but yet is capable of maturing if given the opportunity.

To say that the aborigine is not capable of being raised to the white man's level is but to voice the opinion of the ignorant, and it is to be greatly regretted that the opinion of the ignorant prevails outside Australia Proper. It cannot be expected that a near Stone Age man can be transformed into an intellectual being in five minutes, in five years, or less than in five generations. It took a hundred generations of white men to make a university professor out of the Normans who conquered England: it would take only a few generations to accomplish the same progress with the aborigines. One I know takes his family into Victoria every year and there drives a harvester machine. Not even a lawyer or an author could do that without first being instructed.

4

To Wheeler's Well came to work for a few days 'our old friend, Yorky'.

How long Yorky had been in Australia I do not know. When I first met him he was grey and aging fast. He was a little, dried-up man, and his sight was failing. He had in his time worked on every run fronting the Darling, and on a good many stations west of the river, too, at odd cooking jobs, pumping at wells, off-siding to tradesmen, rouse-abouting at the lamb-marking camps and in the shearing sheds.

He had evolved a really smart scheme for protracting his visits to Menindee to practise which must have required a mathematical mind. With a swag some three times bigger than himself he would arrive at the township and camp beneath a convenient gum tree, or vacant hen house, in order to prevent wicked waste of money on a bed at one of the hotels. He would take his station cheque to one of the stores where, having first settled the year's account, he would arrange with the proprietor to pay the balance at ten shillings a day. For no reason, not even if Yorky went on bended knees, was the storeman to give him more than the ten shillings in one day.

Thenceforth, every morning when the store was opened, Yorky would arise from the veranda floor and enter for his ration of ten shillings. More often than not the money would be spent before midday, when Yorky would look about for someone he knew.

"Have you got any brass?" he would ask.

"Of course. How much do you want?" would be the natural reply.

It might be 'five bob' or 'half a note' or 'a coupler quid'. By this method Yorky's stay in town could be prolonged for several weeks when any other man would blow out in a day or two on Yorky's cheque. In these transactions of 'brass' there was never a record kept outside Yorky's head, yet no matter how drunk he might be he was never known to forget a transaction of 'brass' or to forget to repay the loan. As the loans must have numbered dozens and totalled many pounds, the feat of remembering them all when alcohol is supposed to cloud the mind was as remarkable as was their inevitable liquidation. At the close of these 'busts' Yorky would stagger out of town, bowed beneath his enormous swag, to camp anywhere and suffer the tortures of the damned after he had consumed the bottle or two he took with him.

Sarah once found him asleep in the dead centre of the river road not far from Pluto's camp. A mighty fine woman was Sarah, a dependable homestead help, a woman who knew her way about, too.

Discovering Yorky in no fit condition to be loose in the bush and in great danger of being run over during the coming night. She picked him up in her capable hands and carried him to her tent.

Having laid out the body she fetched the huge swag and the bottles still containing liquid refreshment. Thereafter she proceeded to nurse Yorky towards health and strength, and in this she was succeeding when a jealous lubra speeded down to Menindee and informed the police that a white man was in the blacks' camp.

The senior police officer at Menindee at the time was big and jovial and well liked. He called for his horse and rode to Pluto's camp where he halted outside Sarah's tent, and shouted: "'Lo, there!"

Sarah appeared, to say: "Good day-ee, sergeant."

"Good day, Sarah. I'm told you've got a white man in your tent."

"No fear sergeant, no white feller in my tent."

"Sarah – Sarah! No lies, now. Tell him to come out."

"No white feller in my tent," repeated Sarah with conviction.

"It won't do, Sarah," stated the sergeant. "If he doesn't come out quick I'm going in to bring him out. It's a crime for white man to be in a blacks' camp, as you very well know. Now then: what's it going to be?"

Sarah stuck to her guns. "I tell you sergeant," she shouted, angrily, "there's no white man inside my tent."

She and the sergeant glared each at the other. In the silence accompanying the glare Yorky's snoring could be distinctly heard. Slowly the sergeant dismounted, and, when he strode to the tent. Sarah wailed: "There's no white feller in my tent, sergeant. True, sergeant. Only my old friend, Yorky."

Yorky always had a soft spot in his big heart for the blacks. He was meticulous, and was the butt of other men's chaffing. At first he treated me with suspicion but eventually came almost to be grateful for my interest in him and his history. Once his shyness was punctured he could and did talk with confidence. Compared with him I was a mere new chum tramp. He and another had tramped from Port Augusta to Darwin, twenty-two years before I did the trip with a bike, when the blacks between the telegraph stations were not so kindly disposed as they are to the motor car explorers of these times.

Poor old Yorky! Once when in the course of a long and prolonged 'bender' he thought of his friends, the blacks, and having obtained two bottles of rum, he took the refreshment up river to Pluto's camp. As I have before mentioned, Pluto knew his onions. Two bottles of rum and Yorky were not to be shared with his subjects. When the party was over, when the bottles were void, he generously offered his guest a share in his bed. Yorky cared not where he slept, but Pluto was not so drunk that he overlooked the precaution of being sure that he himself slept between Yorky and his lubra - as though Yorky was in the condition to be interested in any woman, black or white, married or unmarried.

Towards morning Yorky woke with a raging thirst. Unaware of his situation and unable to leave his host's abode from his side of the bed, he began to clamber over the mound of fat in the person of Pluto. And Pluto grasped him firmly and yelled:

"That's enough of that, Yorky. Mary's my lubra not yours." Yorky has passed on to the tramps' paradise where the rivers flow clear and cool, where at every mile peg there is a kindhearted cook, where at every ten miles there is a smiling squatter waiting to hand out a pay cheque, and where there is an old fashioned bush pub every thirty miles.

Of what use was Yorky in the scheme of things?

An honourable man, was Yorky, kind and generous. Of greater use to Australia than any one of those who make a fortune from wool or gold and take it abroad to spend it.

Taking sheep over the Tallyawalka bridge in the mid 1920s.

5

The long, hot summer closed its session that year with a series of heavy thunderstorms. The lightning constantly rang the telephone bell and darted about the extremities of the fans atop the mill. Never liking thunderstorms I did not like those. During them I can brush sparks from my hair. The welcome rain roared on the iron roofs, then eased, stopped, began again when the little drops pinged and the bigger drops thudded until the music became a constant blare of drums. After the first storm there came into the kitchen where I was trying to write a procession of the huge bardee moths, dark brown with black spotted wings. They dashed at the yellow lamp light and fluttered maddeningly over my foolscap. The cats enjoyed much sport. I shut the door and the drop window, but the moths entered through the chinks between the wall logs. I took the lamp outside and set it upon the ground. About it grew a cloud. The cloud became dense and more dense,

New tankstand and windmill at Albermarle Station.

dimming the light. A tiny speck of light lasted for a minute or two before it vanished. The lightning of the next storm revealed a mount about and over the lamp. I gave up writing for that night.

After the second storm had passed to the east and before the third began its uproar I heard the croaking of frogs down in the swamp which had been bone dry for ten months. The day following the storms broke fine and clear and cool. The small flies were no more. Paddy bunted, or tried to. When loosed, the dogs raced madly around the well and mill. There was water lying in the claypans in the horse paddock but the horses had to come tearing to the yards, their manes rippling like sea waves and their tails streaming like the hair from a drowned woman's head. The galahs screamed and beat their wings against the earth and turned over on a wing as though dead. It was the first time they had done this without being urged.

The wind ribbles on the sand-dunes had been beaten out by the rain. The insects that lived in them were busy preparing their bodies for the long winter slumber. The tracks of scorpions were numerous, and those, too, of the fly-catching lizard. All the ants worked with frenzy. From the dunes could be seen countless diamonds lying over the 'vast open space'; water on claypans, water in the gilgie holes, water on canegrass flats.

Thirty hours after the last of the rain fell the sand-dunes burst open like flower buds. The shoots of buckbush and grass, wild spinach and carrot, swiftly painted them a brilliant green. In five days the herbage and grass was three inches high. The mulgas seemed to lose their stringy toughness: the sandalwoods redressed themselves with new colour.

Nowhere out of Western Australia have I yet seen a mulga sapling or a young sandalwood tree. Stock and the rabbits consume them all as soon as they appear. What kind of a land is Australia Proper going to be when the trees living today are all dead?

When the natural wind breaks have died and fallen, when the wild westerlies are uncurbed and scoop up the red sand by the thousands of tons - but why should we be concerned about that which will not affect us? Cricket and football are more interesting than the preservation of a fine country for our children and their children.

My writing was stopped by the lamb marking activities and then the shearing of the 45,000 sheep. Musterers, many of them, were quartered on me as the sheep flocks were passed through the run to the riverside shed and then passed through it again minus fleeces. There would be six, ten, or twelve men to feed, men used to ample and well cooked tucker, who demanded no less.

The nights became cold, colder than nights ever experienced by city folk. Before turning in I would bury a green belar log in the ashes on the open hearth, and, after rising in the dark of early morning, I had only to break open the mound to reveal a heart of great red coals. Wood laid ready, now tossed on to the coals, would produce a leaping, roaring flame before which I would drink a pannikin of tea and smoke a cigarette. Then to wash and dress and begin the day's work.

Six o'clock, and outside the mighty stars gleaming and winking like points of blue ice. All night long the bread batter in a bucket had stood in its cosy of sheepskin near the hearth. Uncovered, its surface was cracked and bubbling. Out it came into a 'dell' of flour on the dough board to be pounded and rolled into a plastic ball, then to be put back into the bucket to rise again, and the bucket carefully placed from the fire.

Phew, it was cold out there at the meat safe, but the trays of chops had to be brought in, half to be arranged on the grills, the remainder to be packed into the frypans. Water in the pot was boiling. Into it goes the oatmeal. Thereafter the chops must be turned and salted and the porridge stirred, the tea made and the table set and ladened with bread and brownie, jam and the inevitable tomato sauce.

Seven o'clock and the dawn painting the eastern sky with gladioli tints. With impish delight I would shatter the quiet with tempestuous beating of iron bar on petrol tin. The dogs would yelp and bark, and, inside the kitchen, up on their beam, the galahs would sleepily object. Men would grunt, yawn, curse, but I would keep on and on until a boot or a piece of soap would drive me into the kitchen. In would then come men to cadge a pannikin of hot water to warm the water outside.

"Hot water! You call yourselves Australian stockmen, and you want hot water! Think a thrice blank cook's got nothing else to do but heat water for a lot of loafing horse walkers? Did the old timers wash in hot water?"

Then: "Now then, you! Burgoo?"

"Yes, please."

"Take it away and may it stick to your stomach all day."

"Burgoo?"

"No."

"What! No burgoo? You must be crook. Chops - grilled or fried or underdone or cold red raw?"

"Grilled and four and not too much lip from you."

"Take 'em away, and think yourself lucky you're working for a squatter and not a dressmaker. What about you? Burgoo?"

Above the clatter of knives and forks on tin plates comes the swift tattoo of hooves on frost-hardened earth when the working hacks come racing to the yard, driven by the rider whose turn it is to go out after them on a flash horse and an empty stomach.

Half past seven and men gather about the tables cutting lunches from loaves of yeast bread, loaves of yeast brownie, blocks of brownie, cold roasts of mutton and compresses of salted mutton. With them I would leave the table wreckage and stand at the door and hungrily wait whilst horses were being saddled, for one of them to buck like hell and toss his rider. All the men thought themselves vastly superior to a measly cook. They told me so when leaving every morning, and when coming home at night I would tell them what I thought of fence lizards. It's a poor world in which men cannot give and take.

At eight o'clock all is again quiet. The cats have been fed.

The hens fed and are freed from their yard: the galahs given their handful of wheat. There is the bread to be punched down and placed in the big ovens and the ovens heated when the dough has risen in them. An eight-pound slab of brownie is another job to be done. Sheep to be killed and dressed must be followed by the mixing of a plum pudding and then vegetables to be prepared. There is no time for writing these short days, and there is no opportunity at night.

What a change has come to the surrounding country! The dunes are now emerald hummocks, while the plain to the east is a great carpet, dove grey in colour and rumpled into folds. The afternoon sun is yellow bright and softly warm. The air is still and so clear that one can see the bullet hole through one of the mill fans. The sun goes down beyond the distant mulgas into a bed of pale yellow, and the smoke from the kitchen fire drapes about the huts and the mill like that from the pipe of a dreamer.

He would jog the riders in the twilight, their tired dogs anxious for food and their warm kennels. Most of the day they have been working sheep but they take no slightest notice of Paddy. Off come saddles and bridles, and then that low rumbling sound of hide being shaken over dusty, sweaty bodies. The horses go off a little way, paw the soft sandy earth, sink to it and roll. One in five or six can roll right over from side to side. The men pack saddles and bridles, and come in for a wash, hungry men and tough and red of face.

"Soup?"

"Too right."

"Take it away. Soup?"

"Of course. What the hell do you think you are paid for?"

"Not to make soup like this for a lot of useless fence lizards. Hey, you! What're you gawking about for? Soup?"

"None of your dish water for me."

"All right. Mutton roast or mutton boiled?"

Good lads, all of 'em. One would offer to help wash up and clear away. Then out would come the cards and the matches and we'd sit in to a game of poker and win or lose match fortunes. They would get a supper of coffee and cakes while I would mix the batter for the bread on the morrow.

Thus passed the lamb marking and the shearing.

Only one man stayed on to ride the nearby paddocks for the summer. I dug in the garden and planted the spring seeds. From six to midnight I wrote.

6

Summer again, again summer in full blast. The sand-dunes had disrobed themselves of their dresses of green, and, in the nude, shimmied and jazzed all day long in the heat. Over the plain rolled and heaved the mirage water. Mirage water lay over the space between the huts and the well. The swamp was covered with mirage water up from which towered masts and poles, the spikes of rubbish now dead upon it.

Daily the mercury rose to 110°, 111°, 112° in the shade beneath the canegrass roof joining the two huts. Poor Paddy panted and grunted, seldom moving. His head languishing, his mouth resting on the ground between his bended knees. The galahs were too busy panting to make a noise. Now and then they would waddle to the dish sunk into the earth and kept filled with water, waddled in their absurd fashion to bathe like other birds. The cats, seven now, lay on dampened ground, their flanks pumping incessantly. Cats hate water! Those cats would lie still and permit me to pour water from the water-bag on to their tummies.

At midday the emus would come stalking through the mirage water, their beaks agape, their throat feathers throbbing. Without fear, even curiosity banished by thirst, they would march direct to the trough and either stand to drink or sit to drink.

The water they would take from the trough was astonishing. Nothing would come to the trough throughout the afternoon, but before the mirage water dried up at evening the first of the 'roos could be seen coming up over the plain like giant fleas, leaving behind them puffs of dust to hang in the crimson air. One, an old grey buck, would always be the first to arrive. When the horses came trudging to the trough, the others would hop away to stand up and watch, but the grey buck would not budge. There were no sheep watering here, but immediately after dark the foxes would arrive to 'quesquex' at each other.

I was once again alone, the stockman having gone to Broken Hill for a month's bender. As during the previous summer, I had my stretcher set up on the short and narrow veranda. Between its foot and the kitchen door stood a home made washing stand constructed of petrol cases, and above it, nailed to the wall, was a fairly large mirror.

This night I had written till midnight as usual, had as usual boiled a small billy for coffee, and as usual had rolled and lit a cigarette immediately before lying down on the stretcher.

The moon was one night from full, its brilliant radiance falling upon the floor and reaching upward to the edge of the stretcher The night was calm, and, save for an occasional 'ques-quex' of a fox at the distant trough, was utterly silent.

Relaxed physically and mentally, I lay on top of the two blankets on the stretcher, knowing that I would not require them throughout the night. The cats at this time did not seek my couch, and I happened to glance towards the kitchen door and saw a man standing before the washing stand and arranging his tie with the aid of the mirror.

The moonlight fell upon him from the waist down. His trou-sers were of gabardine, almost new, creased. He wore a dress shirt. There were links in the cuffs. I could see them although from the waist up he was in shadow. He was tall and lithe and youthful. His face in profile was strikingly handsome, but the back of his head was a little too flat.

Certainly astonished but feeling no alarm, I lay for a little time watching him. The set of his tie did not satisfy him because he untied it and then re-tied it. I expected him to speak and, when he did not, I said: "Good night!"

He did not hear me. I then swung my feet over the stretcher edge to the ground. In the act of sitting up my gaze was averted. When I again looked his way he was no longer there. Continuing to feel no alarm, I called in a louder voice:

"Hullo, there!"

There was no reply. I lit the hurricane lamp and looked for him in the kitchen and then in the empty men's hut. Not finding him, I walked outside into the moonlight and around the two huts. Only then did it occur to me that not one of the three chained dogs had barked: only then did a sensation of pricking run up my spine and come to stay at the roots of my hairs.

A ghost! A ghost be hanged! There are no such things. The night was almost as bright as day. I hadn't tasted alcohol for fifteen months. I had not been living alone for a protracted period. Imagination surely! A mental phantasmagoria, an illusion.

I had never before seen the fellow, but I was sure I would know him if ever I did. And several years later I did see him at Wheeler's Well. It was late afternoon at one of the two Camel Stations owned by the West Australian Government. It was in the room used as a sitting room in winter within the stone built homestead. A young man had arrived on his way to Youanmee, to stay for dinner, and then to wash and begin to dress in his good clothes. I sat on a chair talking with him.

Something made us laugh, and then he turned with collar and tie to the mirror, to stand before the mirror side-on to me. And I recognised him as the man who had appeared to me at Wheeler's Well, and I cried out with astonishment.

The man's name was Snowy Rowles.

He was wanted to hang for murder.

Do we dream when we think we are awake, or do we live only when we dream? Search me if I can tell you!

Upfield's own drawing of Bony

NINE

Fur

I

Early in the 1920s a great flood came down the Darling.

Water swelled over into the billabongs and ran away through creeks to fill long-dry swamps. The flood maintained the requisite level to send water down the Tallyawalka Creek, and the flowing water in the Tallyawalka Creek remained high enough and long enough to send water through another creek into a long chain of large lakes that had seen no water for twenty-one years. With the flood water came the codfish and the perch and the catfish and billions of embryo fish in the form of spawn. With the spawn and the weed came countless ducks and swans and pelicans. The next year another flood came down from the vast water-shed of South-Western Queensland and added yet more water to the lakes so that in Victoria Lake it was fifteen feet deep. Finally there came south huge 'mobs' of water-hens that severely damaged all the homestead gardens.

The Tallyawalka Creek provided a quiet haven for the

water birds. The ducks nested in the box trees and far out on the plains among the grass. It was possible to fill a petrol tin with duck eggs within the hour. The islets of the lakes further east became vast rookeries for the pelicans.

Shortly after the filling of the lakes a rider stationed at Victoria Lake reported having seen a rabbit, and as no rabbits had been seen for several years it was worthy of note. A week later another reported having seen several rabbits, and thereafter swiftly their numbers increased. They set to work digging out old burrows which for many years had been deeply overlaid with drift sand. They began to breed and increase steadily but not with the remarkable fecundity they were to exhibit later.

One night at Wheeler's Well the boss rang to ask if I would cook at Victoria Lake until such time as another married couple could be engaged. If I would he would send to Wheeler's Well 'my old friend, Yorky', to look after the garden, the hens, the galahs, the dogs and Paddy.

In Australia Proper the sun's power of evaporation accounts for five feet of water every year, and there was still ten or eleven feet in Victoria Lake when I went there to cook for one jackaroo and four hands. The homestead is situated on high ground overlooking the fine sheet of water, and as the kitchen door faced over the lake, too, I spent much time idling at it to observe its vagaries and its constantly changing beauty. All day long flights of pelicans sailed the sky like fleets of aeroplanes, and, when the wind blew, the surf along the shore sounded like that on an ocean beach. Men were netting the fish and trucking them twice a week to Broken Hill. Before the water vanished they earned a profit of fifteen hundred pounds.

From the river the station had brought an old flat-bottomed boat, and in this I delighted to explore the lake's shore, the little inlets and islets, and the creeks connecting

Victoria Lake with Waterloo Lake to the north and with Brummies Lake to the south. The entire country was a naturalist's paradise.

Syd Whyte, the jackaroo, who is numbered among my friends, agreed with me that the boat could be made to sail. We fitted a mast and constructed a lug-sail with chaff bags, but as the craft was minus a keel it could never be sailed against the wind on a tack. Still, that did not spoil enjoyment. We used to pull away into the wind early in the evening and come sailing 'home' through the busy ducks and the lordly swans and pelicans as dusk was shadowing the lake.

Then one morning, a Sunday, too, the sun rose above the far side of the lake, a pale-yellow disc in a whitish sky, and the wind rose before I rang the breakfast triangle. By noon the colour of the sky was cadmium in between the enormous billows of red sand sweeping over the house to fall like fog about the distant lake shore.

"What about trying out the old boat?" Syd suggested. "Might sink. You swim?"

"A bit. She ought to travel with this wind behind her." I hadn't seen the sea for years and I had been born within sound of it. Still, the distance across was a little over two miles, and if we foundered mid-way we would have a long swim. But -- "Goodoh! We'll give it a berl after dinner." Dinner on Sundays was at twelve o'clock. At two we went down to the boat.

"You steer her dead before the wind," I commanded. "The sail I'll manage. If we go over, or go down, jump clear."

The boat was pushed off. Round was swung the bow and up was run the rough, home-made sail. Although we were still in the lee of the high ground on which the house was built the sail filled at once and began to draw us away at ever-increasing speed. Fast and faster sailed the old flat-bottomed boat. The cat's-paws became little waves, the little waves big and bigger.

With an oar lashed astern, Syd steered whilst standing like the steersman of a whale boat off to attack a whale. I braced my feet against the thwart and hung on to the sail ropes I dared not lash. I expected the mast to be snapped at any second and had to hand a knife to cut it and the sail free before the wreckage could swing us either to port or starboard broadside on to the following seas. When we were but a third of the distance across it was impossible to see even the house when the boat was in a wave trough. The height of the waves on such a shallow sheet of water was remarkable.

The wind screamed, the water hissed away from the bow and hissed in white foam on the wave crests. The waves were running fast, just a little faster than the boat, and for long we rode a crest or wallowed in a trough. With nothing on bar trousers, we yelled at each other, impelled by sheer exultation.

"There's a submerged fence somewhere ahead of us" Syd shouted. "And there's only about ten feet of water on a calm day."

Help! An old fence! What a nice time to hear about that! Posts sticking up from the lake's bed at least four and a half feet, and only five and a bit feet of water under us when the boat was in a trough. There would be nothing to spare between the bottom of the craft and the top of a fence post should we reach the fence when in a trough.

The sail should come down and the boat's speed be reduced to a minimum with the oars until the fence was passed. Yet where was the fence? Although Syd was familiar with it, it could not be seen and he could not say when we were past it. Chance it! Hang it, we'd chance it. We were still chancing it when the boat slowly sank into a trough to continue speeding at a terrific pace when down in the trough, the fore wave and the one astern seemingly remaining stationary high above us. Out of the foot of the fore wave appeared the top of a post only an inch or two below the surface of the trough. Being further stern Syd could not have seen it in time, and only by chance did we sail between it and the one on the other side. The rusty old fence wire scraped the bottom, halted progress by a fraction but did not prevent steerage way. Then slowly the following wave got beneath us, slowly raised us high and higher to travel for a space on its foaming crest.

The far shore with its background of box trees footing the high ground came out of the red fog to meet us. There were no birds: they had taken shelter in the lee of shore and islets and in the creeks. The homestead was blotted out by the flying sand.

Presently the waves became even higher and their reach longer. We entered the surf proper and flew towards the shore like a bird. Before I expected it we grounded and away went the mast and the sail to drape the bow of the craft. Waves came tumbling in over the stern and filled the boat, and only after much exertion did we manage to heave the craft ashore and then lift one end to empty out the water as we had nothing with which to bail.

The loss of the sail and mast made no difference for we could not sail the boat back, and would assuredly have been swamped even had she been keeled to permit tacking. We had to walk and push the boat along the shallows until reaching the northern extremity of the lake when the wind-created tide swept us homeward.

That such a tide could run, that such a sea could run in and on such a small area of water astonished me: for, as I have said, Victoria Lake is only a little more than two miles in width and some four miles in length. That such an experience could be enjoyed 800 miles west of Sydney was no less remarkable. We stepped another mast and made an even bigger sail. We essayed the trip in weather equally as bad two weeks later when again we were lucky to miss the fence posts.

2

When back again at Wheeler's Well there came one day Moss Jones and Bill Dawes on a truck converted from the very first Ford car ever to reach Broken Hill. It was, indeed, a remarkable vehicle. Moss had driven it over the sand-dunes around the gold diggings of Tarcoola and even over those monstrous sand-waves crossed by the South Australian Border Fence. Dawes and he were on their way to the dams beyond Victoria Lake to trap the rabbits that were beginning to water nightly in their thousands. When they left I wished I was going.

The old accursed wanderlust was stirring again in my blood. For three years I had been at Wheeler's Well, the longest period spent at one job in one place ever. I knew every individual sand-dune within a radius of four miles, almost every tree, certainly every dry water course and canegrass swamp.

I think it was Arnold Bennett who said that if there was anything more difficult than getting a first novel published it was achieving the publication of a second novel. I had taken the first hurdle and was well in my stride to take the second when Moss Jones and Bill Dawes called on their way back to Broken Hill, Dawes being ill. On his way back to the dams beyond Victoria Lake, Jones mentioned his inability to secure a temporary partner and the disabilities he would experience without one.

In Australia Proper trapping is a business dissociated from pastoral activities, as much as is mining, and yet is an important adjunct to the successful production of wool. Success as a trapper depends not only on the number of animals available to be trapped and the world demand for fur, but on the trapper's knowledge of the habits of the animals he traps. He has to be not only a keen observer but something of a naturalist. He must have the enthusiasm of the naturalist to study and ascertain what the animal does when not observed, and what it will do in given circumstances. And to cap it all he must be willing to work eighteen hours of the twenty-four.

I knew something of all this when Jones was discussing the lack of a partner. My knowledge of the business was nil: Jones was an expert. Here was a facet of life in the outback with which I was not acquainted, and here was the opportunity to become acquainted with it. I had observed not a little of the rabbit in Australia, and had been extremely fortunate in witnessing two rabbit migrations, but after all my knowledge of the rabbit was superficial. I was like the sportsman who occasionally goes to sea to hook a few fish in calm weather, and who knows nothing of the dangers and trials of the professional fisherman. It was really the thirst for first-hand knowledge, and not the earning of more money than is earned by a station cook, that prompted me to offer myself for the vacant partnership.

4

The year I joined Moss Jones was the last of several good years in Western New South Wales. The water in the chain of lakes north and south of Victoria Lake was rapidly losing depth, but the number of rabbits living in the vicinity of the lakes was phenomenal. This, however, was the summer when ordinary gin trapping would not pay the tucker bill and when the area of water prevented another method of trapping.

Further east on this run the rabbits had multiplied through out three years, and now in February they were converged on the man-made surface dams, for there was no moisture in the grass and herbage and the rodents had to drink - or perish.

We arrived at the first of the dams early in the month when the daily heat sent the mercury up to the 112 degrees mark, and the nightly coolness permitted the mercury to fall not lower than the 95 degrees mark. We netted the dam and built trap yards on a day when even the crows refused to leave the meager shade of the scrub, and the evening of that day found us at opposite corners of the dam embankment with a shotgun and cartridges and waterbag, for the kangaroos had to be kept from smashing down the flimsy fence and releasing the rodents.

For some two miles out from the dam the country was a Sahara, made so by the passage of sheep and countless animals coming to and going from water. The sheep now had been moved, for there was but a foot of muddy water remaining in the dam and that foot might be sucked up by the sun in any one hour.

Throughout the day of terrific heat not a living thing had crossed the small Sahara from the far-distant scrub, but in the poor shade cast by that scrub panted thousands of rabbits, mobs of kangaroos, small packs of foxes, and several wild dogs, animals waiting for the murderous sun to set when they could leave the shade and travel to the water.

When the sun had gone the sky to the eastern horizon was the colour of blood. It reflected a scarlet light that made of the sandy ground a wind-whipped lake of blood. From all points on the Sahara tiny red objects were jumping like fleas and sending upwards to be suspended in the motionless air fine scarlet veils of dust.

The first of the kangaroos halted a hundred yards out from the dam on sighting we two men on its rampart of mullock, and as the sky slowly was drained of its bloody colour, as though a steel-blue tide was surging from the east to push it down after the retreating sun, there gathered about the dam countless kangaroos.

Dusk was falling fast when the first rabbit slipped over the dam rampart. It took not the slightest notice of me near whom it passed, and continued on down into the now black pit of the dam with a determination, which was both remarkable and terrible, terrible because thirst had made of it a robot. Another appeared atop the bank, to vanish into the pit from the bottom of which gleamed the square sheet of dirty silver. Now others came, more and more, all of them robots, no longer natural. One I easily caught when it was about to pass me. It squealed, not with fright but with anger at having been delayed. When released, it continued its journey to the water.

The fence built round the square sheet of water was erected, about one yard from its edge. Twice along each of the four sides the fence was fashioned into a V, the point of which was within five inches of the water's edge. At the apex of the V the netting was cut to make a small hole just large enough to permit a rabbit to squeeze itself through. At opposite angles of the fence a V pointing outwards from the water led into a large, strongly-built netted trap-yard.

Thus, frantically searching for a way to the water, a rabbit would enter one of the V's, reach its point, poke its head through the hole, and thus bring its twitching nose within an inch of the water it must drink. Thirst burning away suspicion, it would edge further through the hole, and drink with the fore half of its body clear of the V point. Another rabbit coming behind it, hearing it lapping like a cat, would nip it on the rump, whereupon the first rabbit would worm the whole of its body through the hole of the V and, in order not to wet its furred feet, would move to one side or the other of the V and thus find itself in the yard-wide space between the fence and the water.

It was now impossible to see what was going on down there at the fence. Rabbits were trickling through the V's like golden sand-grains in so many hour-glasses, and then, their thirst quenched and their bodies distended with water, there was no going back the way they had come save through one of the two V points leading into a trap-yard.

Now in the dark we could hear the 'swish-perring' of countless rodents running strong and swift over the rampart and down into the pit of the dam. The whispering rustle of furred feet on soft sand was continuous. It pervaded the night. Upward from the fence came the ceaseless murmur of hurrying rabbits, the never ending sharp cries of those bitten on the rump by those so eager to drink, the death screams at longer intervals of rabbits that, having taken their fill of water, were become normal and, in panic, had leaped into the water to swim in small circles till each screamed before sinking to death.

Stationed a little below the summit of the rampart, and on its inside, we would observe on the skyline thus obtained strangely monstrous shapes rising against the dark sky, shapes unimagined in daylight, shapes between a spider and crab. Kangaroos on all fours, creeping suspiciously towards the water, knowing we were there, fearing the loud reports of our guns and yet urged on by the dreadful thirst they suffered. In the dark, unable to see the gun-sights, we shot or drove them off to save the fence, fearing to move from our positions to despatch the wounded in case the other might mistake one for a 'roo and shoot - which has been done more than once.

Foxes and dogs would cross our sky-line too quickly for action. However, they were not a menace to the fence, over which they would lightly leap, and lap noisily as though they never would stop. Perhaps on their way out they would fancy a rabbit, and there would come up out of the pit a low roar of scampering feet when thousands of rodents would rush to escape.

All day long nothing came to drink bar an occasional bird: all night countless animals arrived to quench a thirst which had tormented them all day.

At midnight we would light the hurricane lamps and go down to examine the fence and the catch. Into the radius of the lamp light would come the fence. Along the outside of it rabbits would be packed dense to a width of four and five feet. Inside the fence rabbits would be standing on their hind legs, their forefeet feeling the netting, trying to seek a way over as they could find no way through. As one walked along the fence to a trap yard the rodents would scamper away like leaves before the wind.

And within the trap-yards, each measuring six yards square, there would be a solid block of rabbits two and sometimes three feet deep. Although the point of the V entering the yard was raised a foot above ground, so many were the rabbits packed within that no more could gain entry.

"How many do you estimate are in the Yards, Moss?"

"Oh, about a thousand in each. Enough for us to deal

with in the morning. Raise the fence, and let's get to bunk for four hours' sleep."

The fence would be raised from the bottom to rest along the temporary posts, and the dust would rise in clouds about the lights as thousands of repleted rabbits would rush out and thousands of thirst-maddened rabbits would rush to the water's edge. The kangaroos and the foxes and the dogs could now come to drink without hindrance. They and all the rabbits would come again the next night.

At the first glimmer of dawn breakfast was eaten and the day's labour begun. Fifty percent of the rabbits in the yards would have been smothered to death. The remainder would be killed and tossed to a heap outside the yards at the rate of one per second. Then Moss would skin at the rate of three hundred an hour. Fifty was my first tally for the hour, but after a little practice I raised it to two hundred.

Then all the carcases had to be trucked to a distance of a mile from any of the channels feeding the dam with water - when next it rained. Before the next evening came the sun would dry the carcases to the texture of old leather. Tons and tons of meat were thus destroyed: and tens of thousands in Europe were starving for meat.

All the skins then had to be slipped on to U-shaped lengths of fence wire, fur inside, and set up to dry. By three o'clock the skins would be dry enough to pack into a woolbale, and that task finished, Moss would attend to the re-fixing of the fence for the next catch, and I would do a little cooking.

Rabbit skins fetched £2 per 100 in the Sydney market that year and at that time. The Americans and the Belgians were keen buyers and skins and carcases were fifth on the list of Australia's exports. Today the export is still an important one, and beside 6000 trappers earning a good living, there are the handlers in the markets and the thousands of factory hands turning the fur into felt hats and beautiful Arctic fox and mink furs and coats. Of all Australia's pests the rabbit pest has become an important asset, and should science evolve a means of destroying all the rabbits in this country thousands will lose employment, whilst the damage the rabbit is alleged to have done is past repair.

5

A man on gold never watches the clock. To him Time does not exist: even food is ignored until the body grows weak from lack of it. His mind is illuminated by the magic of golden dreams, and only waning daylight for a space draws him back to reality.

Yet there is no excuse for the prospector on gold working over long hours and starving himself, for the gold, having been hidden in the ground for countless ages, will not vanish in an hour.

To the fur-getter Time is very real, indeed, ever present at his elbow to nudge him on to ceaseless labour. Instead of anxiously watching Time to relieve him of labour, he finds Time always at his heels, always trying to catch up with him, in his mind the ever-present dread that rain will come to stop, or slow down, the flow of fur he is turning into gold. For every rabbit is a grain of gold, every kangaroo is four grains of gold, and every fox is ten grains of gold.

When we moved to the lakes they were as dry as a dog's buried bone. Whilst the water remained in the dams, and the tide of rabbits continued nightly to visit them, we obtained 2000 skins every day. Along the sand-dunes surrounding each of the chain of lakes lived countless rabbits, but other than by gin trapping there were no means of maintaining the mass–production of skins which the netted water at the dams had provided, and it was too early to trap for the coming winter market. However, we continued to earn a good living.

After the sun and the wind had evaporated the water from the lakes on their beds grew a wild profusion of herbage, and nightly hosts of rabbits left their warrens to feed on this herbage.

Every morning the tide mark of the herbage was farther from the shore. When each day came tens of thousands of rabbits feeding along a ribbon of herbage edging the whole, and eagles would fly over this ribbon and send the thousands of rabbits racing to the shelter of the burrows. They would race across the bare ground like sheep, and the eagles would turn back and take their breakfast without trouble or effort.

We built a trap-yard at the foot of the sand-dunes, and from it ran out half-mile wings of netting suspended from light posts. The bottom selvage of this netting was hung up to the post-tops at night to permit the rabbits to pass out to the feed, and then an hour before dawn we let the netting down and roughly pegged it to the ground. At break of day we made a wide detour to reach positions far out on the lake bed and well into the sea of herbage. Beating tins and shouting we advanced towards the distant shore and the trap-yard where the netted wings met, and by this means drove seven and eight hundred rodents into the yard.

This method, however, barely paid on account of the labour and time expended on moving the trap-yard and winged fences, for after two drives the rabbits 'woke up' and moved further along.

We discovered an easier method. On almost every sand-bar running out from the shore the rodents had made warrens close to the surface. Beating tins and yelling, we would drive rabbits into these burrows until no more could get in; and then, risking being clawed by a wild cat or bitten by a snake, one of us would begin to pull out the rabbits after all but one entry had been stopped, and the other would skin them. A burrow would produce up to two hundred. Starting at the entry of the only hole not stopped, all one had to do was to grasp a rabbit, withdraw and kill it, and then feel for the next. When the groping hand could reach no more, with the upward leverage of the forearm the slight and shallow ground crust could be broken, and another yard of rabbits gained. Here and there 'the groper' would come to a small cavern from which radiated runways, and like the runways the caverns were packed with fur. Here, then, were underground cities with their circuses and streets, and unconsciously man has adopted the same planning to escape from air raids.

April came and with April the autumn rains. At once the rabbits scattered over the surrounding country, cleared out old warrens and began breeding. Bill Dawes came back to rejoin Moss Jones, and I went down to Adelaide and bought a utility truck, traps and a camp outfit. In May I began gin trapping. The fur fever burned and burned. Skin prices soared to the average of 80 pence per pound, eight skins to a pound averaging tenpence a skin.

Trapping at the dams is hard, but it is a life of ease compared with gin trapping and fox trapping at the same time. I thought of selling my bed and blankets which became almost useless ornaments in the tent.

By noon every day I had moved sixty gin traps to fresh ground and had set them, thrusting a stick into the ground one yard back from each trap to mark its position. Then back to camp to eat a hasty meal and to stretch the skins obtained the previous day. At two o'clock the first visit to the trap line was made to take up thirty shillings. Back to camp to prepare fox baits of fat balls dipped into strychnine crystals. Then to cook food and, if time allowed, to inspect future trap lines.

At sundown, a hasty meal. As night approaches, a sheep's head has to be dragged over the ground to make a scent trail for the foxes and a mark for the trapper to follow early the next morning, and along the trail two of the baits to be placed every fifty odd yards - two baits making a fox swallow one to pick up the other.

Then out again along the trap-line. Walk, walk, walk! I had been walking at top speed all day. Now with the aid of a hurricane lamp to take up more tenpences. At ten o'clock I would be at the far end of the trap-line, lounging beside a roaring fire or walking round it if sleep threatened to master me. Then each trap to be examined on the camp-ward walk, and more tenpences taken up. Into the blankets at midnight, to sleep with the alarm clock under the pillow to be sure of being awakened at four o'clock.

Four o'clock and bitter cold. A drink of strong coffee laced with brandy, a bite to eat, and a cigarette before the coming of the hurrying dawn. In the half-light of daybreak, ready at the camp end of the fox trail with bags to cover carcases from the crows, ready to beat the crows to the baits remaining on the trail and thus save precious time searching for foxes assumed to have taken them.

Now along the trail. Here a splash of gleaming brown. Over there another. According to the baits taken there must be at least four others. Somewhere they are among the low bush. Walk, walk, walk, quartering the country to pick up ten-shilling notes.

Ah, well, not so bad, this morning. Fox pelts to the value of three pounds. Again on the trap-line, taking up the traps and carrying them to fresh ground, taking out a dozen or two grains of gold - 71 in the twenty-four hours. Say six pounds. Not a bad day, certainly. Nine pounds added to the value of the skins of the skin tent. Not as good as the day before, but a little better than the day before that.

It is noon again and the traps are all re-set along the new line. Confound it, how the sun does flash upward to the meridian! Why won't it stop for a few minutes and give a fellow a chance to regain his wind. At the end of four weeks I was weak enough one afternoon to lie down on my bed - and slept for fifty-two hours.

Henceforth I rigidly kept the Lord's Day and worked the faster during the week.

The new grass came up, and baby rabbits filled the gin traps, stopping the flow of fur. At the end of June the foxes' mating season began when they will eat no meat no matter how carefully served to them. The problem arose - what did they eat during this period? Solve that and it would be possible to continue picking up ten-shilling notes till mid-September. I shot a fox and held a post-mortem, discovering that it had been living on scorpions and centipedes, and because I was a dud at catching these hibernating pleasantries I went back to stock work.

But I watched the rabbits with lustful eyes, and I followed the skin market reports as eagerly as once I read love letters.

Then another drought set in. All the rabbits vanished. The sheep began to perish. The foxes attacked the young lambs, and on one station property I obtained over 800 beautiful fox pelts in a period of ten weeks, making 300 pounds. No rain fell all that winter. I got a job carting water on my truck to perishing sheep, and I carried a butcher's knife with which to slay sheep that were ever so slowly being murdered by the crows and the eagles.

Summer came in hot and filled with wind-driven sand. The kangaroos died. Not one rabbit remained over an area of thousands of square miles. The skin game was finished, and with another man I left New South Wales to drive the truck across the Nullarbor Plain to Western Australia.

Arthur Upfield resetting a section of the Rabbit-Proof Fence, 1928.

TEN

Concerning a Plot

I

Sub-Inspector Coleman was not a policeman but an officer of the Rabbit Department Branch of the Lands Department of Western Australia. He has passed on and, from the point reached after the passage of several years, one is able to appreciate a sterling character. He was of the type so rare these days, a man courageous enough to say yes or no, one who regarded his word as his bond, one ready always to 'give a fair deal'. He hated a liar, and he was generous to the inexperienced and the willing subordinate.

Coleman controlled approximately seven hundred miles of the Number One Rabbit Fence, from the coast near Hopetoun to the 421-mile peg north of the Perth-Kalgoorlie Railway. For many years he inspected his section from the seat of a buckboard drawn by mules, but in 1928 he was doing his work with greater rapidity and additional comfort with a motor truck.

The erection of the rabbit fences to halt the migration of the rodents from the eastern States was no mean task. The first to be put up, the Number One, runs north-south and is a little more than eleven hundred miles in length. The two subsequently built fences join this first one to form an inverted letter K.

The southern section of the Number One Fence has its administrative headquarters at the small wheat town of Burracoppin, situated on the Perth-Kalgoorlie Railway some two hundred miles east of the capital. Here, within a confined area, are built quarters for married men, the inspector's house, quarters for single men, trade shops and the store. In one corner of the cross made by the fence crossing the railway one mile east of the town is the large government farm.

In the year 1928, this southern section of the Number One Fence, under Coleman, was worked thus: The sub-section from the railway to the coast, approximately 250 miles, was controlled by a man using a horse-drawn dray. The sub-section from the railway northward to the 163-mile peg had for a year or two been looked after by Coleman himself as all this section, bar a few miles, ran through salmon gum country and then useless desert lands which had not been taken up by the pastoralists. At the northern end of this sub-section is the government camel station, named Dromedary Hill, where camels were broken in and supplied to the two sub-sections further north as well as for employment on the other fences.

At this time Inspector Coleman was finding that the railway Camel Station sub-section was demanding more attention than he could give it. Shortly after the war a new wheat belt named Campion was opened, and this belt extended through the Rabbit Fence several miles wide. The increasing farm traffic, as well as the destruction of a fence's natural protection against sand, trees, increasingly added to the cost of the upkeep of this short wheat belt section, and so Coleman decided to employ another man to patrol the sub-section from the railway to the 27-mile peg.

The name of the young man who accepted this employment was Harry Watts.

Within a few months Harry Watts pulled this short sub-section into good order, and now Coleman saw that Watts could well undertake the whole of the 163-miles-long section from the railway to the Camel Station. This, however, would mean that Watts would have to discard his horse-drawn dray and use two camels in tandem drawing a much heavier vehicle, the use of camels being dictated by the desert country north of the wheat belt.

Watts had had no experience of camels, and was not keen to be possessed of it, but he was persuaded to 'take them on'. Accordingly, Inspector Coleman temporarily engaged another young man to accompany Watts to the Camel Station, to do as much work along the sub-section as was urgently necessary, and from the Camel Station return with Watts driving the re-commissioned camel team and dray.

The week that Harry Watts and his companion set off for the Camel Station, two men were being detained at the Dalwallinu lock-up to face serious charges, and Dawes and I were trapping along the west coast south of Geraldton. A man named Ryan was following contract work on stations about Dromedary Hill, another, named Lloyd, was trying to obtain steady employment in South Australia, a third, named Brown, was living in New Zealand, and the fourth man, John Lemon, lived in South Australia. And then there was George who was in charge of the Camel Station, and a half hundred of others all of whom were destined to play a part on the vast stage of the Murchison district of Western Australia.

In presenting all these facts it may be thought that I am at the beginning of a detective-mystery story. As a matter of fact I am, but the story to be told is not fictional and will prove how closely allied to real life is the technique of the mystery novel. This one to be related was not imagined by an author, but by Life or Fate, or whatever you may think directs our destiny, that selected its characters and drove them to the doing of those things it wanted done to provide a story which has no parallel in life and none in fiction. For its success it required even a man having the personality of Sub-Inspector Coleman, another man fired with the ambition to make his mark in the writing world, and yet a third man whose natural audacity and courage could prove to be his undoing.

Assuming that Life or Fate is possessed of a personality, it began the action of its mystery drama when it put into the mind of Sub-Inspector Coleman the idea of bringing the Burracoppin camel Station sub-section of fence under the control of a man using camels for transport; and from that moment, like a good craftsman, Life or Fate slowly increased the tempo or action of the drama to an astounding climax.

2

In course of time Harry Watts and his companion arrived at the Dromedary Hill Camel Station where George had been working two selected camels in an open dray. These two animals had been broken in to work, but they had not been worked for several years and required 'quietening' for the track. For several days George coached Watts in their management, and when Watts left they were reasonably tractable. However, they were to be driven to country strange to them from country where they had ranged with their mates, whilst one of them was exceptionally nervous.

The fence track skirts the barrier along its east side, and from the Camel Station to the railway there is not one plain cross-fence to stop camels that, like cattle, are possessed of a strong homing instinct.

About the time that Watts and his companion left the Camel Station the two men in the Dalwallinu lock-up decided to attempt a break for freedom: and, when the policeman entered their cell with breakfast on a tray, one of them kicked the tray and its contents into the policeman's face, rushed by him, and got clear away. The policeman managed to grasp the second man and prevent his escape.

The escapee eventually fell in with another young man in possession of a motor car, and together they broke into several country stores and an ammunition shed belonging to a rifle club. Now in possession of military rifles and an almost limitless supply of ammunition, they reached the fence at the Campion wheat belt, to head north along it to reach the great open spaces of Western Australia.

Over all those great open spaces the winter had been dry, and now in early Spring thousands of emus were migrating southward to strike the Number One Fence and sedately to walk beside it in mobs of hundreds. Thus it was that the prison escapee and his new-found partner met these droves of birds and enthusiastically accepted the opportunity for a little sport. Whilst one drove at reckless speed, the other stood up and fired the military rifle above the windscreen, killing many of the birds and wounding very many more.

Watts was finding his shaft camel most difficult to manage. It was a heavy bullock, quite enough to handle, but exceptionally nervous, one of the worst to place between the shafts of a dray and made to wear winkers like a horse. Nothing would stop it from lurching against the fence, drawing the dray wheel against the netting and ripping it, thus occasioning con-stant stopping for repairs. However, the procession eventually passed the 144 mile peg and entered on country of low ground swells where the road runs straight up miles long gradients and down for miles on the far side.

It was when Watts and the camels, led by the second man with the horse dray, were nearing the summit of one of these ground swells that the two motor car sportsmen were travelling fast to the same summit from the other side. The sportsmen were preceded by whistling bullets which, skimming the summit, screamed over the procession. The animals were stopped, and the two men were about to enter into conference, when they saw appear over the summit a huge flock of emus that came racing down towards them. Guessing what was behind the birds, camelman and horseman urged their beasts into the scrub for protection, and they had gained this protection only a few seconds when the emu mob flashed past on the road between them and the fence. Now came the roaring of a motor engine and the staccato reports of the heavy rifle. Then there flashed past the machine with one man hud-dled over the steering wheel and the other standing up and firing over the low windscreen. After that the air was filled with motionless dust and the sounds of combat gradually dwindled into the low buzzing of a fly.

From this point to Campion, a hundred miles, the man in charge of the dray had to go ahead of the camels and drag off the track all the dead emus and kill the wounded birds before dragging them clear, for Watts' shaft beast would not face a bird dead or alive.

Several days later they arrived at a hut and rock water-catchment at the 69-mile peg. This place is situated half a mile east of the fence and is not a bad camel camp. In fact, during the Spring the surrounding wattles and flowering bush make of it a picture. Here the camels were loosed in hobbles, and Watts set out after them too late to find them. By morning they were beyond tracking.

Well, well! If this was driving camels Watts wanted no more of it. Word was somehow sent down to Inspector Coleman who decided to split the railway-coast sub-section and place Watts on the Burracoppin end with the horse and dray. He then referred to his file, brought to light the application for employment of a man who claimed he had had experience with camels in the eastern States, and so came to telegraph me offering the new post vacated by Harry Watts.

Dawes and I had been doing badly for months. We dissolved partnership and I travelled to Burracoppin.

3

I discovered in this new employment many points of difference from those governing similar work on the other side of the Continent. There I had used pack camels: here I was asked to drive two camels in tandem harness drawing a roomy covered dray. This dray transport was certainly superior to pack camels, for the vehicle provided me with a one-room house giving protection against the elements and the ants.

Further to this mode of transport I found the country itself quite different. The scrub here was thick and composed of trees and bush wholly unfamiliar. I was obliged to learn through observation which of this bush the camels would eat and found they would eat very little of it. I encountered miles-wide belts of scrub which would not support a goat, bush vacant of animal life, alive with ants and almost empty of birds. In fact, nearly the entire length of this 163-mile sub-section is useless for pastoral purposes, the Dromedary Hill Camel Station being situated on the southern edge of the true pastoral country.

Through this dense, useless bush the builders of the fence had cut a ribbon twenty feet wide in the middle of which the fence was erected and the rough track formed along the east side of the barrier. From the summit of one of the many ground swells the cut line appears like a brown ribbon laid taut on a green carpet, a ribbon falling away to rise again in an arrow-straight line to the horizon.

Yet another point of difference. On other fences I had had to travel as much as twenty miles away from the fence to reach water. Here along this one water was conserved in holes blasted in rock, and in iron tanks built beneath roofs of corrugated iron to catch the rain. These waters were situated about thirty miles apart. Every one provided pure fresh water, so different from the bore water to which I had been accustomed, water so laden with soda that one had only to hang a dirty shirt under a bore stream for three minutes to take it out white and clean.

Finally, my solitude here was crowded. I actually met a truck or car on an average once every four days.

It was early in November when I obtained two fresh camels from George at the Camel Station, brought them south to the dray at the 69-mile, and so began my first patrol.

About this time the Rabbit Department sold all its mules and many of its horses to Mr Bogle, the owner of Narndee Station which almost surrounds the Camel Station. Few of these animals had been ridden. Many had never known a breaker. The new owner arranged with the Department to use the Camel Station yards to have the animals broken before being taken away, and accordingly, he engaged a breaker for the work.

Whilst the breaker was 'taking the edge off 'em' there arrived from out of the blue a young man on a motorcycle. He told George that his name was Jack Rowles, Snowy for preference, and that he was looking for stock work on a station. As very many people in this wide district were to do, George experienced a liking for this young man, and he invited him to stay the night. He was fairly tall, splendidly built, rather good looking, fair haired and blue eyed. His disposition was ever cheerful, his manner frank and easy, his voice pleasing.

It was mid-afternoon and George and he strolled over to the yards to watch the breaker at work. The mob of animals had all been handled and were now being accustomed to the feel of the saddle. With George sitting on the top rail of the main yard, Rowles said he would like to ride some of these mules.

" What, do you fancy yourself?" inquired George, to which the stranger replied:

"Oh, a bit. I'll give these a turn if the breaker won't mind." Of course the breaker did not mind in the least. Being a good breaker he was a comparatively poor rider, and was only too pleased for another to do the riding.

Within a minute Rowles proved that he could really ride and during the next day or two he rode the bunch, mules and horses, and offered to ride any of the camels. He was one of the finest horsemen ever to enter the Murchison, and when the new owner came to see how the breaking was getting along he offered Rowles a job as stockmen which he accepted.

"I had a wonderful job once in a buck-jumping show down at the White City, Perth," he told us weeks later. "A cobber and me was paid a pound a night to get on the gee-gees, work 'em up to bucking, and then artistically fall off 'em to make the crowd believe they had fire in 'em. One night my cobber fell awkwardly and got hurt, and he was taken from the arena to the ambulance on a stretcher. They brought him past me, and he looked down right crook and sort of upset me.

"Come on, Snow," says the boss. 'Your turn.'

"I told him I didn't want to ride anymore that night, but he kept on and so I went in and climbed aboard a brown gelding with more vice in him than bucking ability. And after seeing my cobber taken away on a stretcher, I was so frightened that I simply couldn't fall off – and was sacked."

4

Life on this fence was as much governed by routine as that in a city business, but the hours of labour were those best suited to the summer heat which along the ribbon of cut line between the tall scrub was intense.

The day begins when the alarm clock suspended from Curley's neck clatters and bongs as he lurches to his feet when dawn is paling the sky. The early morning is comfortably cool, and before dressing I arrange the filled tea billy on the fire and then loose the animals to get their breakfast in hobbles.

To the hood support of the dray I have fixed a drop table, and, seated on an empty petrol tin, I take breakfast away from the ants before the sun rises to gild the topmost leaves of the skirting trees. Belle emerges from the scrub half a mile towards the Camel Station, and I have not long to wait to hear Curley's bell clatter-bong-clatter when he, noting her desertion, lurches after her whilst venting bellows of annoyance. Three minutes suffice to pack all the gear on the dray, and then with the nose-lines I set off to bring the camels to the harness.

'Never give a camel a chance' is a safety first Motto. The animals are laid down to be harnessed with a collar - similar to a horse collar and worn upside down - and a spider of leather that fits down over Belle's hump. Curley has to wear a back pad to take the weight of the shafts, and, in addition, winkers.

His chief aversion is these winkers, and to get them on his head must be roped short to a tree trunk to prevent him biting. It is the only time he tries to bite, and the roars and yells whilst this operation is performed are alarming.

Already the brake shoes are cramped hard upon the dray's wide iron wheel-rims, and Curley is backed into the shafts the while he tries to chew cud and bellow at one and the same time.

When he is harnessed he stands still - waiting. His black eyes are shining. Belle is placed before him and harnessed to the draw chains. One has now to be careful. With one eye on the nearside wheel of the dray, and legs sprung to heave the body back and away from its path, first Curley's hobbles are removed and then those on Belle's dainty white feet.

"Now then, Belle, I'm looking at you!"

Immediately I stand away and move toward the rear of the dray, both camels in complete unison leap forward into a gallop. As the dray slides past I jump to the brake handle and run with it. However, neither camel likes work, and both understand that their 'bolt' is taking them farther from the Camel Station, and the wheel-locked dray is not pulled far before the team stops, when Belle looks back to inquire with her eyes how I liked it, and Curley forms himself into an S to do likewise.

We now proceed with more decorum and the day's work begins.

Belle and Curley are not companionable but they form the living background of my solitude and make it bearable. Save perhaps the elephant no other animal can reason and plot. All moods are clearly reflected in the camels' eyes, and with their eyes they converse together.

Belle is a matron, but she walks with a mincing gait and

is ever determined to have her own way if seldom she gets it. She is dominated by the homing instinct, and the fact that now she is away from home is torture to her. Curley is young and full of energy. He is like a rampageous boy controlled by his stomach and a passion for adventure. Restraint irks him. Belle knows him very well indeed, and she makes the bullets for him to fire.

Thus, before the sunlight reaches the floor of the cut line, the night camp is left behind. Belle's eyes are flashing with annoyance that once again the wheels were locked against her. Curley, too, is still annoyed. He chews his cud with the energy dictated by temper. Both walk as slowly as they are allowed, Belle because she is ever getting farther from the Camel Station, and Curley because he takes an interest in the scenery and in me.

So the morning passes and we are well forward on this day's inspection.

Now Belle begins to pretend to walk off the track and into the scrub, stopping with her head and long neck thrust beyond a tree trunk and so looks round it and back at me. It is her way of letting me know that the time is twelve o'clock, the official time for stopping for luncheon. The shadow made by the fence posts would not cover one of her feet, but the animals are driven on until a quandong tree, or a wait-a-bit bush, is reached.

Whilst the water in the billy is coming to the boil for tea, the branches of the tree or bush are lopped and dragged to the waiting animals. During any halt along the fence for repairs, if there is a tree or bush they will eat nearby, they are fed like this. I thus kept them with me on this starvation section for seven months, when men before me were obliged to take fresh camels from the Camel Station on every trip.

Now and then we would come to a granite boulder beside the track the surface of which would be several inches above the ground. Belle and Curley knew every one of these partially buried boulders, and both would begin to bolt and draw towards it and thus run a wheel over it in the attempt to capsize the vehicle. Locked wheels only would prevent this. But no amount of planning and argument by Belle would induce Curley to run a wheel against a tree trunk. In his early youth he had been broken in to dray work by the singular method adopted by the breaker. After Curley had been roped and handled he had been harnessed to an old and stout dray and permitted to roam where he willed. It was not long, of course, before the dray became anchored to a tree trunk, and there Curley would stop all night both hungry and disgusted because quite unable to move on after the herbage and bush just beyond his nose. In the morning the breaker would come and set the dray free of the tree and allow Curley his freedom, again harnessed to the dray. After a week of this Curley knew enough not to permit the dray to be anchored to a tree, and always ever after when harnessed to a dray he took exceptional care to prevent it colliding with a tree. Even during his many bolts he would swerve the dray away from a dan-gerous tree trunk.

Belle would watch and bide her time. As has been stated, there was nothing coarse about Mistress Belle. She disdained crudity, such as striking, biting, or kicking. When travelling northward the brake handle would be that side nearest the fence, and as I rode only about one mile in ten, I usually walked between the dray and the fence. Sometimes when thinking of book plots and characters I would unconsciously edge forward to about Curley's shoulder, and then Belle would lurch towards the fence, dragging Curley after her, and, after Curley, the dray. Only by leaping backward, or over the fence, did I escape being crushed by the dray wheel against a fence post. To be injured even on that track at that time of the year would mean the finish. Oh, yes, Belle required a deal of watching.

The night's camp was usually reached about four o'clock, when the camels would be loosed in hobbles. Immediately the edge had been removed from Belle's hunger she would set off for the Camel station, and after an interval poor Curley would go lunging after her, his bell banging, his roars of anger stirring the bush. Scrub would be cut and dragged to partly circle two trees to which the animals would be brought and neck-roped for the night.

If the camp was at a watering place I would bathe from a bucket: if not at a watering place, then with two pints of water in a wash basin for water was as precious as good wine and had to be carried on the dray in a drum.

My leisure began with the setting of the sun, and immediately the darkness banished the flies, I would begin the evening's writing at the drop table in the dray. Sometimes the flying insects about the hurricane lamp would defeat me, but this was not often. The light edge would fall to the ground beyond the dray, and beyond it the bush would be hidden by a featureless black wall or illuminated by the moon into fairy land. The bush was ever silent, save when the wind blew, which was seldom during the summer months. The silence was complete when Belle and Curley slept with their heads resting on the ground and did not ring their comforting bells, so silent that often before turning in on the stretcher set up beside the dray I would sometimes go to them and urge them to their feet to feed and to ring their bells.

The track was long and lonely, but I was treading another that was longer and yet overcrowded, along which the mile stones are bitter disappointments. Whilst on this track I wrote my third novel to be published, when the first and second indicated that not yet would I be promoted to a home on a mountain top with my wife and small son. Still, I had achieved something in being published in America as well as in London. The reviews I was receiving in responsible literary journals overseas were all encouraging, but in Australia my books were being ignored.

5

In the Murchison district towns and settlements are far spaced. From Dromedary Hill Station Mount Magnet is a hundred miles distance, Youanmi some seventy miles away, whilst Burracoppin and the railway lay to the southward more than a hundred and sixty miles. The place takes its name from the shape of the dominating hill, a wrong name for the hill has a double humped summit and its zoological name should be Camel Hill. Our imported ruminant is named wrongly, too, it having but the one hump and being therefore the dromedary.

George, a cheerful and likeable man, was in charge of this small station, and his life was not much less lonely than mine. Other than me he had regular visits from the northern patrolman, but there would be periods of days when he saw no one.

Of necessity all days were alike on the track, and for every Sunday spent beside the netted barrier I was able to take a day off either at Burracoppin or at the Camel Station. Often I spent several days with George, when we would potter about during the daylight hours and play poker with pennies till a late hour whilst both the gramophone and the wireless were working at the same time just to make a noise.

Arthur Upfield, 1929.

Sometimes when I was with George, Rowles would call when on his way to or from the Narndee windmills east of the fence. He was invariably welcomed, and often when coming from his hut on Narndee he would bring a little mutton which would make him double welcome.

He could manage a motorcycle as well as he could manage a horse, and one morning when George and I were playing poker in the kitchen we heard the sound of his machine and saw him, through the window, approaching at his usual reckless speed along the track from Narndee.

"Now we'll have a feed of fresh mutton," George cried with satisfaction. The kangaroos were scarce and we were meat hungry as anyone can be if meat is not eaten for ten days or a fortnight save out of tins. Escorted by a cloud of dust, Rowles arrived, and we went out to greet him with:

"Did you bring any meat?"

His expression became blank and we suffered disappointment even before he replied:

"No, I forgot it. I put some in a bag, and then left it on the table in the hut."

"Well then, you had better go back and get it," urged George.
"Oh, all right! All you fellows think about is meat. Meat, meat, meat! Don't you ever think of nice things like girls and beer?"

His engine roared and he skidded the machine in a sharp turn and then sped down the road to Narndee at a terrific speed. He had ten miles to cover to reach his hut and ten to cover on the return.

"He'll be back in twenty minutes," predicted George. "Get the table set while I clean up the grill. How do you want your chops done?"

"Semi-raw."

"Don't think I'll cook mine at all. Better, I suppose. Even the blacks cook their tucker."

Now and then we would glance at the clock. The time dragged.

We hungrily looked out of the window and down the Narndee track. Fifteen minutes passed. Rowles should soon be back. Then we saw him, coming not along the track, but forming the nucleus of a comet the tail of which was composed of dust. He was riding his cycle at truly terrible speed over the rock-strewn, rabbit warrened, water-guttered flats footing the hill, country on which I would have hesitated to ride a horse.

"What the devil's he doing?" I demanded of George.

We noted then that in front of the comet something was raising spurts of dust, but before we could decide what it was it and Rowles disappeared from our sight behind a mass of low bush.

Thereupon we went out to this bush to observe, and were met and passed by an old man kangaroo closely followed by Rowles on his machine. Snowy mustered the 'roo into the back yard and to the rear of the homestead building where it sat up with its back to the wall and faced Rowles who now sat astride his machine laughing at it and at us.

"There's your meat," he called out, "What's wrong with it?" The next day he came across from his hut especially to bring us a quarter of mutton. At another time he arrived at the homestead to catch George on the open space between the fence and the house. Sending the powerful machine straight at the defenceless George, he skidded it off its target only at the last fraction of a second. George ran for the protection of the house, but before he could reach it Snowy was after him, and on his bike mustered George away from sanctuary and towards the fence. Eventually George was given the opportunity to rush for the kitchen. Behind him followed Rowles on his machine, to bail George into a corner and laugh at him while the exhaust fumes poured out of door and window as though the place was on fire.

Yes, there was much about this laughing young man that was attractive. Eager to perform his share of the camp chores, a cheerful loser at cards, generous in his opinions of others, always nattily dressed and cleanly shaved, he was welcomed wherever he went. There was no coarseness in his character or ever a hint of meanness in his behaviour. It was a shame and a tragedy that Life or Fate should have cast him for the role of villain.

6

On the 10th May 1929, I camped at the 135-mile peg. It rained an inch that night and such was the state of the road the following morning - dangerous to non-gripping rubbery feet of camels - that I decided to remain there that day and cut and renew fence posts.

Towards noon I heard the roaring of a motorcycle engine and, looking along the track to the north, saw Snowy Rowles approaching at fast speed, now and then his machine skidding in the mud, now and then sending outward sheets of puddle water.

Good day," he said, on pulling up. "Have you got the billy boiling?"

"No, but it very quickly will be. How come?"

"I brought a phone message over for George this morning. Inspector Coleman telegraphed to tell him he has to break in a couple of camels for work on the Number Three Fence, away from sanctuary and that you are to stay with him and lend a hand."

"That'll be a change. Decent of you to come down all this way with the road in the state its in."

"That's all right. I skidded into a tree only four times and into the fence only once. You'll have repairs to do at 142-mile. Rain'll do a lot of good."

He stayed yarning for a couple of hours and then departed in the same joyous, reckless manner in which he had arrived. Three days later I reached the Camel Station, and to Belle's great joy settled there for several weeks.

The days were cold and the nights colder. Having 'taken the edge off 'em', we daily drove the two wanted camels harnessed to a buckboard round and round Dromedary Hill. The interesting and exciting portion of the breaking in was past and now this constant driving was becoming boring. We talked out every subject we could command, and during a long silence Life or Fate planted its great idea into my mind.

Before the writing of the psychological study of a lonely man living on a desolate beach south of Geraldton, I had turned out a mystery-story in which was introduced a half-caste detective. The reviews of this book were such as to indicate another about the investigations of this same detective. It was not so much the mystery as the methods he employed which commended him to the reviewers, and for some considerable time my mind had been occasionally occupied in the search for a plot that would in its working out give his methods of investigation further scope.

It appeared to me that such masters of the mystery-story as Wilkie Collins, Edgar Allen Poe, Sir Arthur Conan Doyle and others were all bound by a singular set of rules. The body of a murdered person is found - formerly on the library floor; latterly on the top of a bus, beneath a lift, or some other improbable place - and then the detective examines the corpse and its locality, picks up clues and finally arrests the killer who must be the least suspected person.

It occurred to me: why should there be a corpse? Corpses litter the pages of nearly every murder mystery-story which is why this type of fiction has become hackneyed. Surely it was possible to devise a set of rules differing from those laid down by the masters? Why not date a fictional murder two or three months before the story opens? Why not produce a murder mystery having no poor corpse between its covers? Let us, therefore, completely destroy the body of a victim of homicide, and then permit my detective, Napoleon Bonaparte, to prove first that a murder had been committed, secondly how the crime was committed, and thirdly who committed it. To sum up: produce a murder mystery-story without a murder or a corpse in it.

However, there were many difficulties with which to cope. Many real murderers, including doctors and surgeons, had failed to dispose of the bodies of their victims, despite all their vaunted ingenuity. Crippen and Landru come easily to mind. Of all killers, perhaps the Paris Bluebeard came nearest to success.

It was quite a problem, this. With appliances within reach of the ordinary person, how could a human body be so utterly destroyed that no trace of its existence should remain to damn a killer. A bath of acid, a crematorium, were not within reach of the ordinary person desirous of escaping just punishment. Putting a body down a well, even dropping it down the shaft of an abandoned mine and then exploding tons of earth upon it, would not destroy it. Although concealed it would still exist. If only I could solve this problem I could at once get to work because already I had gathered together a cast of characters and had roughly plotted the action and had gone to the ants to provide me with clues for my Napoleon Bonaparte.

"Say, George," I said, as we drove around Dromedary Hill. "Assuming I killed a feller can you tell me how I could dispose of him without leaving a trace that he ever lived."

"What! You goin' to write another book?"

"Yes. I want to write another Bony yarn in which he gets a job of work worthy of his brains. I want to give him the case of his career, if I can 'nut' out a quite simple way of getting rid of the eternal corpse."

"Well, that's easy enough," he replied without hesitation. "Let's suppose I wanted to do you in. I'd kid you into the bush where there was lots of firewood. I'd probably shoot you, and then I'd lay you on a heap of wood and burn your body. In a couple of days I'd come back with a sieve and get out of the ashes every metal object, such as bootlace tags and boot sprigs, buttons and studs, and every bone which wasn't burned to ash by the fire.

The metal things I'd put into sulphuric acid or scatter down several wells. They wouldn't be very important, anyway. The bones I would put in to a prospector's dolly-pot and pound to dust, and the dust I would throw out for the wind to scatter. So that no chance passer would wonder what the fire had been for, I'd shoot a couple of kangaroos and burn them on the same place."

So that was it! The kernel of my problem was a dolly-pot to deal with the bones that the temperature of an ordinary fire would not destroy; the common iron pot used by prospectors in which to crush stone thought to contain gold. Why, there was one in the blacksmith's shop here at Dromedary Hill.

There was my problem completely solved, meeting all my

few but vitally important demands. One thoroughly burned the body, sifted the ashes, destroyed the metal objects salvaged with a pint of acid used for soldering, and pounded into dust the bones and scattered the dust to the winds. What would then be left of the body to prove that it had existed? Nothing.

The bleakness of the day and the boredom of the incessant driving were banished by my mind that now was fired with this idea. My fictional murderer should destroy the body of his victim in the manner detailed, and then Bony could get to work, and prove --? But what could he prove? With not a particle of the body remaining he could prove nothing, for unless there could be exhibited a body or portion of a body no judge and jury would long listen to a prosecution if my killer carried out George's astoundingly simple method, how could Bony build up a case, be he possessed of superhuman intelligence?

I was confronted by the old problem of the irresistible projectile meeting the immovable object. No matter how wonderful Bony might be as a detective, I could not provide a clue, or engineer one slip on the part of the murderer - unless the murderer omitted to carry out one detail of the process, which, having become possessed of the perfect method, I could not countenance.

The perfect murder had to stand. The killer must succeed in obliterating the body of his victim; but, even so, he must make one tiny and fatal slip. There must be some way to smash the immovable object, because it was difficult to believe there ever was, in reality, a perfect murder. Perfect murders, of course, might be imagined by the dozen, if one took such liberties as locating them where everything is convenient, or luring the victim to where a foreseen meteor is due to strike, or where a professor is experimenting with annihilating rays!

But this murder was to be dealt with seriously. It was to be committed among ordinary, everyday people. But where could a killer make a mistake, and subsequently be visited by the hangman, if he carried out George's so simple method of destruction!

We argued the matter and sought a flaw in the method to be seized upon by my detective, but there was no flaw to be found. The immovable object was not impressed by the projectiles represented by ourselves.

Not unappreciative of the fact that George had given me the basis of a golden plot, I offered him a pound if he could find a flaw in it. I believe he thought that pound was going to be easy money. The fictional killer was to make no mistake when carrying out the method, but yet he was to make one slip.

Time went on and no solution to the puzzle could be found. The mustering and the shearing kept the Narndee hands busy at the western end of that run and we saw nothing of Snowy Rowles. My mind ceaselessly worried the problem. but without avail. And then one night I awoke to hear my companion walking about the house in a most restless manner. It was one o'clock in the morning.

"What's the matter with you?" I asked, to which he replied: "Blest if I can sleep. I'm trying to earn that quid."

Earn it he didn ot.

In July I returned to my fence section, taking as leading camel a lovable matron named Millie, who was really as sensible and as gentle as a dove-like maiden aunt. It was surprising how well Curley came to behave when he found he had no mate to make bullets for him to fire.

One of my friends in Burracoppin was a really clever thinker and an excellent debater. Often we had argued such subjects as Communism and the Authority of Bible Prophecy. Together we tore at and smashed my problem, but found no solution. I think that a congress of barristers and expert criminologists would have been no more successful. It was the perfect murder, provided the murderer carried out the remarkably few and simple details. Finally I gave it up in despair.

Meanwhile, George was out on horseback one day when he met Snowy Rowles riding his motorcycle on his way to pay us a visit. It happened that George was unshaven, hatless, and that he carried a rifle with the intention of obtaining meat should he come across a kangaroo. Still intent on earning my pound, he said to Rowles: "Hey! Snow! If I was to shoot you dead, drag your body to all that dead wood, properly burn it up, and then go through the ashes with a sieve and get out all the metal from your clothes and boots, which I'd shove down a well, and get out all your bones which I'd dolly-pot to dust, how could I make a slip and get caught?"

Greatly astonished by this somewhat involved and abrupt question, seeing the rifle George was carrying in his right hand, and knowing that too much solitude is apt to send a man crazy, Rowles said something about being in a hurry, and forthwith skidded his machine in a short half circle and roared away back towards Narndee, expecting - he afterwards told me with a grin - to feel the impact of a bullet in his back.

The humour was deepened by George's genuine surprise at Snowy's exit from the scene of an imagined crime, and by his not realizing the cause until he had nearly reached home. One of his many good points was that he delighted in telling a joke against himself.

The early spring weather was superb, and the desert bush

became a garden in which the wattles and broom-bush bloomed and the everlasting flowers covered the ground by the square mile. The buttercups flowered *en masse* all over Dromedary Hill when next I saw it. I halted the camels and stood entranced by what had become a stupendous nugget of gold all gleaming in the sunlight beneath the blue dome of the sky.

Sometimes I worried the problem produced by George's perfect murder. Then I would resolutely thrust it from my mind and employ it on the fashioning of another plot. The weeks passed and the evenings again became warm to permit me beginning the writing in the cart, effort that had had to be suspended during the cold nights.

One morning Curley was particularly cross and offered objection to being pushed back into the shafts. He bellowed and spewed cud disgraceful, and it was whilst looking down his throat beyond his evil-smelling teeth that like a comet there flashed into my mind the solution of the problem I had so vainly sought.

I admit that the solution did not budge the immovable object, but it did permit my fictional murderer to carry out George's plan in every detail. Even so could make a fatal mistake. Bony could arrive on the scene months after the crime had been committed, and from the very sand of the locality he could dig up clue after clue to establish that a man had lived, had been slain, how he had been killed and by whom.

Snowy Rowles with Ryan's utility, as photographed by Upfield; Rowles' rifle and dog with Ryan's utility, on the road.

ELEVEN

The Second Act

I

George had been in charge of the Dromedary Hill Camel Station for several years when Inspector Coleman decided. to reverse our positions, a decision welcomed by me as I itched to begin the writing of The Sands of Windee. The change would mean enhanced comfort, to write on a wide table in a real room beneath a real roof, to be uninterrupted by flying insects and the spring and summer thunderstorms.

The handing over of the stock and plant was to take place on October 7th, and the previous day, a Sunday, there were gathered at the homestead: George, Dave Coleman, Lance Maddison - the northern patrolman - Snowy Rowles and myself. The day was cold but clear, and we spent the afternoon in the sitting room before a fire of mulga roots.

We talked about many things before someone mentioned that a certain overseas author did something extraordinary to obtain local colour for a new novel. I said I would not mind spending a month or two in a first class gaol to obtain local colour and to study the psychology of the inmates. George then said to Rowles, his small eyes beaming:

"Tell 'em how you got on in gaol, Snow."

Rowles flushed to the roots of his fair hair. I liked him the more for this, and I thought George unwarrantably indiscreet. We in the bush are a tolerant people with whom a man's past weighs as nothing in the balance with his behaviour in the present, but it seemed unfair to raise a man's record before people in whom he had not confided. We had known Rowles now for more than a year, and he had proved his integrity.

This is the story he related that afternoon.

"At the time I was riding the gee-gees at the White City I was getting around with a tart who I thought was all right, but who I threw down when I learned she was fishing with other blokes. Some time after, she wrote to say she was going to have a baby and that, as I was responsible, it was up to me to do something about it. Me responsible!" The naive manner in which he refuted such an extraordinary idea created a roar of laughter. "Anyway, I let her know she's after the wrong bird this time, and I heard nothing more until one afternoon when I met her on the street. She was carrying a baby in her arms, and she said that if I didn't come to light with a wad of cash she'd sue me for maintenance.

"Where was I to get a wad of cash, even if the kid was mine which it wasn't. Cash doesn't grow on lamp standards. I didn't take no more notice of it until one day my grandfather, who lived with us, says to me:

"'Come down the garden a bit. I got something to say.' Down the garden he looks hard at me and says: 'What are we going to do about this girl who is blaming you for getting her into trouble?'

"'Do! Nothing, of course! I'm not to blame. She's been running around with half a dozen fellers. That's why I threw her down. I'll go to gaol before I pay a zac.'

"'That sounds all right, Snow,' says he, 'but we got to consider others in this house. As a fact she called here yesterday to see me especially. and we talked things over. She's got you in a cleft stick, Snow, and as you never have any money I suppose I've got to pay. Now here's a cheque for two hundred pounds. Make an appointment with her and settle with her.'"

We had heard about Rowles's grandfather, and the sum he now mentioned was not beyond probability. He went on:

"So I wrote her a note fixing a date and place in Hay Street to meet me, and when I did meet her I took her into a furnishing shop and bought her a pram with the money I got at the bank with grandfather's cheque. Then I took her to a tea shop where I slipped her the balance. She wasn't a bad looking tart, you know, and anyhow we had been cobbers although I was wild that she was getting all that money so easily. We parted without words.

"Well, then, time goes on, and after a couple of months or so I met her accidentally in Murray Street. She's got the baby in the pram.

"'Hullo, Snow!' she says, without smiling. 'What d'you think of your son? He's the dead image of you, isn't he?'

"'You're a liar,' says I. 'He's not like me and he isn't mine.'

"'Oh yes he is, Snow,' she says. 'You can't get out of it like that. When are you going to begin paying me maintenance?'

"'There's nothing doing. Grandfather, through me, settled with you.'

"'Settled with me,' she says, as though she had never seen me before. 'Why you haven't paid me a penny maintenance. Settled with me, indeed. If you don't begin to pay the proper amounts I'm going to take you to court.'

"Then I saw what I had done. When I paid her the money I hadn't troubled to get her to sign a receipt for it. I was well in the cart and she knew it. I had no proof that I bought her the pram or paid over the balance of the cash.

"After a fortnight I got a lawyer's letter, and grandfather wanted to pay again a lump sum through a solicitor this time. But I wouldn't have it. Into court I went and told the tale. The P.M. didn't believe a word of it, said he didn't disbelieve grandfather giving me the cheque but didn't believe I paid over the money. I refused to pay, and eventually a D. took me up in Hay Street, and down to Fremantle I went. I was there for nearly ten months before grandfather persuaded me to let me pay the blackmail. Course, when I came out there was no jobs going easy, so I borrowed the brother's bike and came up here."

For an hour Rowles described his life in the Fremantle gaol, and it did not occur to me, or to the others, that he knew a great deal about it for one incarcerated only for debt.

2

On the tenth of the month the others departed their several ways, and this night I began the writing of The Sands of Windee, using in the foundation of its plot George's perfect murder. On this I erected an edifice truly Australian, substituting hackneyed clues for others produced by the ants and the trees, and rigorously avoiding blood and bellow drama. I relied on our natural fauna and on the personality of my detective for success, and I achieved it. Pardon me for blowing my own trumpet, but I intend doing so when referring to The Sands of Windee.

For me, life at the Camel Station became governed by different routine. I made and fitted several new gates, sometimes rode a horse round the 33,000-acre property, maintained the old mill in efficient order, visited the drying waterholes at which stock might linger and perish, and carted firewood on a small dray hauled by five donkeys.

Every second night the camels would come to the well troughs to drink, these troughs being situated inside stout yards which thus acted as traps when animals were wanted. At intervals of many days someone passed through on his way to Youanmi, Burracoppin, or Perth. A prospector had lunch with me, a tough, bearded man who used an extraordinary car for transport. After leaving me he sold the contraption to Snowy Rowles for fifty pounds. Another came and stayed the night and took away his two camels that had been roaming on the property for some time. James Ryan, chosen by Life or Fate to play a tragic part in this play came one afternoon, had tea and yarned for an hour, and departed for his camp on Narndee where he was putting down bores on contract.

Summer arrived one morning to cover the westward flats about Dromedary Hill with a thick layer of shimmering celluloid, to burn away the golden buttercups and reveal the hill's khaki uniform, to send the emus by day to the troughs in their hundreds and the rabbits in their hundreds by night.

Then one morning when I went along to the mill to overhaul it I discovered in one of the yards a solitary camel lying down. It was odd that this camel in the prime of life should be there alone, and going into the yard I 'shooed' him to his feet, when I saw that his near-side hind-leg was injured so severely that he could not support himself on it. Unable to travel on three legs as a dog can, he lay down again with a grunt of pain.

It was obvious by the fresh tracks that a bunch of camels had entered the yard some time in the night for a drink, and that during a fight the leg had suffered a strain or other injury.

There being no crush in this set of yards, and no means of communicating with the outside world from which to obtain assistance, it was not possible to examine the leg, and I was quite unable to decide whether it was a break or a strain.

The following day the leg was no better. The animal's big black eyes regarded me pathetically, and, seeing that there were hollows in front of the hip bones denoting an empty belly, I cut a quantity of saltbush and dragged it into the yard, where the camel at once began to eat.

By the following Sunday I had become sure that the leg was broken. For a week now every day I had cut scrub and dragged it to the yard, and had watered the animal from a bucket. The Inspector had gone south before the accident, so that I could not get his directions about destroying the camel. According to regulations I could not destroy a government-owned camel unless there was a Justice of the Peace present, but there was not a J.P. within shouting distance.

Another difficulty was presented. I could not destroy the injured camel where it was in the yards, because the carcase would have to be removed, and not all the King's men could have harnessed a couple of camels or a horse to drag it away to the distant bush. And to leave the carcase within the yard to pollute the air would have prevented any live animal from coming there to drink.

Thinking of this difficulty from all its angles. I saw a way of getting the camel out of the yard before destroying it. I made an opening in the yard fence, and every time I fed the camel with saltbush I placed it a little nearer to the opening in the fence. When the camel wanted to reach the fodder, it had to scramble forward on his fore-knees: and in this manner, after five days, I got it through the fence and fifty yards beyond.

At the close of the tenth day, I decided to put the animal

to sleep. Since the Inspector had gone south I had not seen a soul, and now not all the government regulations and laws in the Commonwealth should prevent an act of common mercy. Selecting three cartridges of the larger shot, I walked to the yards with a twelve-bore shot-gun. At the yards I loaded the gun, and when walking from the yards to the camel I decided to aim from behind just back of an ear.

I had not fed and watered the camel since early that morning, and the animal looked round at my approach and gurgled its pleasure at seeing me, expecting, of course, to be fed as usual. Well, it would require no more saltbush. The western sky was blood red, indicating another hot day on the morrow. I came to stand within a yard of that camel, to make certain sure, and the big black eyes gazed at me and said:

"Well, it's been pretty lonely here all day in the hot sun."

I went back to the house for the axe and the water bucket.

It was not until the following Sunday, fourteen days after the leg had been broken, that Snowy Rowles arrived in his newly acquired car. Hearing my trouble, he said:

"We'll soon fix that up."

Snowy mercifully shot the beast, and then we had to cut the carcase into two portions for the car to drag away into the bush.

3

A week or so after the destruction of the injured camel, Snowy Rowles left his employment on Narndee Station, and took up the work of fox trapping for a living. He camped with me several nights at different dates on his way to various points many miles distant.

I arrived home one evening after a long day in the paddocks to find his old car over the pit, and he himself tinkering with the entrails. About the pit was nearly every tool on the place, and the manner in which he reassembled the engine proved him to be no novice at such work. During this period, while he did a deal of travelling about, he did not accumulate many fox scalps, the payable bonus on which was two pounds.

"Fetch me half a dozen plugs of gelignite, a length of fuse and a detonator, and watch me blow this junk to splinters," he shouted when I was returning to the house after having loosed the hack. Then, when I stood peering beneath the machine at him: "I'm losing too much time pottering about with this thing. A feller ought to be able to buy a tip-top secondhand utility for a couple of hundred."

Having made the few preparations for dinner, I called him to it, and work on the car was suspended till the next day, when I lent a hand. He got the engine running about four o'clock, when he announced that he would start off for Youanmi that evening. By the time I had ready the simple dinner, he had showered and shaved, and I joined him in the spare room when he stood in a smart pair of gaberdine trousers, a silk shirt, and polished shoes. I guessed his errand to Youanmi.

"Ever hear the yarn about the feller who was in the habit of winking his eye at the girls on the street?" he asked, that slow smile lighting his handsome face, his collar and tie held idly in his hands. "A tart reported him to a policeman who ran him in. The next morning the beak said: 'I cannot understand such behaviour. You must get a lot of rebuffs.' 'Too right, your worship,' says he, 'but I get a lot of tarts, too.'

"I've often borrowed a few quid off the old grandfather, often I've got a rebuff, too. Reckon I'll write to him and explain about that car and how I'm losing so much time messing about with it. Then I'll put it to him for a couple of hundred. I could pay him back inside a year. With a good utility I could do much better."

He turned then to the mirror, leaned towards it a little and began the small task of fixing collar and tie. His face to me was in profile, and it was as though my mind received a blow. There was the identical man whom I saw at Wheeler's Well one moonlit night looking into my mirror above the washstand at the foot of the stretcher.

"Well - that's peculiar to say the least," I gasped, and then had to explain it all.

"Trick of the mind - fancy," he said carelessly.

Other comparatively frequent visitors were Emily and Larry, two full-blooded aborigines who got about in an old jinker. Both were young, both were happy, both dreaded the day when Emily's former husband, a bad black, was released from a prison compound. These two indulged in swift and energetic fits of temper, when Larry would thrash Emily. And then Emily would wait her chance for revenge: throwing scalding tea into Larry's face, or cracking him with a waddy when his back was towards her.

About the 24th November James Ryan arrived at my homestead in a newly acquired utility car. He was a welcome visitor, for he was blessed with a fund of dry humour, and his store of anecdotes was inexhaustible. He was on his way to Burracoppin for stores and two new wheels, and said he would be back within a week, and consented to bring me stores and my mail for which I was starving as I had been without mail for seven weeks.

About the first day of December Rowles came again to the Camel Station, and he asked if Ryan had returned, saying he wanted to meet him when he did as he understood that Ryan intended leaving Narndee for the far north-west of the State, and he, Rowles, thought of offering to go into partnership should his grandfather return a rebuff instead of the desired two hundred pounds. I did not know that Ryan contemplated leaving the district and was not much interested, because Ryan was not a Government man and his movements did not concern me.

Ryan was certainly overdue from Burracoppin. Rowles was apparently anxious to settle matters with him, and he decided to travel south along the fence to meet him coming north. He got down as far as the 100-mile peg when his old car broke down, and in the flaming heat he walked the four miles to the 96-mile hut and rain shed where he found Ryan and another man, and George with his truck.

About two-thirty on the afternoon of December 7th I saw Ryan's utility pull up beyond the netted fence gate, and from the house veranda observed Ryan alight and open the gate for a second man to drive through. The driver was a stranger to me.

Poor Ryan had been at the bottle, and his short-clipped beard was untidy, his eyes were red, his hands were trembling. He said:

"Meet George Lloyd. He's come up to join me in the great open spaces."

Lloyd was a man of about twenty-eight. Clean-shaven, powerfully and athletically built, he was quite sober and bore no physical evidence of alcoholic indulgence. It transpired that he was a teetotaller. There was about him that indefinable something that distinguishes the farmer from the bushman, and I learned that he recently had arrived from South Australia and had gone to the Burracoppin wheat belt in search of employment. Meeting Ryan at Burracoppin, Ryan had offered to take him into partnership.

"Have you seen Snowy Rowles?" was almost my first question. "Yes. His car broke down at the 100-mile. He's coming up with George."

Of course Ryan and Lloyd were invited in to a hastily prepared meal. Despite the time they had been 'delayed' on the track, the yeast bread they had brought from Burracoppin was quite edible. Lloyd, I saw, was concerned about Ryan's condition, and only after much persuasion from Ryan did he produce a bottle of whisky.

He was playing a brand new accordion and Ryan was singing when George arrived with Snowy driving the truck. Immediately on their arrival I sensed that Rowles was angry at the situation created by Ryan bringing with him a new partner in the person of Lloyd. Sometime during the evening he expressed annoyance, saying:

"What the devil did Ryan want to bring that feller up here for? He knew I wanted to go with him to the north west, before he went down to Burracoppin."

Like many a man recovering from drink, Ryan appeared to favour the acceptance of small services from Lloyd who unpacked the utility and made up Ryan's and his own bunks. I could see that Lloyd was desperately anxious to please Ryan, and with the prospect of permanent employment and good money this is not surprising. He was the kind of man to whom unemployment would come very hard.

The next morning Rowles departed with Lloyd and Ryan for the latter's camp on Narndee Station. That was the last time I was to see Ryan. The day following, Lloyd and Rowles came through on Ryan's utility and went south to tow back the breakdown which was left at the Camel Station. Lloyd and Rowles then departed for Ryan's camp, and that was the last I ever saw of Lloyd.

Three days later George drove northward along the fence to see a man who was fencing on Narndee country and was camped at a well named Watson's Well. Yates reported that he had seen Rowles, Ryan and Lloyd who, instead of passing the Camel Station homestead, had skirted the northern boundary of the Government property and so came to the netted barrier opposite Watson's Well, at which place they passed through a gate and so continued northward. According to George, they had taken this course to avoid him for some reason. Yes, they were all headed for the NorthWest where work was plentiful and the money good.

The writing of The Sands of Windee was proceeding smoothly despite the heat which this summer was abnormal.

Two days before Christmas, Maddison, the northern patrolman, arrived. At this time Maddison was using an old utility car named The White Ant due to its coat of new white paint. Unlike Rowles's car it did go, and without doubt it must have been a vastly improved method of transport to that of the camels, even if dearer to run.

"I ordered a sucking pig from the store at Youanmi," he said with his usual unfailing cheerfulness despite chronic war injuries which made us wonder how he could carry on. "We'll go for it tomorrow evening in the cool. Might as well have a decent Christmas dinner."

Youanmi is a derelict mining town, where the superstructure of the one time valuable gold mine was being rapidly dismantled by the westerly winds, and where all that remains of many business premises and houses is a few scattered bricks or sheets of twisted, rusty corrugated iron.

Greatly to my surprise Snowy Rowles came to the entrance of the one hotel to greet us. "Hullo, Snow! What are you doing here? Thought you went to the Nor'-West with Ryan and Lloyd."

"They're over at Mount Magnet," he replied in his easy

manner. "We messed about in that district for a while and then Ryan decided to spend Christmas in the township. You know what Ryan is. Get to a pub and not leave it until broke. I'm trying to get him to sell me his utility, and meanwhile I borrowed it off him to run over here for Christmas to see a girl."

All of which appeared to us as being quite in order. We knew Ryan, knew his type would not leave any hotel until broke, knew it likely enough that Ryan would even sell his utility for more money to spend on grog. His affairs were not ours: neither were Snowy's affairs ours.

At the beginning of January Rowles arrived at the Camel Station accompanied by Larry and Emily, the aboriginals. He said he was selling them his old car as he had purchased Ryan's utility, his grandfather having sent him money. Within the hour he got the old machine to run. There was no laudatory eloquence from Rowles or any haggling over the price by Larry. Money, or money values, meant very little to Larry. He owned so many fox scalps, each worth two pounds, and he knew easy methods of securing the balance required to complete the purchase money.

Larry climbed in behind the steering wheel, and Emily, his wife, dressed in a cotton frock, silk stockings, and shoes, occupied the rear seat. I did not think Larry could drive a car, but he could well enough to get the vehicle on the move. He was still grinding in the gears without mishap when the car disappeared over a shoulder of the hill with two summits. He went on driving it, even after all the tyres were ripped off the wheels weeks later, for such obstacles as fallen tree trunks and casual boulders did not deter Larry. And those were wonderful weeks for Emily, too.

4

When the blast of the depression fell upon Western Australia the organisation of the Rabbit Fences was altered, and all men not returned soldiers were put off. Before this I returned to my sub-section, and under the re-organisation I was relieved of the camels and given Harry Watts's horse and dray and two hundred miles of the fence to care for - a hundred miles to the north of Burracoppin and a hundred miles to the south.

Not being satisfied with the first writing of The Sands of Windee I re-wrote it during 1930. In 1930 Sub-Inspector Coleman died. In him yet another of the old brigade passed on, to our personal regret. No boss was ever better liked.

In 1932 I took my annual leave during the first fortnight in June, and, with permission, occupied the house at the Government Farm near the railway, where I wrote from morning to late night throughout the fourteen days. Never before or since have I worked harder than I did during those 'holidays'.

As I have already stated , I am going to blow my own trumpet when writing of The Sands of Windee. In the newspapers of June 6th appeared the following paragraph:

London, June 5 - The Crime Book Society has selected as the month's best book, The Sands of Windee, *to be published by Hutchinson on June 19.*

It is, I am aware, the fashion among highbrow authors, whose work has never received such notice from a book society, to sneer at this method of increasing public interest in books. Any method of increasing public interest in books is good. The judges of this particular society at this time were well known English literary people upon whose necks I would have fallen in gratitude for the crumbs of help and encouragement for which I was starving. They selected my novel as the best of the month, and they put in second place, as recommended, three books by authors whose names are known all over the world. In Great Britain the book was quite a success: in this country, outside Western Australia, it was ignored until a year later when the case of Snowy Rowles gave it an undeserved reputation.

For me that case began months before the public heard about it, began in February, 1931, when I was camped forty-six miles north of the railway. There the inspector arrived from a trip to the north, and, as the day was late, he camped with me.

"When I was at the Camel Station two detectives came there in a car," he said gravely. "They are looking for the possible remains of a man known as Louis Carron. Do you remember ever having met a man named Jack Lemon?"

I did. I remembered Lemon telling me that a few months before I met him he had come from South Australia by boat, and that during the trip he had become friendly with a fellow from New Zealand. The two had tramped from Geraldton in search of work. A job had been offered and accepted by Carron on a station west of Narndee, and Lemon, tramping on to Narndee, had obtained the job vacated by Snowy Rowles.

The Inspector went on to explain that Carron had left his employment, or was put off, ten months before this meeting at the forty-six mile peg. He had then fallen in with Snowy Rowles and visited Jack Lemon at the hut on Narndee before he and Snowy left for the new mining town, Wiluna, to hunt for work. Since leaving Jack Lemon, no one had seen Louis Carron nor had Carron communicated with his fast friend, Lemon. Added to Lemon's uneasiness occasioned by Carron's silence, enquiries were being made for Carron by people in New Zealand. The Inspector could not learn much beyond these meagre details, but he did learn that Rowles had cashed Carron's pay cheque with the proprietor of the Paynesville Hotel, another old mining town then in the doldrums. Rowles had bought, it was said, a case of beer to take out to their camp - which was certainly not near Wiluna. Another point the Inspector found out was that months earlier Lemon had sent a reply-paid telegram to Rowles at Youanmi asking where and when he, Rowles, and Carron had parted company. When Rowles called at the Youanmi post office, the postmaster, knowing the contents of the telegram, said to Rowles as he was leaving: "What about sending the reply to that telegram?" To which Rowles answered:

"Oh! I'm in a hurry now. I'll send it from Mount Magnet."

But he sent Lemon no telegram.

And now the police were scouting all over the country looking for Carron's possible remains, and from the Inspector they obtained a rough map of all the old tracks leading off the Rabbit Fence, and all the waterholes. Rowles was working on a station several hundred miles farther north, and there was no hint that the police were even approaching him for information.

"It looks bad for Snowy," remarked the Inspector. "The police seem almost sure Carron is dead."

"Perhaps they both got drunk on that case of beer." I suggested. "Perhaps they fell into a brawl and Snowy accidentally killed him."

"Maybe something of that kind."

"And perhaps, having realized that he had killed Carron, Snowy remembered our discussions of the murder plot of what has become The Sands of Windee... If so, they won't get anything on him. On the other hand, what is much more likely, the police are barking up a wrong tree and Carron will be found alive and working somewhere."

Three weeks after our conversation at the 46-mile rain-shed, the Inspector found me at work 68 miles south of Burracoppin, and his first sentences to me were:

"Ryan and Lloyd are missing now. They haven't been seen since they left the Camel Station when you and George were there."

I gaped. The Inspector went on: "They have found Carron's charred remains near the 183-hut - bones, a ring, teeth."

"Go on! Anything more?" I asked with forced calmness.

"And when they went to arrest Snowy Rowles they recognized in him a man who escaped from the Dalwallinu lock-up where he was held with another man on a charge of burglary in 1928. They haven't arrested him for murder, but for gaol escape, so that they have whips of time to complete their investigation into the disappearances of Ryan, Lloyd and Carron."

It was all so incredible that for many minutes my mind refused to accept it. I found it much more difficult to believe that Rowles was a burglar than a suspected murderer. No man was less like even my modern conception of a burglar. He had never stolen anything from me, or from anyone else, or as little as a piece of hoop iron from the Government whilst I had been in charge of the Camel Station. It was infinitely easier to think that he had killed Carron during a drunken brawl than that he had killed three men - Ryan for his utility, Lloyd because he was in the way, and Carron for his poor station cheque which in those parts form common currency.

It was all unnatural, monstrous. The detective had found where Carron's body had been burned, and all they found were a ring, a few small bones, and human teeth. Rowles must have gone through those ashes with his hands to get out the skeleton but missed the items found by the police.

The police found other fires, several of them, in the vicinity of Ryan's camp on Narndee, and here Rowles had been more careful, for all that the police could find by sieving the ashes which might possibly form the remnants of two human bodies were placed in a small essence bottle. They did find what was unmistakeably kangaroo bones resting on the top portion of the ashes of each fire - a belt buckle, and the rib of an accordion, doubtless that same brand new accordion Ryan had purchased at Burracoppin and on which Lloyd at the Camel Station had played whilst Ryan had sung.

Urged by the Inspector and several friends in Burracoppin, I typed a two thousand word statement detailing the basic plot of The Sands of Windee and the movements of people at the Camel Station during the period of Ryan's and Lloyd's visit there. I thanked God I could say nothing with reference to Carron. I expected an immediate police interview. Nothing happened.

A cloud fell upon the Murchison district and for months nothing could be learned by the Inspector. We began to believe the police had failed to gather together sufficient evidence to warrant a charge of murder. In the meantime Rowles had been charged with burglary and had been sentenced to three years' imprisonment.

5

The English success of The Sands of Windee came at a time when I was experiencing domestic difficulties, and my wife and I having saved money we decided that the day had come when I might break away from my beloved bush and begin to earn a living with my pen. That was in September, 1931, when my fifth novel was with the publishers and I was in the middle of the sixth.

We were living in a suburb of Perth when one day a car stopped outside the gate and a tall handsome man came to the door and knocked. Upon my opening it, he asked:

"Are you Mr Arthur W. Upfield?"

"I am."

"Good! I am Detective-Sergeant Manning, and I've called to have a little talk with you."

In my writing room, I said:

"I assume you have called on me about that statement I wrote for you many months ago. I was beginning to think you had dropped the investigation."

At this his eyes opened so wide that they appeared to me to be as large as saucers.

"Dropped it!" he exclaimed in astonishment. "That was a rattling good yarn you wrote in Sands of Windee."

"I'm glad you like it. A bookseller told me that several detectives had bought it."

Manning smiled. I liked him instantly. There was nothing of the bull about his neck and third degree methods in his manner. "I think every detective in the State has read your book. I was wondering if you would come along to see the Crown prosecutor. There are several points in your book he wants explained further."

"Very well. When shall I see him."

"Tomorrow if you could."

"What about right now? You have a police car outside."

"Good. We shall want as much assistance as you can give us as we will be calling you as a witness."

"As a witness! Whatever for?"

Again the enlarging of the eyes in astonishment.

"I have discovered everything about you and that murder plot you and George discussed. No harm in it, of course. Free country and a good one for normal sane men. We think that Rowles put that book plot into practice and at the coming trial we shall base the charge of murder on it."

Like an octopus the law thrust forth its feeling tentacles and caught in tight hold a jeweller, a dentist, doctors, hotel proprietors, a postmaster, a bookkeeper, a station owner, station and stockmen and fence riders. The law brought all these people from as far afield as New Zealand to gather them in array to prove that Snowy Rowles killed Louis Carron. The preparation of the case was a monument to the law's slow but inexorable movement to achieve justice: whilst Detective-Sergeant Manning's intricate and thorough investigation has never been surpassed by any writer of detective fiction.

Although Rowles was brought to trial for the murder of Louis Carron it was impossible for any of us concerned with his trial to dissociate the disappearance of Louis Carron with that of James Ryan and George Lloyd. The several big fire sites found in the vicinity of Ryan's camp on Narndee Station provided no other logical reason than that two men were burned there.

The Crown based its case against Rowles on: (a) property belonging to Carron found in the possession of Rowles, (b) no person had seen Carron after he left Lemon's camp in the company of Rowles, and (c) Rowles knew of a method of destroying a human body through discussion of it with Upfield who incorporated the method in his novel The Sands of Windee. The case was remarkable on many counts, the most important being the extraordinary similarity of the investigation of the fire sites conducted by Detective-Sergeant Manning to that investigation conducted by my fictional detective, Napoleon Bonaparte, into similar but fictional fire sites.

MANNING

Police found ashes of a large fire 10 months after Carron disappeared.

Manning found in ashes human bones (very small portions), false teeth, dental plate, Zip-fasteners, a wedding ring.

Manning found in the ashes a piece of melted lead of weight equal to a 0.32 bullet.

Manning found among ashes a large number of whole animal bones.

Manning found an iron camp oven which was alleged to have been used to smash to small pieces the bones of poor Carron.

Manning investigated a careless attempt to destroy a human body utterly.

Manning found in one of the small heaps of ashes carried away from the main fire site bone which he took for finger bones.

Manning had to convince a real life judge and jury that Carron had been murdered and his body partially destroyed by fire.

Manning is par excellence a bushman.

BONAPARTE

Bony examined the ashes of a large fire two months after a man disappeared.

Bony found in ashes one boot sprig. Also a silver disc in the fork of a tree some distance from the fire site.

Bony found in ashes three pieces of melted lead, each of equal weight to a 0.44 bullet.

Bony found in ashes no likely human bones but plenty of kangaroo bones.

Bony found that a prospector's dolly-pot had been borrowed and used for this purpose.

Bony investigated the almost perfect murder, the body having been utterly destroyed.

Bony found in the ashes bones which he despatched to Headquarters to determine if they were human finger bones or the bones of the jaws of kangaroos.

Bony was diverted from bringing his case to a judge and jury because he would have failed to convince them.

Bony, having the tracking ability of his aboriginal mother and the reasoning power of his white father, was a super-bushman.

Bony's protagonist carried out the method to the last detail, but Rowles did not. He had not provided himself with a sieve, and even had he possessed a sieve he doubtless would not have delayed about the site of his crimes painstakingly to sieve all the ashes. Even when engaged with his fires at Ryan's camp he was interrupted by the arrival of the station owner who came there to see Ryan, and who did not see Ryan because Ryan was supposed to be cutting a fence line through heavy timber some miles away. Rowles dared not linger long at the 183-mile hut on the Rabbit Fence, for although this hut was very rarely visited by Maddison, the patrolman, he could not know the moment when Maddison would arrive at the gate, see his car tracks through it, and so himself pass through to visit the hut hidden among the scrub.

It was the wedding ring that Carron was known to have been wearing, regarding which he had sought information as to a method of removing it as it was becoming uncomfortable, which really hanged Snowy Rowles - according to a juryman who subsequently wrote of the jury's deliberations.

From all the evidence it could be reasonably deduced that a human body had been destroyed with that particular fire although there was not one whole bone discovered among the ashes or portions of bone which could be reconstructed into a whole. The Crown had to prove not only that a body had been destroyed, in that fire but that the body destroyed was that of Louis Carron. It was the ring which proved it.

In December 1925, Carron and the woman he married purchased a wedding ring from a jeweller in Auckland. It does not concern us how, but when Carron left New Zealand for Australia he was wearing this wedding ring.

On the stand Mrs Carron said that the wedding ring produced was hers. The ring fitted her finger. Counsel for the Defence finally shook this witness's definite statement that she knew the ring as that formerly belonging to her, and she altered her assertion to the generalization that the ring produced was like that her husband had purchased for her in 1925. Counsel for Rowles was right, of course, in pinning her to this, although one might expect a woman to know her own wedding ring.

When Mr. Long, the jeweller, was called he was asked to examine the ring, and this he did through a glass. He then related the sale to Carron, and stated that he remembered both Carron and his future wife entering his shop to buy it. He pointed out to the court the maker's mark on the inside of the ring, and said he had for years bought wedding rings only from this particular firm.

"I suppose," Rowles's Counsel began his cross examination, "that the makers of this ring turn out hundreds of them in any year?"

"Yes."

"You yourself have sold many of these rings during your trading life as a jeweller?"

"Yes, I have."

"The makers of this ring - do they trade with Australia?"

"They may do, but I don't think so."

"Then, as there must be many rings bearing this registration mark being worn by people in New Zealand, and most probably by people in Australia, it cannot be possible for you to state that this particular ring was that which you sold to Mr and Mrs Carron. You say you remember cutting this ring to make it fit Mrs Carron's finger, but that is an operation which you would undertake for many of your customers, is it not?"

This argument had been raised by Counsel for the Defence when other witnesses related how they had sold to Carron shirts made only in New Zealand, a hat bought in New Zealand, and he had won on the fact that many articles of similar make must be in use in that country and, most probably, in Australia. But Mr Long leaned back in his seat and began a technical discourse on the art of the goldsmith.

"When I examined this ring just now it was for the second or third time. I noticed then that about it which recalls to mind even more vividly the business of selling this ring to Carron. At the time I was rushed with work, and I was employing an assistant who although a good jeweller was not an expert goldsmith. Mrs Carron said that the ring did not fit her finger, and I had no other rings in stock which would fit her finger.

She consented to leave the ring with me to cut, remove a segment, and rejoin the ends to make the ring fit. I have said I was rushed with work, and, having cut the ring and taken from it the required segment, I handed it to my assistant to solder the ends together.

"This is an 18-ct. gold ring. An expert goldsmith would have used an 18-ct. gold solder, but my assistant used a 9-ct. gold solder. When I found this mistake I would normally have dropped the ring into the melting pot and cut another one for Mrs Carron, but I did not as she was anxious to have the ring and I was very busy with rushwork. I should not have done so, but I let the ring go from the shop as it was. If you examine this ring you will see clearly that the solder joining the cut ends is lighter in colour than the gold of the ring itself, meaning that the ring is 18-ct. gold and the solder used is 9-ct. gold. There can be no mistake. This is the ring I sold to Carron and his wife in December, 1925."

During his last days Snowy Rowles made what was an extraordinary confession. He said that he had returned from cashing Carron's cheque at the Paynesville Hotel to find that Carron had accidentally poisoned himself by eating butter pats containing strychnine which had been made for poisoning foxes; and that, on account of his police record, he feared he would be accused of a crime he did not commit and so burned the body at the 183-mile hut on the Rabbit Fence.

Examining this confession in the light of dates establishing Rowles's movements at this time, in conjunction with the mileages from several points to several other points, it is impossible for this to have been the truth.

He was silent about Ryan and Lloyd, save to deny knowledge of their fate.

6

Had Snowy Rowles been mentally normal he might well have risen higher than his environment at the time I knew him.

He came from a good home. His education was that of the youth of the country. He was physically perfect and quite good looking. His disposition was ever cheerful, and he was attractive both to men as well as to women - to the latter exceedingly so. He was, too, fearless, as was evidenced by his readiness to ride any kind of a horse and by the manner in which he habitually rode the motorcycle. He was diffident in another's home or camp; was ever ready to do another a good turn.

In his make-up, however, the desire to dare was strong, and this desire was based on vanity. He was in no need of money, he was willing to work to earn money, and yet he dared himself to snatch from a girl a bag of money she was taking from a bank to her employer's office. For this he served a sentence of three years.

To see himself as a hero had become with him an obsession, and he simply had to dare and do to prove to himself that he was a hero; for there was no necessity for him to take to crime, to risk his neck by riding stupid horses and mules, and by so rashly riding his motorcycle. With Snowy Rowles, however, vanity was never to be observed by others. Even when on the witness stand during his trial for murder there was no visible hint of vanity in his demeanour. Then, as well as when we knew him, he comported himself with modesty. He seldom talked horses and never boasted of his riding ability.

He was remarkable for the success with which he kept his left hand ignorant of what his right hand was doing. His vanity was as successfully hidden as were his past and his plans.

No one knows from whom or where he obtained the motorcycle on which he arrived in the Murchison. From that day until he left the Camel Station with Ryan and Lloyd his living was exemplary. He stole nothing, not even a bolt or nut belonging to the government, as a subsequent check of the inventory proved. He was never violent, never overbearing. He lived decently among decent people. He earned fairly good money and could have gone on earning good money. At the time he killed Ryan for his truck he could have borrowed enough money from half a dozen of us to have enabled him to purchase a utility.

Unmasked, he showed himself to be cold, calculating, cunning.

He prepared my mind, and the minds of others, to accept his possession of Ryan's truck as due to money he had solicited from a grandfather. He prepared my mind, and the minds of others, to accept the fact of Ryan's disappearance as due to Ryan's determination to seek fresh fields of employment in a distant part of the huge State. He selected his victims from a class of bush worker whose comings and goings are erratic and unregistered: for had he killed George for his truck, Maddison for his car, or me for my pay cheques, a hue and cry would have risen within a fortnight.

To his hands was a method of utterly destroying a human, and his vanity led him to believe that he could put this method into practice. Like all men damned by his kink he thought himself superior in everything as he had made himself superior to us all in horse riding and motorcycle riding.

The obstacle he encountered in the person of George Lloyd was to him an unimportant one. How he killed him and Ryan was never made public, but it is probable he used strychnine as he was possessed of this poison with which to trap foxes. He wanted nothing bar Ryan's truck. He did not want the new accordion Ryan brought with him from Burracoppin, and on which Lloyd accompanied Ryan's singing, and the ribs of this instrument were found among the ashes at Ryan's camp. Having consumed the bodies with fire, he went carefully through the ashes with his hands, for a sieve is not a common object outside a station trade shop, and the purchase of one would have been traced to him. For a prospector's dolly-pot - an iron cylinder not unlike a gun shell - he used Ryan's heavy iron baking oven. Then he dragged to the fires the remains of kangaroos Ryan had killed and brought to his camp for meat for himself and his dogs.

He was careful to salvage from those fires objects of human identification, but he omitted to salvage objects establishing an existence of articles which neither Ryan nor Lloyd would have discarded as of no further use.

He shot poor Carron, and from the remains of the great fire he made to consume the body he carried ashes in the camp oven to other points in the vicinity and threw them down cold on to grass which was discovered by Manning as unharmed. When he killed Carron, five months had passed since Ryan and Lloyd had allegedly gone to the north-west of the State, and, as nothing was afoot to trace them, Rowles was become confident. The ashes of the fire near the hut at the 183-mile hut on the Rabbit Fence succeeded in keeping from him the dental plate, teeth, and the gold wedding ring.

Rowles was very clever. He was cold and calculating. But he was not patient. He dreaded that someone would visit Ryan's camp while he was dealing with the remains, and, in point of fact, the owner did visit Ryan's camp whilst the fires were burning.

The sound of the owner's car engine warned Rowles of the visit long before Mr Bogle arrived there to find him calmly baking a damper. Where was Ryan? He and Lloyd were out cutting a line through the bush for a new fence. They would be three miles away. That meant that Mr Bogle would have had to walk three miles to see Ryan and then walk three miles back to his car. He decided to call on Ryan another day, and that decision without doubt saved his life.

When dealing with the remains of Carron he dreaded that either Fence-rider Maddison or the Inspector would arrive at the gate in the Rabbit Fence opposite the hut hidden in the bush, and there see his utility wheel tracks passing through the gateway. The hut was very seldom visited as the water in the small iron tank against the wall was seldom renewed and soon gave out, and wheel marks leading to it would most certainly have caused Maddison or the Inspector to investigate.

A significant point in these dreadful crimes is one which escaped notice prior to and during his trial. It dawned on me several years afterwards that George's method of the perfect murder was not perfect. Had Rowles sieved the ashes for every scrap of identifying material, and had he pounded the bones to dust in a prospector's dolly-pot, he would still have done something for his own undoing. What that something is I am not going to state.

There is no such thing as a perfect murder, for there cannot be a perfect human mind. After all, my immovable object never existed even as a problem, but the irresistible projectiles do exist in men having the probing minds of Crown Prosecutor Gibson and Detective-Sergeant Manning. Unsolved murder mysteries are due not to the criminal's cleverness but to the lack of ability in an investigator.

Arthur Upfield with his only son James, and wife Anne; Anne and Arthur Upfield, on the road 1935.

TWELVE

Interval

I

Some men are gifted for storing money in property or in a bank, others are gifted in spending money. Many men occupy the major part of their lives in the acquisition of money; and, whilst I am not so foolish as to decry this devotion to money making, I am going to say that there is something very much better, which is the storing of memories.

I am going to write finis to this volume when at the age of forty-five, when I have one storehouse filled with memories and look forward to filling another before the era of the carpet slipper is reached, when I have arrived at the end of one phase of life and look forward to another. At forty-five I have found myself and have achieved ambition, and henceforth I have to develop myself and my ambition. To stop still is to die. Man has never done anything well that could not be done better still, for nothing can be perfect. Man nears perfection not by achievement but by his endeavour to achieve. Achievement is a rotten apple: the endeavour to achieve is the honey of life.

The greatest of men is not he who has amassed almost unlimited wealth, the man who controls almost unlimited power, the man who has a fame world wide, but the tolerant man, the man who is able clearly to see the good in others and is able equally to shut his eyes fast to their faults. No one of the heroes in this volume was without his faults, but I steadfastly refuse to acknowledge them, even to see them. They were all fine men and women: even the terrible Snowy Rowles had his good points.

War teaches men to be tolerant, and your ex-soldier will gladly relate the humorous and the pleasant incidents of his army life, and seldom the terrible things. So it has been with me. My life on the tracks of inland Australia, and with men and women having wide, fearless tolerance, has made me tolerant, too. I bend the knee to no one in this world, and I expect no one to bend the knee to me. That is not pride, unless it is the pride of regarding all men as human beings - not as halo-owners or microbe-carriers.

Even after this excursion into the realm of philosophy you who have read thus far might say I have not given much away of myself. True, brother, true! There is nothing more boring than to listen to anyone trying to prove what a mighty fine fellow he is.

So, even to the end, I intend talking about others. An age produces its special type of men and women, and it is the duty of anyone with a flair for writing to do his utmost to fix a type before it fades into the blur of time. Which is why we are so indebted to Henry Lawson. There never again will be such men and women as those who lived in Australia Proper before the arrival of the internal combustion engine, and I count myself lucky to have come to Australia a few years before Cobb & Co's coaches disappeared from the tracks. In many respects the people in Australia Proper today are no different, but swift transport and wireless have exerted influences tending to make them suburban. The increasing airlines will draw them ever nearer to the cities which in the coaching days were almost as far distant as the planets.

As for me, I have changed, too. I feel much like a man who has deserted his mates at the front. I have arrived at my home on the mountain top where life is green and profuse all the year round, but I feel that my right place is in Australia Proper which has not been deserted by the One Spur Dicks and the Marys. Doubtless they are wiser than I, doubtless they know they would feel as I do did they desert, would know that they would cry for the sand-dunes and the claypans and the mulga forests all dancing beyond the mirage.

Often I walk the few hundred feet to the mountain summit from which I can gaze across blue space to and beyond Melbourne, as far as Mount Macedon. In a direct line beyond Mount Macedon lies Australia Proper and the great Murchison district of Western Australia. I sit and dream of men and women who lived there, and of those who still live there and are supremely happy. I was born in England, England is in my blood, but I would rather follow my imaginary line to its terminus than I would travel to England. People going to England and America do not arouse envy in me, only a soft pity that they can be so easily thrilled.

And now I have to plant daffodil and iris bulbs, for the winter is not far away. How One Spur Dick and Jake the Hangman and the Storm Bird would chuckle did they know that Hampshire was about to plant flower bulbs! But yet they might not. They might say:

"Didn't think Hampshire would ever become so ruddy soft."